ANTIGONE'S SISTERS

SUNY series in Theology and Continental Thought
———————
Douglas L. Donkel, editor

ANTIGONE'S SISTERS
On the Matrix of Love

LENART ŠKOF

Cover image: "Matrixial Web," from the series *Elartemis#ses3* by Maja Bjelica

Published by State University of New York Press, Albany

© 2021 State University of New York

All rights reserved

Printed in the United States of America

No part of this book may be used or reproduced in any manner whatsoever without written permission. No part of this book may be stored in a retrieval system or transmitted in any form or by any means including electronic, electrostatic, magnetic tape, mechanical, photocopying, recording, or otherwise without the prior permission in writing of the publisher.

For information, contact State University of New York Press, Albany, NY
www.sunypress.edu

Library of Congress Cataloging-in-Publication Data

Names: Škof, Lenart, 1972– author.
Title: Antigone's sisters : on the matrix of love / Lenart Škof.
Description: Albany : State University of New York Press, 2021. | Series: SUNY series in theology and continental thought | Includes bibliographical references and index.
Identifiers: LCCN 2020024808 | ISBN 9781438482736 (hardcover : alk. paper) | ISBN 9781438482743 (pbk. : alk. paper) | ISBN 9781438482750 (ebook)
Subjects: LCSH: Antigone (Mythological character) | Femininity (Philosophy) | Love.
Classification: LCC BL820.A68 S56 2021 | DDC 128/.46—dc23
LC record available at https://lccn.loc.gov/2020024808

10 9 8 7 6 5 4 3 2 1

CONTENTS

Acknowledgments · vii

PRELUDE: The Matrix of Love / Ettingerian Matrixial Web · 1

PART I: COSMOLOGY / THEOLOGY OF LOVE

1 Antigone / Savitri · 13

2 Metis / Lepa Vida · 37

3 Bethlehemite Concubine / Mary · 49

INTERLUDE: Interval / Time of Love · 71

PART II: PHILOSOPHY / ONTOLOGY OF LOVE

4 Clara / The Matrix · 89

5 Beyng / Sister · 111

6 Irigaray / Breath · 145

POSTLUDE: Jesus / Antigone · 163

Notes · 171

Bibliography 215

Index 229

About the Author 237

ACKNOWLEDGMENTS

There are many philosophers and theologians that should be mentioned at the beginning of this book. I hope that my humble indebtedness to all them is visible throughout the book. First of all, let me thank Tine Hribar for his encouragements and support to embark on another philosophical journey—this time by writing a book on Antigone. Among my main influences, I wish to highlight in particular various encounters with the thoughts of Luce Irigaray, Bracha L. Ettinger, John D. Caputo, and Clemens Sedmak. Without them this book could not have been written in its present form.

I would like to thank my dear colleague Maja Bjelica from the Institute for Philosophical Studies at Science and Research Centre Koper for the beautiful photos from her *Elartemis#Ses3* series, which express our philosophical correspondences and our *ethical conspiracy* in a beautiful way. Also, I thank her cordially for all her assistance with the editorial work.

I also thank Vlasta Pacheiner-Klander for her illuminative reflections on Savitri, and also my sincere thanks to Robert Faas for sharing with me his careful translations of insightful mystical materials of Jakob Böhme. I wish to express my thanks to my friend Jeff Stewart for allowing me to publish from his unpublished work. I want to thank three anonymous reviewers for their criticism and extremely valuable suggestions for improvements of my arguments in the book. I also want to express my gratitude to SUNY Press editors Doug Donkel and James Peltz—for their editorial support and care for this project, and to Eileen Nizer for taking care of the publication process of the book. Finally, I am indebted to my colleague Gašper Pirc for helping me with the final version of my index.

Some chapters and sections of this book were previously published in the following journals and edited collections:

"Antigone / Savitri": short parts of this chapter (also without the appendix on Alcestis) were published as "On Sacred Genealogies in Antigone and Savitri," in *Poesis of Peace: Narratives, Cultures, and Philosophies*, edited by Klaus-Gerd Giesen, Carool Kersten, and Lenart Škof, 68–77 (New York: Routledge, 2017). Materials reprinted with permission.

"Metis / Fair Vida": an earlier and shorter version of this chapter (also without appendix on Favour) was published as "The Material Principle and an Ethics of Hospitality and Compassion: Requiem for Lampedusa," *Annales, Series historia et sociologia* 25, no. 2 (2015): 263–72. Materials reprinted with permission.

"Bethlehemite Concubine / Mary": an earlier and shorter version of this chapter (also without the appendix on Sophia) was first published as "God, Incarnation in the Feminine, and the Third Presence," Sophia 2018, doi: https://doi.org/10.1007/s11841-018-0646-9. Materials reprinted with permission.

"Interval / Time of Love": originally published as "An Interval of Grace: The Time of Ethics," *SpazioFilosofico* 17, no. 2 (2016): 211–24. Reprinted with permission.

"Irigaray / Breath": an earlier and shorter version of this chapter (without the appendix on Chora) was published as "Breath as a Way of Self-Affection" in *Bogoslovni vestnik* 77, no. 3/4 (2017): 577–87 and in *Atmospheres of Breathing*, edited by Lenart Škof and Petri Berndtson (Albany: SUNY Press, 2018), 51–67. Materials reprinted with permission.

The following chapters and sections of this book were translated into English by Petra Berlot Kužner: Introduction, part on Savitri, all supplements to chapters, and chapter "Beyng / Sister." Also attributed to her are the translations of Irigaray's later works in Italian and selected translations of Claudel's poetry in the book.

Finally, I want to thank to Suzana, Lucijan and Lev, for providing me with the most elemental matrix of all matrixes—our family.

Lenart Škof, January 2021

Photos by Dr. Maja Bjelica: *Elartemis#Ses3*

The photographic series *Elartemis#Ses3* is one of the rings of the chain project *Elartemis*, in which the author researches the visual worlds of the elements, emotions, and echoing experiences. Images are created out of analogue unedited black and white photographs that she takes randomly and intuitively. The photographs are then digitally reframed and presented in print after a playful mirroring process that brings the eye unimagined realities and sp(l)aces.

The sequence presented here was inspired by thoughts on the feminine and matrixiality by Lenart Škof, which the author was following through her postgraduate studies in philosophy and anthropology. The title of this sequence, the third one of the larger ongoing project of fourfold symmetrals *Elartemis*, is constructed as *Ses3*. This, in the Slovenian language, the mother tongue of both authors, reads as "*sestri*" and carries a double meaning, "two sisters" and "to (a) sister." It derives directly from the inspiration of Lenart Škof's present work, which gives voice, voice in *différance*, to the sisters of this (and other) worlds. Intuitively selected, the images offered in this book are a result of both authors' mutual commitment and meeting expressions.

unending matrix

PRELUDE

emanating love

The Matrix of Love /
Ettingerian Matrixial Web

This matrixial awareness accompanies us from the dawn of life.

—Bracha L. Ettinger, *The Matrixial Borderspace*

Christ and Mary, differently and together, recognize, in short, the sovereign lucidity of Antigone . . . And they invite all women, natural mothers of the species, not to halt the flow of childbearing but to join with them (Jesus and Mary) at one of the possible crossroads of Greek and Jewish memory.

—Julia Kristeva, "Antigone: Limit and Horizon"

O my daughter! O little child like my essential soul, you whom I must again resemble. / When desire is purged by desire. / Blessed be God, for in my place there is born a child without pride. . . .

—Paul Claudel, *Five Great Odes*, trans. Edward Lucie-Smith

This book is about Antigone and the related cosmic, philosophical, and theological possibilities for a new thinking on the matrix of love. Antigone is thus put in dialogue with her genealogical sisters; among them are ancient mythological and cosmological characters on one side, and various philosophical and theological feminine figures on the other side. For this purpose, a series of readings, relating to Antigone and her unconditional ethical gesture, is offered in this book. This attempt rests upon a belief that a shift from the ontology of violence to the ethics of love and tenderness would only be possible through an enhanced matrixial[1] identity as developed and defended throughout this book: by matrixial identity, we point to the ontologico-ethical core of the feminine identity, whose lack or even absence in our cultures of intersubjectivities and/or communities is visible in numerous sufferings of women, children, and men throughout history and in every culture of this world that we are sharing. According to Ettinger, an ethical difference that is *feminine*, and will guide us throughout this book, is explained as follows:

> I propose departing from a difference that is feminine from the onset, from a *rapport* of *borderlinking* in an originary psychical sphere that I have named "matrixial." In the matrixial sphere, *not-knowing* the feminine difference is impossible inasmuch as this difference in itself is a *co-naissance* (knowledge of being-born-together). . . . This cross-inscription is transmitted by matrixial effects such as empathy, awe, com-passion and compassion, languishing, horror, and maybe telepathy. *However, the transgression itself is a bridging and an accessing to the other already in the feminine.* . . . The matrixial designates a difference located, in its originary formation, in the linkage to invisible female corporeal specificity, to the archaic enveloping outside that is also an inside: the womb. However, by matrix I do not intend an "organ" or an "origin," but a complex apparatus modeled on this site of a female/prenatal *encounter* that puts in *rapport* any human becoming-subject-to-be, male or female, with female bodily specificity and the mother-to-be's encounter-events, trauma, jouissance, phantasy, and desire.[2]

While women might evidently be the privileged holders of this Ettingerian matrixial core, it is important to know that, broadly, and as argued in this book, the matrixial identity is also equally available to men and thus forms the primordial ethical core of humanity.[3] Relational ontology in this book becomes a trinitarian process in which women, men, and children are ontologically co-created and ethically co-related in a new way. *Antigone's Sisters* is therefore an attempt at a genealogy of love, a reflection about a lost opportunity in theology and philosophy and of essentially violent mythological, philosophical, and theological modulations that have persisted for centuries in the oblivion of something primordial that we possess—the memory of the beginning, out of and in love.[4]

It seems to be impossible to define Antigone: Hegel has compared her to Socrates and Jesus, and numerous philosophers have interpreted her in various ways—using the languages of psychoanalysis, feminism, philosophy, political science, law, theology, etc.—only to elucidate her story as an example of a revolutionary mission toward justice, care, or supreme love.[5] With her archaic but also universal *maternal* gestures of care and tenderness (Kristeva), with her resolute but again sublime gestures of compassion for her dead brother, Antigone transgresses the alleged dichotomies of this and the other world, love and death, but also of balance and madness, subjectivity and community, or autonomy and law. With her words "My nature is for mutual love, not hate,"[6] Antigone paves the way toward the logic of the Gospels, and installs both a new ethics and a superior, or even an eternal logic into the world of injustice, suffering, and any of the forms of tyranny.

From Plato to Maximus the Confessor, from Thomas Aquinas to Hegel, or from Kierkegaard to Lacan, love has too often been philosophically and theologically appropriated, even metaphysically abused. Love could not become a way of cultivating our Being as self-transcendence and was too often guided and appropriated by a preestablished idea of the supreme Idea / supreme divine / supreme God—all these being generally represented in one of the elevated forms of a monarchic principle, predominantly male, and existing for us in one of its metaphysically stable forms. Here we wish to analyze the primordial and immanent nature of love in its own archaic temporality and show that it is only through this ontological preeminence of love that the divine can be revealed to us. This book is in search of an original code of love and its *matrix*—traceable in *chóra* as a primordial place of equality—and thus matrixiality is revealed as a key concept. As absolutely powerless and peaceful presence, this primordial place hints at cosmic pregnancies and its plentiful springs of life, which we need to respect, fully protect, and nurture. Matrixiality is first unveiled in *chóra*: the secret remainder in ourselves, which reminds us of an abyssal *womb-matrix*, as an eternal germ of Being, before even the first division of Being and non-Being, or before all things were ontologically divided.

But there is another genealogy that this book addresses—more hidden, perhaps, yet also visible and clearly traceable in this book—the reflection on the idea of a child. If philosophy today is still lacking one gesture, it is that of the concretization of ontological reasoning that can encapsulate the thought of a child, or natality.[7] As Luce Irigaray states—perhaps again prophetically (as she was prophetic with her *Speculum of the Other Woman*)—in her latest work *To Be Born*, philosophy has the task to secure the coming into the world of a child's singularity—by granting it ontological belonging—in such a way that it secures this singularity, while allowing and enabling her/his self-transcendence.[8] According to Deleuze, this thought is present in a beautiful and simple way in very small children who "all resemble one another and have hardly any individuality, but they have singularities: a smile, a gesture, a funny face—not subjective qualities. Small children, through all their sufferings and weaknesses, are infused with an immanent life that is pure power and pure bliss."[9] We shall see that love can only develop from such an environment; therefore, the thought of a child must be the primordial gesture of any future philosophy.[10]

And there is a third ethical thread in this book. It is very thin and gentle (and extremely vulnerable to various outside conditions) in its core, but still ethically powerful in its message; it permeates and nurtures the entire ethics as its own breath of life. The material signifiers that gently flow throughout this book are all related to this emerging plane of ethics of compassion and protective justice. The elements of this ethics are comprised of *tears* and *laments* upon the vulnerability of the other; of *touch*, a silent *embrace* or a hospitable *lap*—all plentiful of compassionate *caress*; of pulsation of life springing out of cosmic and feminine pregnancies, beyond lives of fear and violence; and, finally, of mildness of being/Beyng and exuberance of love, both coming out of the receptacle/wetnurse/genetrix/matrix—of powerless, yet invincible *chóra*. This ethical constellation is now tied to the hope that in this world that we are sharing, it would still be possible to recognize our own weakness and vulnerability, or *ethical humility*. It is often an impossible thought, or extremely onerous in itself—and in its negative side it might even be destructive to our ethical selves—as it exposes us in the very ontological core of our personality and our being.

In his essay on the imagination of peace, theologian Clemens Sedmak describes a story about a newborn named Issa Grace, a little girl who was born with a severe genetic disorder (*trisomy 18*) that would prevent her from ever living a decent life without extreme suffering. The doctors predicted she would live for a few days at the most.[11] But her family virtually did the impossible in their care for this little girl and spent nine months with her, from June 2013 to March 2014. On the horizon of insight into the utmost vulnerability of human existence, the care for this child, says Sedmak, revealed the truth about our own vulnerability. The care that many people, from the closest relatives to a broad circle of family friends, dedicated to this child is the reflection of the most powerful "element" that we possess: a mysterious exuberance of love, which is born from something utterly vulnerable, demanding nothing, yet giving us what is most precious—connectedness in a community. The care and compassion extended into a communion of love that rose around Issa: wanting to help the parents get at least a few hours of sleep, their relatives, friends, acquaintances, and others lovingly took care of their baby. *Gestures of love, wanting nothing in return.* To explain the internal logic of these developments, Sedmak introduces here a term which he, in a lucid way and in accordance—and simultaneously, counterpoint—with the famous Rawls principle of justice (*veil of ignorance*), calls the *wound of knowledge*. The wound of knowledge tells us we should try to imagine how it would be if any of us *knew*, right from the start, that something similar to what Issa Grace's family experienced would happen in our lives. How would we live our lives then?[12] What would it mean to live with such latent, yet potentially present knowledge about our own vulnerability: would we be touched by such knowledge, would it change us? In this frame of reference, Sedmak speaks about *the pedagogy of the weak*.[13] The vicinity of weakness teaches us about humble listening, about learning out of love and closeness, about thoughtfulness and compassionate affection—*all* this in full respect for the freedom and full autonomy of the individual. Building on the awareness of one's weakness and vulnerability for a community's life in compassion, Sedmak eventually offers for consideration the following words: "A wound of knowledge makes it easier for us to accept that 'behind our roles and masks we often wear, we are all vulnerable and struggling human beings whose hearts are more needy than we would dare to admit at times.'"[14] This is where the mystery of love, its *exuberance or hospitality in excess*, is concealed. The present book intends to point to some of the origins and margins of this exuberance—in mythological, cosmological, theological, philosophical, literary, and cinematic contexts.

To sum up: according to Elizabeth Grosz in her *The Incorporeal: Ontology, Ethics and the Limits of Materialism*, philosophers such as Descartes or Hegel "have tended to privilege ideality over materiality."[15] The energetic and ethical forces, hidden in the human body, were only revealed with thinkers such as Spinoza (immanence), Schopenhauer (will), Feuerbach (sensibility), or Nietzsche (the body), and since then it is difficult to follow any path of the alleged spirituality-materiality divide. This book offers a novel ethics, which as such also aims at a new mode of ethical transformation within intersubjective encounters among mortals, a transformation in which birth and death are taken as two margins: both form an unsurpassable horizon of *ethics of life* as revealed through gestures of compassion, caress, and hospitality. Antigone, her genealogical sisters as presented in this book, and Jesus all stand on the precipice of this ethical horizon. The ontological margins of birth and death marked by all of them thus point beyond any metaphysical or ethical duality and inaugurate a new plane of ethics of intersubjectivity at its very limits—stretching toward the exuberance of love, or its matrixial core.[16]

∽

This book is written for Antigone and her philosophical-cosmological-theological sisters. It is a series of dialogues with key thinkers, such as Böhme, Schelling, Feuerbach, Heidegger, Derrida, Caputo, Kristeva, Ettinger, and Irigaray. Just as Jesus represents Christianity, Antigone stands prepared at the origin of ethics in the earliest European Greek thought: uniting the ancient unwritten laws (*agrapta nomima*), primordial ethical principles (burial of the dead), and the highest law of love. To reinterpret or understand Antigone in a new way on a horizon determined by Hegel, Heidegger, Lacan, Butler, Kristeva, Ettinger, and Irigaray and their explanations of this Greek myth—is a near impossible task. For this reason, our interpretation of this Greek myth at first glance distances itself from its immediate environment and thinks it through the platform of the so-called matrix of love and the related cosmological, theological, and philosophical genealogies. The dialogue with Antigone draws in some of the ancient deities (such as Metis) and ancient cosmological matrices (such as the ancient Greek notion of *chóra*), as well as figures of "heroic" women, such as Savitri from the Indian poem *Mahabharata*, Alcestis from the homonymous Euripides tragedy, and Fair Vida from Slovene mythology. The book also centers on the relationships between feminine figures (such as the concubine of a Levite), the eternal feminine from the Old Testament (Wisdom or Sophia from the Proverbs), and the figures of Mary in the frameworks of the New Testament and contemporary (feminist and philosophical) theology. We also wish to explore philosophical interpretations, such as those found in Schelling and his sensitive character Clara, in many ways one of the most sublime creations in the history of philosophy and literature, as well as Binswanger's and Heidegger's reflections on the exuberance of love and Being/Beyng—also in reference to ancient Greek contexts of cosmological thinking in Sappho and her Aphrodite as Being's/Beyng's sister. Finally, in the conclusion of the book, we focus on Luce Irigaray, whose name in the final chapter is interpreted as the code of a new philosophical theology and at the same time a transition to a newly legitimated thinking of the approaching Age of the Spirit/Breath, all nearing the horizon of the forthcoming and anticipated philosophy of proximity, sensibility, and compassion.

praying sisters

PART I

COSMOLOGY / THEOLOGY OF LOVE

walled rocks

1

ANTIGONE / SAVITRI

In this chapter, we wish to delineate new ethical spaces, by following the deeds of two heroic women from the literary and religious tradition—Sophocles's Antigone and Savitri from the *Mahabharata*. What they have in common is that in their lives and/or deaths, and in their heroic deeds, they were in a close relationship to the deceased and to death. But also to life. In this, they were guardians of cosmic laws, with their sacred sexual and generational genealogies. Despite their tragic fates, they were and remained sacred guardians of basic cosmic laws, related to the living and deceased, heaven, earth, and the underworld. In Heideggerian language, they were, as it were, in a close proximity to the elements of ancient cosmic order and cosmic laws; in their deeds, they acted and spoke out of a belonging to Being (to *deinon*).

Today, it seems that we have lost our relation to the cosmos and its ethical order. We live in a civilization offering us a plenitude of earthly goods, including various ethical and political laws, and justice in one of its forms. In this fabricated world we (who are we?)[1] (un)willingly tolerate evil and violence in one of its varied forms and are thus not able to posit an unconditional ethical demand against them. Being subjected to different forms of power, we cannot find a peaceful repose, a place to host (hospitality) and protect peace for the concrete living others. This chapter wishes to place Sophocles's *Antigone* into a new ethical framework and point toward some elements for a possible new cosmico-feminist interpretation of justice. It will elaborate on the logic of *agrapta nomima* (unwritten/divine laws) and the logic of ethical gestures toward mortals (both deceased persons and living beings). It will show how Antigone's sacred duty was to preserve the equilibrium of the cosmic order (with its sexual and generational genealogies), and how this equilibrium has been lost in our times, in fact, how it has been subjugated to various forms of power since Creon's political act. According to Luce Irigaray,[2]—whose teachings have been my inspiration for years—this was possible only with the Greek substitution of ancient law and cosmic justice with an inauguration of new political laws, as defended by Creon, who finds ancient unwritten laws obsolete. We know that even Hegel—by fully acknowledging this shift and by highly praising Antigone for her acts—was still not willing to support Antigone's adherence to those ancient laws, representing a sacred order of femininity. New ethical gestures and a new view of justice are thus needed in our times; gestures that are more closely related to the human body, deceased (as in Polyneices), but also gestures for the living corpse (Agamben), any child, or a (wo)man on the very edge between life and death, or any other living body in pain. Universally then, no duty and no justice can be more important than our adherence to the deepest cosmico-ethical layers of both our faith and our knowledge, an awareness rooted in our bodily sensibilities and interiority.

Antigone

From Hegel to Irigaray, Sophocles's *Antigone* has provoked major thinkers and raised key ethical questions: from divine law to human law, from ethics to morality, from cosmic awareness to modern political life, in all these contexts, interpreters and authors such as Hegel, Lacan, Butler, Irigaray, and Žižek have searched for the proper *measure*, delineating the most sensitive space of all—the space of proximity between the sexuate subjects, between kin members (even hinting at incestuous relationships between them), or, as in more politically invested readings—among the members of a political community. The languages of psychoanalysis, ethics, theology, and law were used and merged in the many and varied readings of this ancient drama. But originally, *Antigone* is a tragedy about cosmic laws and hospitality toward others as members of a kin, but also others as strangers.

According to Irigaray, unveiling the meaning of Antigone is not an easy task in our culture.[3] It is a task requiring from us a descent into entirely different modes of our intersubjective thinking as we inhabited them from our predecessors. Clearly, this also is an intercultural task, since Western man cannot find the way by himself. Irigaray's awakening through Yoga testifies to this. And there are only few contemporary philosophers that are sensitive to this task in its entirety. We would dare to (in this sense) only add Jean-Luc Nancy (perhaps Agamben) to Irigaray. Now, at the very beginning of his *Being Singular Plural*, Nancy cites Nietzsche from *Thus Spoke Zarathustra*:

> Like me, guide the virtue that has flown away back to the earth—yes, back to the body and life: so that it may give the earth its meaning, a human meaning! . . . Let your spirit and your virtue serve the meaning of the earth. . . . Human being and human earth are still unexhausted and undiscovered.[4]

Nancy is right in his diagnosis: this earth—now at this moment—"is anything but sharing community of humanity."[5] There is no compassion on this earth, no sense of an *être-à-plusiers*, as he states. Moreover, in his *Corpus*, first by enumerating the atrocities committed in the last century against the humanity, Nancy—by reflecting the jurisdiction of bodies—rightly observes that we'd need a *corpus*, namely "the areality of corpses: of bodies indeed, including the dead body."[6] What Nancy is aiming at is to delineate spaces, places, topics, perhaps new grounds for bodies, being able to go beyond mere "dialectical respiration from the 'same' to the 'other.'"[7] Here we can already sense another *justice*, coming from this sense (or sensitivity) for the bodies and their places. But we will stop here and return to *Antigone*.

What kind of love and justice is then revealed to us in this play of Sophocles? Authors of an excellent study on Antigone—namely, Max Statkievicz and Valerie Reed, state that Antigone is "'the turning point in the ethical thinking of our time' and 'an embodiment of the ethical value of the community,'"[8] in a sense of Agamben's *coming community* (*communità che viene*). Is it not that out of the Hegelian claim on the collision between two equally valid claims (Creon versus Antigone) there comes our uncertainty regarding justice: "familial love, the holy, the inward, intimate feelings—hence known also as the law of the nether gods—collides with the right of the state."[9] To be able, then, to view justice or *Gerechtigkeit* not as one-sided, but as an integral ethical law, we have to admit the inner logic of this collision. *But this is impossible*. Antigone's faith and her radical ethical care for the other, the brother-as-corpse, is deeper than any one-sided view as proposed by Hegel, Lacan, Butler, Žižek, or many others. Antigone's ethics is best understood when confronted with Heidegger's and Irigaray's ontologies on one side, and Levinas's and Derrida's views of justice on the other. These are all thinkers, being in the close vicinity of an ancient Greek and Indian (Presocratic: as Heidegger and Irigaray with her relation to pre-Vedic cults and sources and Yoga) or divine (as in Levinas and Derrida) justice: this is the realm of divine law and *agrapta nomima*.[10]

According to Rémi Brague, we can understand the divinity of Greek law only beginning with Sophocles. For Brague, these divine laws (and accompanying justice, of course) are so old that "they really did not appear, since they are so obvious, that there is no beginning in them"[11] (*qu'elles n'ont pas de point d'émergence*). For the double setting of an *ethical archeology* and *ethical anatomy*[12]—or relation between morality (with justice) and ethical gestures toward the other *in* her body, the other in pain, and equally the deceased and dead bodies—this simple but pregnant observation by Brague is indeed of key importance. *Agrapta nomima* can only be inscribed in our hearts and our bodies. We all are the inheritors of this sacred message, being inaugurated by Antigone's act and—as we shall see later—having also important intercultural consequences. Divine laws and our bodies as sacred stelas, furthermore, the logic of a sacrificial body, the body as a tabernacle (M. Douglas);[13] this also is an inauguration of a plane where Derrida and Levinas meet with their interventions into the very logic of justice. In this tradition (Ancient Near East and Old Testament), washing the body—a living body—is "an enactment that replicates atonement for restoring the sanctity of the tabernacle."[14] The same holds for Antigone's now ancient Greek ancestral care for Polyneices's corpse: it is an act, necessary in order to regain the lost cosmic order, to remove, or to wash out the impurity brought into this world by Creon's political act. This is why there is no antagonism between two different ethical worlds (according to Hegel and his followers, *eine sittliche Macht gegen die andere*) in Antigone: her act rests in divine law and divine justice; it is an act inscribed in the feminine body and as such it is *an-archic*. In the body as a microcosm a "shared background knowledge"[15] is stored. According to Levinas, these ancient rights of the other person, and their justice, are apriori: they have an *ineluctable authority* and demand from us an *inexhaustible responsibility*, one compared to Antigone's claim.[16] Phenomenologically, they lead us toward radical proximity in intersubjectivity, toward the event of meeting, goodness, and peace.

In the pre-Homeric Greek world, the guardians of these ancient cosmic laws were Erinyes (and along them Gaia, Hades, Persephone/

Demeter, Kore, etc.). In the pre-Vedic, and later in the Vedic world, this place had been secured by deities from the Proto-Shakta-Tantric cults on one side, and later from the Adityas—Varuna, Mitra, and Aryaman—on the other. But let us hold off for a moment with the intercultural aspects and first reflect upon the world of pre-Homeric deities and Irigaray's interpretation of the tragedy. According to Walter F. Otto,[17] pre-Homeric and pre-Olympic deities of the ancient chthonic religion testify for the close proximity of the Greek (wo)man to the elements of nature. These elements appear philosophically in the world of both pre-Socratic and Upanishadic philosophers, but later they reappear only in Schelling, Feuerbach, Heidegger (via Hölderlin), Irigaray, and Caputo. Caputo, for example, pleads for greater respect for intuitions, based on the ancient mythic elements, forgotten all the way in our philosophies and theologies, and in our view of justice—human and divine. Invoking Irigaray, Caputo mentions "sun and eye, air and breath, wind and spirit, sea and life, rock and god"; we may add, for the sake of our reading of Antigone—earth and the netherworld.[18] Now, to return to the Greek world: it seems that Antigone is a guardian of this sacred cosmic order, as represented within this elemental world. Otto mentions in this sense ancient laws, or, better, ancient justice, as an interruption into this world. The gods that belong to the Earth, argues Otto, all belong to the principles of femininity (perhaps matriarchy)[19] and stand against the later masculine orders of the Olympic gods. This ancient earthly order is a place where also Antigone's act is rooted. This is a magical world: with the corpse of Polyneices lying there on the earth, unburied as prey for dogs, and any corpse or living dead (Agamben) in *our* world not being cared for, or being *deserted, betrayed, forgotten*, the sacred equilibrium of the cosmic order is broken. This intrusion of an injustice into the cosmic order means that sexual and generational orders, and of course also natural orders of fertility (food, grain), are unsettled and broken. The basic principles of *a life* are endangered, including death as its part. Twins (as Indian Yama and Yami), brothers and sisters, sharing the same womb, as in the case of Antigone and Polyneices; mother and child . . . This now is not yet a world of morality (or, not any more), nor any form of "justice"; we may add that it is this cosmic order that is the meaning of apriori in the above-mentioned Levinasian sense, including the phenomenological consequences.

But before we approach Irigaray's understanding of Antigone, we need to delineate the tragic paradox of Sophocles as understood by Hegel in his *Phenomenology of Spirit*. Hegel positions Antigone in the spiritual world of the pagan (Greek, therefore not yet Christian) morality in which the family (as represented by Antigone) and the *polis* (as represented by Creon) are mutually exclusive; the particularity of the family life cannot be reconciled with the universality of the *polis* and Sophocles's play is thus caught in this tragic dichotomy, according to Hegel.[20] The Greek Penates stand opposed to the universal Spirit of Hegel. The spirit *must* become incarnated within the political community and its citizens (men—in the case of the Greek world, but also in the case of the modern, yet still predemocratic Christian and Western world). And thus the conflict between divine law and human law is actually the conflict between the two sexes in their predefined roles within Hegel's *grand œuvre*. While men are destined to become full citizens, women are limited to family life—sister must now, as wife, become the head of the household. The relation between husband and wife therefore takes precedence over other familial relationships (such as between brothers and sisters, or parents and children). With her decision to resist Creon's famous edict, Antigone enters forbidden territory in morality, and Hegel will never be able to reconcile himself with this move by Antigone (and Sophocles). In Hegel's own words:

> Since the community only gets an existence through its interference with the happiness of the Family, and by dissolving [individual] self-consciousness into the universal, it creates for itself in what it suppresses and what is at the same time essential to it an internal enemy—womankind in general. Womankind—the everlasting irony [in the life] of the community—changes by intrigue the universal end of the government into a private end, transforms its universal activity into a work of some particular individual, and perverts the universal property of the state into a possession and ornament for the Family.[21]

Still, for Hegel, under the heaven of his concept of *Sittlichkeit*, Antigone *is* manifesting the Divine Law: as a woman, she stands in the vicinity of divine laws—the feminine, for Hegel, possesses the highest intuitive (but not conscious)[22] awareness of the ethical. While in her role of the wife the ethical life of a woman is not pure, this changes in her relationship to her brother. Hegel tried to repair his otherwise masculinely appropriated notion of sexual difference by representing the relation between brother and sister as an ethically pure example of an equilibrium between the sexes, based on their shared blood and their mutual lack of desire (later, the lack of physical passion will become an ideal within the spiritual bond of Christian marriage). In this view, for Antigone the loss of her brother is irreparable; but, again, this relation is itself limited—ideally, brother necessarily passes from the divine law into the sphere of the human law, *polis*. Antigone may act from pure ethical intuition as related to unwritten divine laws, but again, she cannot (or is not allowed to?) move beyond her own limitations, for Hegel. We may now ask ourselves: Was then Antigone's act of burial of her deceased brother not a *double intrusion* into higher spiritual orders? First, by not obeying Creon's state orders, as a woman, she transgresses the ethical order of the hegelian *Sittlichkeit*; secondly, by remaining (allegedly) caught in her feminine-intuitive ethical drive, Antigone, as it were, *redeems* (and not only takes care of, as this divine obligation falls naturally to the sister—as ordered by divine laws operating within the family and thus positioning also the family within the universal) her brother('s corpse) and inaugurates a new transethical order that was not accessible either to her sister Ismene or to any of his male relatives, or, ultimately, to Creon.[23] *Antigone transgresses the limits of both life and death.* But this could not be allowed—either in the Greek *polis* or in the Hegelian (-Christian) world. As argued by Patricia Mills, Antigone clearly and openly "transcends the limitations of womanhood set down by Hegel."[24] In the concluding part of the book we will address these highest redemptory traits in Antigone's acts, which were therefore not accessible to Hegel. We may now conclude our reading of Hegel by stating that Antigone brings an alien law into this world—a new law, also inaugurating new ethical standpoints in this world—of remembrance and forgiveness.[25]

Now, for Irigaray, Antigone represents a key point in the history of mankind; as a woman and as a sister she incorporates in herself three orders: of life and cosmic order, order of generations, and order of sexuate differentiation. This is how Irigaray summarizes this task:

> The law or the duty Antigone defends at the risk of her life includes three aspects that are linked together: respect for the order of the living universe and living beings, respect for the order of generation and not only genealogy, and respect for the order of sexuate difference. It is important to stress

the word "sexuate," and not "sexual," because the duty of Antigone does not concern sexuality as such, nor even its restraint as Hegel thought. If this was the case, she ought to have privileged her fiancé Haimon and not the brother. Antigone undertakes the burial of her brother because he represents a singular concrete sexuate identity that must be respected as such: "as the son of her mother." For Antigone, human identity has not yet become one, neuter, universal as Creon's order will render it. Humanity is still two: man and woman, and this duality, already existent in the natural order, must be respected, as a sort of frame, before the fulfilment of sexual attraction or desire.[26]

Antigone's decision (famously, she gives precedence to brother over the potential child or husband) shows her cosmico-ethical intuition: she cannot substitute a potential other to the concrete living other, or, even more radically, to his corpse. She must also secure an identity for herself, for her self-affection. But she must protect her dead brother, not only from decay but principally from his wandering as a ghost, being deprived of his memory, his past, and, paradoxically, his future. For Irigaray, brother and sister represent two horizontal identities: "She must secure for her brother the memory of a valid sexuate identity, and not just of an anonymous and neutralized bodily matter."[27] Again, she thus wants to preserve life and cosmic order.

This is why we cannot relate to the interpretation by Martha Nussbaum, who in her *Fragility of Goodness*, while reading Antigone and leaning (too) heavily on Hegel and other critical interpreters of Antigone's gesture, maintains that both Creon's and Antigone's acts are products of "a ruthless simplification of the world of value, which effectively eliminates conflicting obligations." Paul Ricoeur's interpretation is very close to that.[28] Nussbaum is right, of course, when she ascribes Creon's insistence on the ban on Polyneices's burial to his concern for the state: according to the Greek law, which grades the culpability of a traitor above the culpability of a foe, the traitor could not be buried within the outer bounds of the city state, as this would have credited them with a dignity they did not deserve following their offense. But Creon, on the other hand, although as a ruler he wished to ensure the welfare of the state and thus be fair, was not under any obligation to ban the burial as such—which could translate as interment outside the city boundaries and concurrent commitment to a burial organised by the victim's family (part of which includes himself; in this consists his tragedy). Creon undoubtedly took a bold and ruthless stand against the gods—albeit in the defence of the polis. Nussbaum, on the other hand, ascribes to Antigone—based also on her famous words in which she ranks her love for her brother above her love for a husband or child—"a strangely ruthless simplification of duties, corresponding not so much to any known religious law as to the exigencies of her own practical imagination."[29] So even if Nussbaum does not wish to appeal to the unwritten law according to which it would have been necessary to at least protect the exposed body of Antigone's brother, in the interpretation of Danae's suffering and reading of the fourth choral ode she nevertheless writes the following statement that puts her interpretation of Antigone in question:

> In a world, where fathers, seeking safety and control, imprison daughters and attempt to prevent the birth of their grandchildren, salvation would have to come from an extra-human source.[30]

Luce Irigaray understood Antigone precisely in connection to unwritten religious or ethical laws and family genealogies, which comprise not only relations between parents and children, but also between siblings. At first glance, Antigone may indeed be focused on darkness and death and, as Ismene also believes, is closer to the dead than to the living; but Antigone carries inside herself something very much alive, something she will not allow to be taken from her (or to be relinquished to the world) at any cost—only this can be her "madness" and at the same time her close link with Jesus: Antigone stands beyond the ontology of life and/or death, light and/or darkness, good and/or evil, and she cannot be reduced to a dichotomy or the sphere of family—and/or state. Her fundamental message is that of the exuberance of the demand for love, its excess and singularity precisely because of this incomprehension. Her demand—despite the appearance of unyielding obstinacy or unreasonable insistence—is an ethical demand made by *a daughter* and *a sister*. We shall see, later on, the interesting parallels that we can draw between Antigone and the Indian divine-heroic figure of Savitri.

Antigone's famous words, "It is my nature to join in love, not hate,"[31] represent the peak of the tragedy. Not only Hegel but also Irigaray thinks that her mission might even be higher than that of Christ. Again, Antigone's problem stays at "the turning point in the ethical thinking of our time,"[32] being in the closest vicinity of the place of *hospitality*, perhaps the central topic of all today's ethics. *Hospitality, clearly, is justice.* Hospitality is closely related to the problem of Antigone: within ancient Greek, ancient Near Eastern, Vedic, etc. contexts, hospitality clearly played a prominent role. Philosophically, hospitality first means that we are willing to acknowledge the other in his or her autonomy, without appropriating his or her subjectivity to our place, our interiority; this is what Derrida understood by unconditional hospitality. We also know that already for Levinas, the very essence of language *was* hospitality, but Irigaray, being heavily influenced by the teachings of Buddha and Yoga, will say that this place can only be secured from the *silence*.[33] Now, for Derrida, Antigone clearly had to transgress written laws "in order to offer her brothers the hospitality of the land and of burial."[34] This offering of an ultimate hospitality is furthermore accompanied with the possibility of its radicalization through what Anne Dufourmantelle has called in her commentary to Derrida's text *hospitality toward death*, which means, a hospitality offered to the dead one (as a burial), an act that of course can never be reciprocated. This act—hospitality toward death—testifies how closely tied Antigone was to the gods of the netherworld. This is also the essence of Patočka's reading of Antigone.[35] But it is not the night and death, which is feared by Creon, it is principally Antigone's mode of silence, her language, and her values that he cannot understand or, ultimately, bear.

Savitri

> Then Savitri made her husband sit close to her, and sat down on the ground herself, taking him in her arms, and laying his head in her lap.
>
> —*The Story of Sāvitrī*[36]

We now wish to move into the sphere of ancient Indian ethics and religiosity and ponder the meaning of Antigone's world through the perspective of the legend of Savitri (Sāvitrī), from the *Mahabharata*. Although the tale of Savitri is part of ancient Indian epics, it describes events from the Vedic cycle. All the gods and all the sacrifices in it, therefore, are

Vedic. The legend about Savitri is the following: Ashwapati, king of the Madra Kingdom (in the present Pakistani Punjab), is a lover of truth and peace. With his life in truth and ascetic devotion, he is a symbol of the ideal sovereign who rules with justice and love. Notwithstanding that, king Ashwapati is childless. In the hope of issue, he worships the goddess Savitri through sacred "Savitri" verses for several years, asking her for a son. The Savitri mantra (also known as the "Gayatri" strophe) is the most revered verse from the Vedas, dedicated to the sun deity Savitar, and can be found in the third book of the *Rigveda* (RV III,62,10).[37] Finally, King Ashwapati has a child—a daughter granted to him by the god Brahma and his spouse, goddess Savitri, after whom the girl receives her (divine) name. Savitri grows up to be a splendid woman of every virtue (knowledge, devotion to asceticism, honesty, truthfulness, . . .), but the father is unable to marry her off. Savitri is given permission by her father to find a husband for herself. She sets out on a journey and visits the ascetics living in the forests of the neighboring kingdom. This kingdom used to be ruled by King Dyumatsena before he was afflicted by two calamities: he went blind and lost his kingdom. But the king has no inkling of the third and greatest tragedy that awaits him. His son Satyavan (whose name means "One who speaks truth" or "Devoted to truth"), it has been predicted, has only one year of life left. After meeting Satyavan, Savitri decides he will be her husband. Although the sage Narada tells Savitri that her noble husband is destined to die one year from that day, Savitri marries him. She calculates the date of his expected death based on the prediction, and three days before its arrival takes on a strenuous ascetic or yogic fast involving meditation, vigil, and continuous standing. When the day of her husband's death—known only to Savitri, her father, and Narada—arrives, Savitri accompanies Satyavan into the forest, where he goes to gather fruit and collect brushwood. While gathering and splitting wood, Satyavan is struck with a terrible headache. Savitri appears next to him and Satyavan, in agony, lays his head in her lap. At that moment, Yama, the god of Death, comes and with his *pasha* (a sort of lasso, originally linked to the branches of a fig tree) pulls the breath out of the man, and he dies. Yama carries him toward the realm of the dead, but Savitri follows him. Her perseverance—Yama promises her various boons, from restored eyesight and a kingdom to a hundred sons for her father-in-law and a hundred brave sons for herself and Satyavan—eventually convinces Yama to allow her husband to return to life, as without him the *dharma* of her family life cannot not be fulfilled.[38]

The Story of Savitri features at the point of departure for the works of the Vedic symbolic cycle, but much of its content dates back to even earlier periods of ancient Indus Valley civilization (Harappa, Mohenjo-daro) and its contacts reaching all the way to Mesopotamia. The gods and people in it are still part of the process of creating and preserving life as a broader cosmic principle of reciprocity and interconnection through sacrifice, while death (and the related knowledge about immortality) in the context of this late-Vedic period (the time when the key *Upanishads* were formed, as well as the *Mahabharata* and the Samkhya-Yoga school), slowly transformed into a fundamental philosophical and theological/eschatological problem.[39] Gradually, the first elements of the later Hindu (mono)theistic religiosity, which would bring gods such as Brahma, Vishnu, and Shiva to the forefront, also take shape. But *The Story of Savitri* is still set at the margins between these two periods (Vedic poly- or henotheistic Brahmanism and subsequent theistic Hinduism) when, for the first time in the history of Indian philosophy and religion, there also emerges the ethical principle of karma as the scale of the afterlife based on the positive or negative consequences of acts. Owing to the difficult time of transition, the roles of the gods in the story are not clearly defined (in later Hindu religion, the goddess Savitri is the partner or spouse of the supreme god Brahma, but in our narration she is probably still the daughter of the Sun deity Savitar; nevertheless, in this tale, the goddess Savitri appeals to the mercy or grace of the heavenly father), so the legend should be taken as part of the early cosmological Vedic cycle despite the presence of certain later elements in it.

The crucial passage in *The Story of Savitri* is the point where Satyavan, after leaving for the abode of the dead (i.e., when he actually dies), returns among the living through the intervention of his wife. Savitri expresses that with the following words, which clearly convey what we wish to be understood in this book under the term *matrixial logic of love*:

> You have indeed slept for a long time on my lap, noble sir. And the blessed god Yama, the constrainer of mankind, has gone.

Satyavan, who is unaware of what occurred that evening, responds:

> I came out with you, graceful lady, to collect fruits, and then while I was chopping wood, a pain arose in my head. . . . I

fell asleep in your lap—this is all I remember. And while I was embraced by you, my mind was stolen away by sleep.[40]

The expressions that *The Story of Savitri* has put before us are here manifestly connected to the feminine logic of the lap, embrace, and care for the other, which shifts the logic of heroism from the sphere of war and violence into the firmament of love and tenderness. In her dialogue with Yama, the god of the dead, Savitri speaks about love, mercy, trust, selflessness, justice, and kindness in a language of a radical and superhuman/divine ethical perseverance-for-the-other and thereby supreme *hope*. Yama thus brings Satyavan back from the realm of death and returns him to Savitri, divinizing them both, as he predicts both will live until the age of four hundred years. While *The Story of Savitri* and the motif of resurrection (not only the motifs of rebirth/reincarnation or redemption in death) represent a unique Indian version of the gospel story of Lazarus, its ethical precept about the superiority of love over vengeance and hate stands side by side with Jesus's New Testament teachings about the predominance of love and compassion over the language of hatred, violence, and revenge. In his reading, the Indian interpreter Deshpande sees in Savitri an avatar of the homonymous goddess, who came into the world to save *dharma*. At the same time, Vlasta Pacheiner-Klander, a Slovene Sanskrit expert, recognizes in the so-called truth sayings from *The Story of Savitri* that which decisively defines a righteous or virtuous man (*sat purusha*): this is the highest Indian ethical teaching (which is only present in this form in Buddhism and Jainism) of *ahimsa*—non-harming or nonviolence in relation to any creature, compassion for one's enemy, and, ultimately, acting without any thought of reward.[41]

But let us return to the key question in this story: Why did Savitri need to bring her husband back into life? Why was it not possible for Satyavan, in his own death—the death of a righteous man threatened by no karmic punishment in the afterlife since he was, as a mortal, unblemished—to be left in the realm of the dead?

In his explanation of *The Story of Savitri*, the Indian interpreter Subhash Anand may perhaps have gone a step farther than some of his colleagues: to him, Savitri's action is simply, yet extremely subtly, an expression of *the love that conquers death*.[42] This is no doubt a powerful thought: How is it possible for a conception like that to emerge in the midst of ancient Indian religiosity, which has always been (but for a few bright exceptions, such as Gargi Vachaknavi's role of wise arbitress in the *brahmodyas*, theological discussions, in the early *Upanishads*) dominated by Brahmanic masculine logic? The answer is concealed in the hidden matrixial logic of *The Story of Savitri*, and we believe that its message transcends its time and reveals to us even today in a singular version of the old myth from the pre-Vedic as well as Vedic cosmic cycles. The myth guided by Savitri is a unique act of a mortal/immortal (Savitri in both her roles; it seems, and numerous interpreters have emphasized this, that Savitri is at the same time a mortal and an incarnation of the Goddess), who wants to establish, once and for all, a cosmic order based on justice, love, and peace. Only Savitri as a woman can understand this cosmic constellation and put it into effect, thanks to her exceptional insight into and perception of the hidden logic of the link between life and death *in love*. Only love in its abundance or excess can bestow immortality (Skt. *amrita*) on people.

To understand this special and singular role of Savitri as a heroine and a savior, it is necessary to set her act into a somewhat broader cosmic/mythological context. But let us return to the initial question: Why was it necessary to bring Satyavan back into life? Satyavan and Savitri are a couple living a life of complete commitment, mutual respect, and affection, of the *dharma* fulfilled in a man-woman relationship. The prophecy that allots Satyavan, the one who is devoted to truth, only one further year of life is unjust, and Savitri cannot accept it. As Deshpande finds, "This cannot be accepted as the eternal fact of existence."[43] It seems that Savitri was born (or reincarnated on the Earth) to transcend suffering and grief and reveal a path of hope. In this, her role is close to that of Jesus, or Joshua, if you wish, as the one who was able to show people the superiority of love and hope over hatred and who could also convey the promise of immortality. In a somewhat more symbolic reading, which is frequent among Indian interpreters, Savitri, as a member of the Sun genealogy (with the Vedic gods Surya and Savitar in the forefront) is that light of the spirit that can conquer the darkness of ignorance, falseness, and related eternal suffering, misery, even hatred among people. In this account, Savitri is associated with the power of *knowledge* and the related faith, which only can lead the way toward overcoming ignorance. Her cosmic genealogy and mission were described by Sri Aurobindo in his famous poem with the following glorifying words that place her, in a unique way, in the sphere of the divine-maternal. Aurobindo's characterization of Savitri comprises all the aforementioned elements, linking them with a deep philosophical, cosmological and theological meaning that is difficult to match, even in the Indian tradition itself:

> Calm was her face and courage kept her mute.
> Yet only her outward self suffered and strove;
> Even her humanity was half divine;
> Her spirit opened to the Spirit in all,
> Her nature felt all Nature as its own.
> Apart, living within, all lives she bore;
> Aloof, she carried in herself the world.
> Her dread was one with the great cosmic dread,
> Her strength was founded on the cosmic mights;
> The universal Mother's love was hers.
> Against the evil at life's afflicted roots,
> Her own calamity its private sign. . . .[44]

In this exceptional excerpt from his poem, Aurobindo knew precisely that Savitri—now already in her divine-human likeness—was the bearer of the earliest genealogical order, that is, of the ancient or archaic ontology of love, which derives from the very germ of primeval being that was there even before the split into being and nonbeing, good and evil, life and death, and even divine and human. Savitri, who feels all Nature inside her, was sent into this world to found a new lineage of people existing out of this germ of primeval love, and this is exactly what makes up her love, which our Indian poet calls the love of the universal Mother. This is an original thought that cannot be recalled to pre-Vedic, Vedic, or post-Vedic periods (for example, Samkhya-Yoga), as, in it Savitri is understood and presented as the deliverer of justice and hope into this world.

It is important to take into account two other significant aspects of this story. First, that what Luce Irigaray designates with sexual difference and (divine) couples, is in the ancient Indian religions already represented in the form of divine couples, among them Brahma and Savitri (Yama and Yami are also in close relation to this). It seems that Indian religiosity of the earliest age (including the pre-Vedic cults and Shaktist traditions, regardless of the concurrent Brahmanic ideology and its masculine genealogies) is closely associated with the task of gaining sexually defined identity through religion and is thus in the very proximity of the ideal of justice. Second, it is also important to take into account that after king Ashwapati had wished for a child and worshipped the goddess Savitri with a poem about her, he was granted *a daughter*. Luce Irigaray believes that daughters play a special role in cosmic and generational orders: they are women born from women and, as such, bearers of a different type of genealogy compared to men, a genealogy that is not accessible to men.[45] The princess/goddess Savitri undoubtedly represents this genealogical element. And then there are other genealogies, the kind that are presented within the rules of kinship that Savitri abided by (some of these worked analogously to Antigone and were stigmatized as incestuous relationships);[46] nevertheless, the autonomy of her acts links her to the autonomy of the argument of key Upanishadic women, such as Gargi Vachaknavi from the Upanishadic theological tradition, or *brahmodyas*.[47] And ultimately—this will be our next point—the Savitri legend is characterized by similar cosmic relationships or cosmic symbols to those from the religious background of *Antigone*. This makes it possible to go a step farther: according to Asko Parpola, Savitri as a goddess and daughter of the Sun (the god Savitar) is connected to "the first dawn." She is called *prasavitri*—for her roles of "procreatrix, mother, bestowing progeny."[48] As such, she inhabits the threshold between night and day, between not-yet-life and life, between death and creation/resurrection, with femininity and masculinity represented in their different roles, but undoubtedly with a powerful message of cooperation or interplay between the sexes in this cosmic game of creating and preserving life.[49]

In her role, Savitri as a person will now come closer to what Luce Irigaray anticipates as the future task of philosophy—not the one presented in the works of male philosophers (Irigaray mentions Sartre, Merleau-Ponty, and Levinas), in which the woman is reduced to a certain state of passivity and the man (or at least philosopher) to activity. In her role, Savitri represents the ancient cosmic generational and sexual orders, cognate with the elements of female action that Luce Irigaray propounds in her interpretation of *Antigone*, and, especially, in her work *The Mystery of Mary*. Irigaray's interpretation of Mary will later be highlighted; suffice it to say that extremely interesting parallels are already outlined here with Savitri, particularly if we take into account that in her work, Irigaray frequently makes direct references to Indian spirituality, including ancient traditions of the pre-Vedic proto-Shaktism, which come to the fore in reading Savitri.[50]

Irigaray's Mary is a completely new cosmic/theological savior figure. As we shall see—and here we are only referring to her in the context of a contemplation about Savitri—she can be comprehended in broader terms than those proposed by current dogmatic explications, although even these contain a wide range of possible interpretations and reinterpretations of her veiled ontological edifice. Irigaray's interpretation opens with the following words:

> The angel reminds Mary of the fact that she will be unable to give birth to a divine child, and in particular a son, without committing herself to being faithful to the virginity of her own breath: a reserve of soul capable of receiving and of sharing with the other, and of respecting its difference, as such, without betraying her own spiritual life.[51]

In Irigaray, Mary is closely connected to breath: as we know from the Old Testament texts already, God creates with his breath. Due to the precedence that the spiritual/metaphysical principle held over corporeality in Western Christian tradition (and, consequently, with masculine genealogies firmly *immobilizing* breath into stable spiritual categories, beginning with Plato and then all through Hegel and Husserl), breath has been allotted relatively little space. The exception that deserves to be mentioned here is the case of Christian Hesychasts, among them primarily St. Gregory Palamas. His mystical physiology (cf. Indian chakras) and the theory of breathing (cf. yoga) are most certainly a well of spirituality too often neglected or forgotten in the course of history. One chakra is located in the thorax, and it is the focal point also mentioned by Irigaray in her Mary—as she, with her hands folded on her chest (and her closed lips expressing silence, contemplation, and concentration), according to Irigaray's interpretation, preserves and protects her vital breath and thereby her autonomy.[52] For this reason, as Irigaray perspicaciously finds, some icons depict the Infant Jesus in this very spot. Breathing in Mary is what connects her with the entire cosmos; her breathing "unites, without rupture, the most subtle aspects of the cosmos and body with that which is most spiritual in the soul."[53] Thus, even in the Christian context, the holding of breath can signify that this breath that inside our body transforms into love can be shared with others—and Mary's virginity (now understood as a protected place of spiritual autonomy of a young woman) is to Irigaray the original code of this process. The sacred possibility of breathing may also be found in Saint Teresa of Avila, who cultivated special methods of calming the rhythm of breathing. There is another thinker close to the sacred breath who knew this—Paul Claudel, who described it in his poem about Saint Teresa of Avila:

> To illuminate the clay and make it capable of heaven and hell,
> God joined to it, outside time and place in itself,
> yet in a primordial relationship with our flesh,
> that knowledgeable soul in us that makes of our body an instrument of desire,
> constantly busy breathing so as not to die . . .
> Thus, once odorous vapour and now the sun of our night,
> Therese is resplendent in the breath of the Holy Spirit![54]

Like Savitri and Mary, Saint Teresa of Avila is here linked with breath as well as with light and the highest spiritual realization. In Savitri, who led an ascetic life and before her act performed a difficult yogic meditative fast with nocturnal vigil, which later became known under the term *vata-savitri-vrata*, the focus was on the meditative breath, and precisely because she kept a reserve of this vital breath in her, she could, at the moment of Satyavan's death (when Yama, with his lasso, extracted breath from Satyavan's body), recover his soul (breath) and give him his life back—her essential mission.

Let us, in conclusion, return to Savitri one last time: justice can only be established where care and compassion exist in the world. This has nothing to do with the *sati* ritual or a heroic death, as it is understood later in Hinduism through the act of the wife's departure into death together with her husband (that is why the ritual is also called *sahagamana*, lit. "departing/going (away) with"). In this ritual, the ancient cosmic respect for sexual difference is already lost. Deshpande is therefore right to present the message of the legend in the sense of incarnation of the goddess Savitri, who enters this world with the purpose of saving *dharma*. In Deshpande's eyes, Savitri is a symbol of Mother Nature (*prakriti*), which has to be understood not through some philosophical explanation (such as, for example, the ontology of the mentioned Samkhya-Yoga school), but rather in a more primary, cosmic/ethical way, as caring for life, the different generational orders, their issue and prolific growth. In Indian tradition, just as in all other world traditions, the sensibility in regard to the feminine aspect that was present in the original cosmogony (cf. for example Metis, Demeter, and Kore in Greek mythology or analogous Middle Eastern genealogies) was later lost or covered by the thick detritus of Brahmanic ideology and its variant of *dharma* based on the submission and oppression of women.

Savitri is thus for us a cosmic/divine figure of the highest faith in love, its power that extends above death itself, a co-savior and deliverer of hope into a realm beyond the life and death dyad, or, as Deshpande says: "She has established something new in the process on this earth."[55] To conclude: we are inhabitants of a world in which suffering, death, and evil form an equal part. Our task as humans, in our masculine and feminine identities, is to secure in our interiorities (through ethical gestures such as caress and compassion) and in our intersubjective relations the hospitable place for the others/guests/enemies, including animal others in this world. Only in this care has a cosmic justice the possibility to emerge in spaces between us—and enliven and ethically trespass the sacred threshold between Gods and mortals, nature/earth/nether/world and heavens. There is only one transcendence, then: the transcendence of a cosmic order, securing to all cultures and all persons their identity, their unique, respected, and hospitable place within the cosmos, and one *justice*.

(Alcestis)

In closing this chapter, we would like to tie in our thought with the Greek heroine Alcestis, who might, in her mythological and social roles, seemingly paradoxical and difficult to understand, represent a bridge in the relationship between Antigone and Savitri. While Antigone with her suicide protects the unwritten law, thus establishing the ground zero of ethics, Savitri is the one who, as a woman, reclaims her husband's life and thereby secures him progeny. Antigone and Savitri appear at the very boundary between life and death, and while Antigone crosses this boundary, Savitri returns from its margins into life. Alcestis's place is next to Antigone and Savitri at the same time, as she dies (by way of a mysterious self-sacrifice), but resurrects or is brought back to life, although, as we shall see, not entirely. We can say that, besides

Antigone, it is precisely Alcestis who stands as the example of the Greek heroine acting out of the highest cosmic/ethical principles and whose act (her dying for her husband and the related ontology of life and death) can through Euripides's otherwise idiosyncratic play nevertheless suggest a deeper message than we are willing to acknowledge at first glance.

Alcestis was a daughter of the famous King Pelias, associated with the story of the Golden Fleece—it was he, in fact, who sent Jason on a quest for this precious treasure. Upon Jason's return, Medea advised Pelias's daughters to cut and boil their father in magic herbs to rejuvenate him. But that was a trick; Pelias's daughters followed Medea's counsel, but instead of thus restoring their father's youth, they killed him. The only one who did not take part in this was his daughter Alcestis. This already seems to indicate that she will not accept the irruption into the principles of cosmic justice and the inherent laws of life and death. Because of that, she is considered the most compassionate among Pelias's children. One of the Argonauts was Admetus, king of Pherae and Alcestis's husband, and his story, too, has to do with the laws of life and death. Admetus welcomed the god Apollo at his court when the latter was banished from Olympus: Apollo was being punished for killing the Cyclopes—which he did in revenge for Zeus's having killed his son the god-healer Asclepius, who was able to resurrect the dead, by striking him with the thunderbolts forged for Zeus by the Cyclopes. Admetus offered Apollo shelter, and in return the god conferred great benefits on him—even possible help in becoming immortal. When Admetus married Alcestis, he offended Apollo's sister Artemis (by neglecting to make the required sacrifice to her at his wedding) and thus brought down upon himself the wrath of the goddess, who in revenge sent a nest of snakes to the bedchamber to kill Admetus; but Apollo came to his aid.[56] This is where Euripides's play begins: the Moirai have now decided that Admetus's fated day of death has come, but Apollo persuades them to reprieve Admetus if he can find someone to die in his place: "[T]hey promised me, those goddesses of fate, that Admetus should escape the impending doom, if he found a substitute for the powers below."[57] This is where Alcestis steps forth. First, Admetus tries to persuade his elderly parents to go into death for him, but with no success, so his wife offers to die in his place. In this way, Alcestis decides to save her husband. But since she is also a mother—she has a son and a daughter—she demands from the husband that he provide unconditionally for the future of their children (royal honors for the son and a noble spouse for her daughter, i.e., she wants them both to become sovereigns) and that, after her death—again in protection of her children—he never take another woman into their house: "Take thou my place and be a mother to these babes," she says finally and leaves into death.[58] At the end of the play, after Alcestis's death, the hero Heracles defeats the hound of Hades and Thanatos (Death) itself, and brings Alcestis back, unrecognizably covered by a veil and mute. Alcestis thus passes from death back into life. There exist various interpretations of her act, and we would like to highlight the one by Svetlana Slapšak, who recognizes in Alcestis's actions and words a political act of establishment or self-constitution as a wife and citizen. Slapšak says:

> The unnatural wish of a citizen to prolong a life determined by fate—and this aspiration is to a Greek a *hybris*, for even gods defer to fate—is being rectified by a woman who is introducing balance. . . . Alcestis's demands are in truth an establishment of new rules and new criteria–the rights of a wife, the rights of a mother, the rights of a woman to full citizenship.[59]

By extending the duration of his life, Admetus tried to outsmart destiny, but the price for that is extremely high: the sacrifice and thereby death of another human being, in his case, the very mother of his children. Besides Alcestis's above described *demand*, the key point of this Euripides play (which some classify in the cross-genre of tragicomedy) can be understood from the following passage from the play, specifically, from the dialogue between the father and the son, in which the son is trying to convince the father to die in his place. The father answers:

> Die not thou for me, nor I for thee. Thy joy is in the light,
> think'st thou thy sire's is not? By Heaven! 'tis a weary while,
> I trow, that time beneath the earth, and life, though short,
>   is sweet.
> Thou at least didst struggle hard to 'scape thy death, lost
>   to shame,
> And by her death dost live beyond thy destined term.

> Dost thou then speak of cowardice in me, thou craven
>   heart!
> No match for thy wife, who hath died for thee, her fine
>   young lord?
> A clever scheme has thou devised to stave off death for
>   ever,
> If thou canst persuade each new wife to die instead of thee.[60]

Considering all the known elements—Admetus's most cowardly cunning, expediency, absence of moral shame and sense of piety or respect for divine laws, as well as the fact that he breaks all his promises to his wife—there is another element, related to Alcestis's demand and her act, and for which she can be considered a feminist heroine. Alcestis's deed is of a cosmic/ethical order and therefore comparable to Antigone's and Savitri's: through his gesture, Admetus conveys much more than is suggested by his apparently egoistic artifice, which might in truth originate from fear alone—when his father tells him that he could negotiate immortality this way, he exposes the core of the problem of this extraordinary Euripidean play. With her act, Alcestis not only protects her children against becoming fatherless and against Admetus's cowardice, but by dying for the other she joins the order of those divine and human beings, heroes and heroines, who do not allow irruption into this world that would perturb the unwritten laws of life and death, and thereby intimacy and loyalty and, as a final consequence, love. Therefore, although some interpreters (including Plato in *The Symposium*)[61] say that Alcestis sacrificed her life out of supreme and absolute love of her husband, such an idea would be essentially antiethical and destructive to the thinking of sexual difference and the related respect for sexual and associated family orders or genealogies. In reality, Alcestis—as a woman, mother, and citizen—gave her life *for* love; her demand, which now dwells hidden behind the shroud of appearance (her veil) and language or voice (silence), comes precisely from the exuberance of love, and she, the noblest of her sex,[62] after resurrecting from the grave and coming back into life, is no longer the same Alcestis as before. Having touched Death, she can now serve as an admonition, and not only to Admetus, who is forlorn after the subsequent encounter with her uncanniness and, indeed, destroyed as a human being.[63] Alcestis is an admonition, and for us, mere mortals, a fearsome and an uncanny specter of love.

Antigone . . .
    who has lived in the vicinity of elements,
close to vegetal beings and little animals.
    Touching sand and earth, giving alms to the poor . . .
Antigone who liked it so much
to share her tender words with her little dog.
And who buried her dead brother with the baby shovel
that once belonged to
    him . . .
In this world ruled by too many Creons,
    Antigone cannot live anymore.[64]

elemental drops

2

METIS / LEPA VIDA

The Tragic Death of Fair Vida and its Ethical Consequences

In a story from Slovene folk tradition, an original mythical ballad titled *Lepa Vida* (*Fair Vida*) a young mother is searching for genuine—or absolute/unconditional—hospitality for her child and family; but being only a woman, she is forcibly taken away into a foreign land under the guise of hospitality. The central message of this literary motif, which refers both to individuals and cultures that are victims of threats or kidnapping (or colonization—in political terms) at the hand of the more powerful and are personally, culturally, or politically subordinate, essentially points to the lack or void in the very structure of world community and to its violated laws of justice and hospitality in every historical period. The legend about Fair Vida, a young woman with a sick child, originates in the Mediterranean and dates to the Early Middle Ages (between the ninth and eleventh centuries). Driven by pure maternal wish to help her sick son, Fair Vida boards the ship of a foreign merchant who promised to give her a medicine for her child. Instead of giving her the medicine, the merchant tricks her, kidnapping her and taking her away from her home. When Fair Vida realizes the horrible truth and its fatal consequences (she will never see her child again), in one of the variants of the poem preserved, she jumps overboard in despair and drowns in the middle of the Mediterranean Sea. In the variant recorded in writing by Slovenian ethnographer Anton Breznik in 1898 in Ihan (Slovenia), Fair Vida, in the culminating moment of the poem, thinks about her child and how he would grow up motherless, makes the sign of the cross, and plunges into the sea.[1] The story about Fair Vida and her tragic death holds much more than we might be willing to admit. It is an expression of the mythological thinking that reaches past usual explanations. Fair Vida is a point of special mythological *marking* or reaction to the interruption of the old genealogical orders (mother-daughter/child) that have been disrupted throughout history by essentially violent modes of dwelling. As such, Vida's act transgresses or excludes any gesture of an absolute sacrificial womanhood: it rather gestures toward an absolute ethical demand of Antigone.

But what is the connection between femininity and water? This reflection takes us first to the ancient Greek goddess Metis, one of the first Oceanids and according to certain traditions also the first love of Zeus. Metis is also the goddess who suffered the untimely fate of being obliterated from mythology in the worst possible form of divine cannibalism (theophagy), and, consequently, of seeing her primary maternal role exiled. Shé Hawke explains that Metis met with "ontological and epistemological extinction"[2] or persecution, because Zeus (who suspected she was a threat to his future) devoured her when she was pregnant—carrying her daughter in her womb—and declared that he gave birth to Athena from his own head, resulting in the "maternal loss of Metis, and the advance of the masculine enterprise."[3] Thus, in the earliest phase of Greek religion, Zeus violently and unambiguously interrupts the fundamental genealogical/cosmological connection between the mother and her child or, more specifically, daughter (cf. Demeter and Kore-Persephone) and grounds the antimatrixial[4] logic in the very nucleus of Greek mythological thinking—emphatically even, by taking over the role of mother/procreatrix himself. Once the new order of Olympus is established Metis is not mentioned again in popular myth. Her fate is thus similar to the fates of the Erinyes, who could, in the context of the early mythological era, still accompany Antigone, but later completely disappeared from the sphere of the divine. Creon, too, is heir to these developments. But if Zeus belongs to the fifth (Olympian) generation of Greek gods, then it is Metis the goddess who still preserves the direct link with the first generation of pre-Olympic (Orphic) deities, with the first, primeval era of origination and creation of the world. Metis is thus the primordial feminine divine, connected to the very beginning of the world or cosmogony.

Part of ancient Greek mythology links Metis to the "primordial moisture emanating from the splitting of the 'Cosmic egg'"[5] into the tripartite Phanes, Metis, and Erikepaios. This is mentioned in Orphic theologies, and other, more modern sources. Some versions describe Aether and Chaos as primordial Water and producers of the Cosmic Egg. Other versions predate Chaos as the origin, referring instead to the primordial form of the first triadic principle Phanes/Metis/Erikapaios.[6] Hawke, who chooses to await Metis's return by way of contemplating the coming God/dess, says that she is thus seen as the "maternal water deity of All, and mother of Athena, contrary to popular myth that references Zeus as ruler, father and mother to Athena and the world."[7] That is also why Walter F. Otto rightfully states in his work *The Homeric Gods* that "in prehistoric religion the feminine essence was dominant."[8] Marcel Detienne, eventually, says about this myth:

> The Orphic theologians gave the name of Metis (and those of *Phanes*, the Dazzling one, he who appears and makes things appear, and *Protogonos*, the First-Born) to the great primordial deity which, upon emerging from the cosmic egg, carried within it the seed of all the gods, the germ of all things, and which, as the first creator, brought into the light the entire universe.... For the Orphics, Metis is no longer regarded as female.... Metis now becomes an androgynous god with a twofold nature, being both male and female.... Metis is no longer a woman and subordinate to Zeus.... In the fifth generation of the gods, (the sceptre having passed from Phanes-Metis to *Nux* or Night and thence through Ouranos and Kronos into Zeus' hands), Zeus swallows Phanes-Metis and deposits it inside his stomach.... In this way a "second creation" can take place, similar to the first, the creation of Phanes-Metis.[9]

Because Metis has been appropriated and removed from story in this way, she therefore suffers from the early form of what Luce Irigaray understands in her work as *matricide*—the displacement and appropriation of the original space of sexual difference by patriarchy and its power relations. The result is the disappearance of female genealogic orders—a "maternal asylum,"[10] which, as we have seen, still defined the earlier mythological era.[11]

But if we return to Fair Vida—her death is not natural. It is an act closely connected to Antigone's claim. On the surface level it first reveals as an act of desperation, a suicide out of despair, but—once we relate it to the Antigone's act—it becomes an ethical deed with one sole purpose: to prevent—once and for all—the brutal irruption of injustice into this world. According to Patricia J. Mills, already Hegel fails to discuss Antigone's suicide, and as argued:

When the chorus declares: "What woman has ever found your way to death?," it reveals Antigone as unique, as the exception to female behaviour, and therefore as a transitional character, not the paradigm of pagan divine law as represented by woman. While embodying the tragic conflict between particular and universal, Antigone also represents the history of the revolt of women who act in the public sphere on behalf of the private sphere, the sphere of inaction. She is the precursor of the women who, in the recent past, proclaimed the personal as political.[12]

Now, Fair Vida also cannot accept that the fundamental cosmic laws (life as a maternal genealogy, taking of a child, interruption of the mother-child link) be so viciously attacked or violated. By her act she demands the restoration of the eternal justice that at that moment cannot yet be guaranteed to her child and family—as it was not to the numerous victims in the Mediterranean Sea and anywhere else—but there is hope that in the future, an eternal justice might be present among women and men. The early Greek goddesses could still be the guardians and representatives of the ancient orders that constituted "a bond between parents, children, and siblings."[13] These goddesses were still able to protect pregnant women and their unborn children, daughters and sons, brothers and sisters in regard to their authentic birth and genealogical rights. But they do not appear any more in the world of Antigone and Fair Vida. In this sense, the ultimate protective act of Fair Vida is connected to the sphere of the divine.

Forgotten Layers of Ethics

The proto-ethical thought of ancient cosmologies (of Egypt and Mesopotamia, ancient Indo-European cultures, and other unjustly marginalized civilizational and cultural loci throughout world history)[14] was therefore forgotten or suppressed by new masculine orders in order to ground and develop new ontologies in ethics. These ontologies have destabilized the world, suppressed and forgotten the ancient proto-religious/ethical criterion, and established and inaugurated a world of unjust justice,[15] being ignorant of cosmic, sexual, generational, and cultural differences. In this world, the monosubjective Self governs and guides both epistemological as well as ontological enterprises. Our gods remain distant and do not want to accept our offerings—the many compassions and many hospitalities we offer. In Sophocles's *Antigone*, Creon is haunted and cursed by Erinyes, the goddesses, whose altars were polluted by his acts:

> Then know thou—aye, know it well—that thou shalt not live through many more courses of the sun's swift chariot, ere one begotten of thine own loins shall have been given by thee, a corpse for corpses; because thou hast thrust children of the sunlight to the shades and ruthlessly lodged a living soul in the grave; but keepest in this world one who belongs to the gods infernal, a corpse unburied, unhonoured, all unhallowed. In such thou hast no part, nor have the gods above, but this is a violence done to them by thee. Therefore the avenging destroyers lie in wait for thee, the Furies of Hades and of the gods, that thou mayest be taken in these same ills.[16]

The understanding of this world is marked by its feminine cosmic character: whatever disturbs cosmic laws not only disturbs the sacred order of life and death, but also transgresses an ancient order of hospitality—the sanctity of the dinner table[17]—which relates to the care of those who seek refuge and shelter in our house, at our hearth. In his reading of Antigone, Heidegger interprets the hearth as Being: not our stranger, whom we did not invite to our home and offer the hospitality of our dinner table, but we ourselves have been expelled from the hearth (*der Herd ist das Sein*) and now "stand outside of Being."[18] It is thus our own strangeness, the strangeness of our being, which leads us to ignorance for the life and for the being of the other—on which we will elaborate later. The Erinyes are thus the highest ancient guardians of the cosmic genealogies—those of life and death, of hospitality, and of generational orders (parents and their children, brothers and sisters).[19] We have forgotten those laws; we have also lost our relation to the elements, to the earth and waters, wind (breath) and fire (Sun) as begetters and guardians of our lives. Even Prometheus, in his suffering, calls upon these elements—as witnesses to the injustice he has been enduring, and as witnesses to his broken being:

> O you bright sky of heaven, you swift-winged breezes, you river-waters, and infinite laughter of the waves of ocean, O universal mother Earth, and you, all-seeing orb of the sun, to you I call! See what I, a god, endure from the gods![20]

There is a need for new ethical criteria in today's unjust world. Since the early times of the history of philosophy, Western philosophers have been in a search of a new ethics. In a series of attempts to ground a new ethics, these efforts resulted in the history of ethics, culminating for the first time in Kant's system of morals.[21] Later, nineteenth- and twentieth-century critical thought (Feuerbach, Marx, and Nietzsche; intercultural philosophy, feminism, postcolonial philosophy, liberation philosophy, deconstruction, and phenomenology) convincingly showed the insufficiency of the Western ethical model with reason/rationality as its sole criterion. Thus, as a result, Enrique Dussel points out (radically, but correctly) that today, neither in Europe nor in the United States, "an absolutely postconventional morality [is] possible."[22] For Dussel, the possibility of this other or new morality builds on the "'great critics' (Feuerbach, Schopenhauer, Nietzsche, Horkheimer, Adorno, Marcuse, and particularly Marx, Freud, and Levinas) and the Latin American experience"[23] with its inherent criticism of Modernity and any form of domination (in the systems of ethics, politics, and economics and in relations between "races," dominant and marginalized cultures, between sexes, hierarchies of age, etc.). However, to this group of thinkers it is important to add Schelling, who stood at the very beginning of this critical line of thinking and whose influence, as Dussel shows, spread among the many immediate listeners of his Berlin lectures—such as Feuerbach and Kierkegaard, or Engels and Bakunin. In his lectures from 1842–43, Schelling approached philosophy from the "positive" point of view and declared old ("negative") metaphysics as positing the "first source of knowledge in the pure understanding."[24] For Schelling, the new approach is now to be referred to under the heading of "metaphysical empiricism" and is in its essence directly linked to the content of *life*.[25] But not only life, for death also constitutes part of this logic; in his *Clara*, Schelling argues: "Shouldn't we generally more often observe the same sensitivity to the departed that we believe we owe to the living?"[26] With this, in the midst of the critical and positive era of philosophy, Schelling already knows intuitively that in order to secure peace for future generations, we have to secure peace for those that passed away. Our care is for them and our hospitality also extends its sensitivities to their dwellings.

On Hospitality and Ethical Symptomatology

In order to proceed toward the new ethical criterion that we intend to present and defend in this book, we offer the following hypothesis: there are two ontological genealogies guiding our ethical lives—the first is the ontology of thinking (which is transcendental) and the second is ontology of love (which is empirical). The topic of hospitality—which represents one of the key questions in today's world—can be a part of both ontologies but it only expresses itself in a "material" way within the latter. We will see that hospitality builds upon compassion; both must be understood and felt as a part of a new material-maternal-matrixial ethics. According to Derrida—and this indeed is the secret core of compassion—"one doesn't know *why one trembles*."[27] Ancient Greek, Semitic, and Sanskrit words for compassion all testify equally for this ethics of compassion; they all relate us to the most intimate bodily phenomena of trembling for/with the other, such as Greek verb *spagkhnízomai* ("to be moved by visceral compassion"), the Hebrew word *rakhamim* ("matrixial compassion"), or the Sanskrit Vedic and Buddhist terms *ridudara* and *anukampa* ("compassionate inside" and "compassionate co-trembling"). All these sacred words testify for the *inside* as a locus of compassionate feelings, and also as a locus of hospitality.[28]

We pay homage to *our* civic laws of compassion and *our* civic laws of hospitality, but these were not *their* laws. In the future, we must bring our laws of compassion and hospitality to bear upon this difficult—indeed, impossible—thought. The philosophical genre that testifies to this intrusion we will now refer to as *lamentation*—the lamentation for the thousands of deaths. In *The Gift of Death*, as already noted, Derrida inaugurated the philosophical discipline that can now be put in the closest vicinity to the new material ethics or thinking of the body: this is *philosophical symptomatology*. We need to come to that "cause closest to our body, that which means that one trembles or weeps rather than doing something else," as he puts it.[29] Interiority and exteriority, inside and outside; our tears (and their hidden memory of the primeval and all-encompassing cosmic waters) are able to transgress this invisible border between the body and soul, debordering them at the very threshold, which is pain, in its most elemental form; lamentation, tears, and our sadness—our longest compassion for the pain of mothers, fathers, and children at the shores of this world, for the hospitality that did not come, with Derrida: "God is the cause of the *mysterium tremendum*, and the death that is given is always what makes us tremble, or what makes us weep as well."[30] But let us now continue with this questioning of hospitality and compassion with the following words of a great Tibetan philosopher, Dzong-ka-ba, on compassion:

> Candrakirti's homage to compassion observing phenomena is: Homage to compassion viewing migrators as evanescent

or momentarily disintegrating, like a moon in the water stirred by a breeze. His homage to compassion observing the unapprehendable is: Homage to compassion viewing migrators as empty of inherent existence, though they appear to exist inherently, like the reflection of the moon in the water.[31]

According to the Buddhist philosophy, sentient beings do not have a permanent nature; they are composed of impermanent aggregates, based on the Buddhist Mahayana theory of dependent origination and the emptiness (*shunyata*) of all existence. This is the Buddhist metaphysical-material view of the human person and compassion. But there is an intrusion into this logic, which requires from us another view of justice, of compassion, and perhaps hospitality. The intrusion transfers migrators to concrete migrators; we all have been distant witnesses of their deaths, of children, little sisters and brothers, of their mothers and fathers, being drowned in the water, disappearing from the surface, becoming only a reflection for us, being reflected in a terrifying way; disintegrating in front of our eyes, they are the worst possible intrusion into the cosmic order, as depicted by the Buddhist and other ancient cosmologies (Metis and Erinyes, but also other similar genealogies in ancient Greek, ancient Near Eastern, and ancient Vedic religions).[32] Already Sophocles's Antigone testifies to this kind of violent death: being violent even toward dead bodies, which are prevented from finding their rest in peace—this is what dangerously interrupts the cosmic order. Without hospitality, there is no peace. Hence, gods refuse to take our offerings; our lamentations, sorrows, they all come *plus tard* (Levinas). For us, the bodies and the souls, as forever lost in the Mediterranean Sea, and elsewhere, were emptied of inherent existence, but in a manner that perverts the ontological and ethical order. Between them and us there was a bond that has been broken; between us and them there was a threshold, but as a place without our visitation: first designating *cháos*, or a primeval gap, difference, grief (*der Schmerz; das Unter-schied*),[33] as in the ancient Greek (Hesiod) or ancient Indian (Vedic) cosmogonies—as a threshold, this dwelling on the plane of the first ontological difference between Being and non-Being, which can only be secured and, as it were, carried over with love and hospitality, our welcome of the other. There was no compassion or hospitality offered for them when they needed it, nobody was able to give them shelter in the moments when they needed it most. Who is able to liberate us from this ignorance? According to Bracha Ettinger and her ethics of femininity, compassion and hospitality are related to the matrixial (womb/mother) sphere: what must become our home, habitation, and what, at the same moment is the most vulnerable of all, is a "creative gesture in *copoiesis*"—of me for the (m)other, which only brings care to this world.[34] This care, feminine or maternal (*rakhamim*) in its character, is represented by the primeval compassionate and corporeal relation of the infant and its (m)other. As such, then, our compassions and hospitalities are primary and an-archic; together they represent what could be called *misericord*: being compassionately hospitable for the other. Misericord is proximity and home, primarily being home on the most intimate plane—that of our "flesh and breath"[35]—and at the same moment offering our place to the other; here, Irigaray also rightly observes that what we offer in our everyday hospitalities are empty places and empty gestures, giving to the other what we already and always possess: we offer them "empty territories,"[36] our own traumas, our own possessions. In this sense, the hospitality offered by Levite to the stranger ("In the morning . . . with her hands on the threshold"; Judges 19:27) is also false hospitality. Moreover, to return for the moment to Chandrakirti, we are not yet able to empty our own compassions of their masculinities, directednesses, gravities, all enclosed by a desire we nourish for ourselves; only then, sharing with the others becomes the most precious gift we possess—the offering of the place we yet have to inhabit, our unlimited *misericord*, beyond the interiority-exteriority divide, beyond *our* time, beyond *our* place:[37]

> Mercy alone is seen as the seed
> Of a Conqueror's rich harvest,
> As water for development, and as
> Ripening in a state of long enjoyment;
> Therefore at the start I praise compassion.[38]

Absolute hospitality, then. We pay homage to *our* civic laws of compassion, and *our* civic laws of hospitality, we said, but these were not *their* laws. We offer them territories, but they are not their territories; what we offer to them instead of our subtle selflessness is our unhomeliness (Chandrakirti), gathered around the hearth of Being (Heidegger),[39] which should be no one's possession. According to Derrida—and here we return to the problem of justice—"justice is an experience of the impossible,"[40] and law is not justice. In a Levinasian voice, Derrida speaks of that justice, which is only possible when its essential or constitutive part is an ethical relation to the other, as a promise of *sainteté*, a promise, which paradoxically and anarchically comes before all philosophy and all theology.[41] This emanation of holiness from the ethical plane of *misericord* (as hospitality and compassion) is what now, finally, designates the very materiality of the human person and its ethics, understood within the ethical cluster of *Maternity—Matrix—Material—Matrimony*.[42] The dignity and the future (*avenir*) of humanity rest on this thought.

(Favour)

There was a Nigerian girl, called Favour. She was only nine months old and her mother died on the way toward the Mediterranean Sea during the difficult voyage from Africa to Europe. While dying, she gave her vulnerable child to a stranger—to another mother—to carry with her, to her new life. Thanks to this gesture of pure hospitality, claiming nothing as reward (which *hospitality-toward-the-dead* cannot expect), Favour survived, while so many other children did not, because they were not offered hospitality, either by their home countries or by their possible future hosts. Her name testifies for all these absent and hospitable gestures of strangers to strangers. If we are searching for a genre within philosophical theology and its ethics, saturated with ethics of proximity and compassion, and able to encapsulate such a difficult thought on the matrixial core of ethics, then the book *Tears of Salt* is one of a kind.[43]

Pietro Bartolo is a medical doctor, specializing in gynecology. But he also is an intiator of a new ethics, which is fully attuned to the logic of his medical vocation, and thus to the logic of matrixiality and to its inherent idea of the child—because both his practical wisdom as well as his agapeistic compassion spring from his exuberant love for the living and for the deceased alike. Wanting nothing in return, he knows, as Antigone did, that it is his duty, based on eternal unwritten laws and as inscribed in our hearts, to bury the dead bodies of children, women, and men on the shores of Lampedusa. Because they could equally be our children, sisters, brothers, or parents. We could say that, as a man, Bartolo reveals to us the feminine core of ethics. In his own way, Bartolo thus rescuscitates Metis from oblivion and brings her sacred presence back into this world full of suffering. This ethical cardiology was also at the bottom of the words of Pope Francis when he visited Lampedusa and remarked: "Has any one wept? Today has anyone wept in our world?"[44] But the doctor from Lampedusa knew already how dangerous any sea journey can be: he nearly died at sixteen, on a fishing boat, when he was saved at the last moment from the night sea by his father. *We all are equally vulnerable.* Bartolo now testifies to what would otherwise be forgotten, and there is no ethical theory or ethical temporality that could prescribe this, for these ethical gestures originate from a more archaic/hidden core of ethics that is not accessible to everyone. There are also things too sad to be described: victims of wartime rape, with their saddest pregnancies; boys and men, girls and women, physically mutilated with their lives' futures destroyed permanently; families separated forever; impossible choices—a father forced to decide between keeping his nine-month-old son and his wife in his arms and letting his other three-year-old son drown only because he cannot save them all in the rough sea. Pietro Bartolo knows: one can never become accustomed to seeing the dead bodies of newborn babies, or women who died during childbirth at sea, with their suffocated offspring still linked to them by their umbilical cord. *Requiem eternam dona eis, Domine.*

There is a new ethical genre that needs to be developed in order for us to be able to think, meditate, and pray on these thoughts ethically. It is called ethical anatomy of the body: one trembles from the outside (the role of skin and touch: Feuerbach, Mead, Chrétien) to the inside (viscera, bowels, womb: Schopenhauer, Ettinger, Wu),[45] and vice versa; one laments in the eyes (tears; Derrida) and in the heart (opening of the heart to the other; *kardia*: Caputo); then, finally, one breathes with lungs full of the wind of alterity in an inspiration which is yet to come (*pneuma*: Levinas, Irigaray). The main disciplines of ethical anatomy therefore consist of: *ethical neurology* (empathy, compassion science, and neuroscience),[46] *ethical cardiology* (agapeistic compassion), *ethical pneumatology* (sharing breath with others), *ethical dermatology* (haptology and the logic of proximity with mirror-touch synaesthesia[47]—in its extreme form St Francis's *stigmata*), and *ethical gynecology* (with wombing motherliness at its core), linked to the hidden matrixial core of all life, protecting the vulnerable. Cognitive science and neuroethics already provides evidence for this novel ethics. But philosophy and theology must work on new material/matrixial *ontology* and thus prepare the grounds for this ethics on their own.

Favour has survived. But it is our duty to nourish these thoughts in ourselves and pray for all the departed not to forget them. This highest form of ethical thinking is called *remembrance*—which should be enhanced to be able to become an ethical principle of its own. And no one else will ever take this responsibility from us.[48]

flaming love

3

BETHLEHEMITE CONCUBINE / MARY

*Dedicated to the Yezidi girls and women—
and all other victims of war rape.*[1]

In Utero

Our times are times of great sadness. From day to day the world is witnessing the most horrible images of the sufferings and tragic deaths of numerous migrants—children, mothers, fathers—in their extreme vulnerability, and the fragility of their existence. "We"—if we may use "we" for all of *us*, who are sensitive to extreme suffering of numerous individuals in the world—are also facing in the last decades horrific scenes of sexual violence and war rape in various regions of the world, where masculine power and quasi-religious ideology have taken control over communities, and have thus been annihilating the last remains of an ethical life. As members of a global community, we all have been affected by this. It is our opinion that within contemporary feminist theology we indeed can search for new evidence, ideas, and arguments that might help us to become aware of these tragic events, be our guide in the most difficult processes of mourning, and also enable us to imagine a better and brighter world for future generations.

    The spiritual world that we might share (our point of departure here will be the Judeo-Christian religious environment) is in need of a new embodiment of the divine, indeed a new theology of Incarnation. Too many mortal bodies have been, as it were, immobilized by supernatural tendencies, and too many of us have forgotten to listen to the most intimate layers of our being-in-the-world. For Luce Irigaray, our future dwelling in the world will thus have to be related to our spiritual becoming, which thus cannot be a task of only one sex, or even one single culture or civilization. It will require a dialogue of spiritual traditions both within ourselves as well as between different civilizational circles—the task is to become enlightened enough to be able to open ourselves toward the new epoch in thinking. The ancient cultures of America and Africa, the old Indo-European cultures (Greek, Slavic, Indo-Iranian . . .), and the cultures of the Middle East and Far East must guide us in following this spiritual task.[2] As this chapter will begin by focusing on Christianity and its transcultural and transcivilizational environment, let ancient Middle Eastern and ancient Greek cultures be our point of departure.

This chapter wishes to argue for a new *matrixial* theology—as a theology of the maternal body and a theology for the maternal body.[3] According to Irigaray, thanks to her spiritual virginity and for the purpose of protection of the living, a woman must be capable of being a temporal bridge between the past, present, and future, and a spatial bridge between all the cultures of the world.[4] The futurity of this thought refers to the transformation of our bodily/spiritual energies, which is closely related to the awaiting of real presence of a feminine figure in the midst of the religious world. This gesture, for Irigaray, is marked by the progression from a young girl to the most important feminine figure in the religious history of Christianity—Mary, the mother of Jesus. We know that throughout the religious history of *man*kind (with few exceptions), women have been deprived of their proper spiritual identities; and, clearly, the concept of a Godhead—ontologically, linguistically, and physiognomically—has been designed as a role model predominantly for one sex. Monotheisms have traditionally developed into stories of totality, of a monarchical and patriarchal One, and have been searching for epistemologically, ontologically, and linguistically stable derivatives of one Truth, and thus forgetting in this process the multiple incarnations of the divine. In its character, this process is marked by its porous nature and is basically interconnected to the world of the living.[5] If Mary has been denied her own incarnation,[6] or, to be more precise, her own ontological and/or theological dispositive, we need to ask ourselves what role she will play in the future for our redemption, and, especially, what will be her possible future role for the redemption of little girls and women (but also boys and men) subjected to power and extreme (gender) violence. To recover this ontologico-ethical dispositive, Elizabeth Johnston has beautifully altered Irenaeus's *Gloria Dei vivens homo* into *Gloria Dei vivens mulier*, which now for her means: "The glory of God is women, all women, every woman everywhere, fully alive."[7] It is only in this sense—i.e., of "full flourishing of women's bodies, as much as any other bodies within creation"[8]—that redemption of little girls and women, as well as boys and men, and thus all of us, will be possible.

The truth of Antigone is hidden in the *body*: as a woman, but first as a sister, she had shared the same maternal place (*womb, matrix*) with her brothers and sisters (Polyneices, Eteocles, and Ismene), and she had been carrying the memory of this *place* in her feminine body until the end. Like Mary, she has preserved the unique symbolic sexual identity and autonomy of a virgin. It is thus not a coincidence that in her redemptive role for the world Irigaray (also by referring to Hegel) thinks that her mission might even be higher than that of Christ himself.[9] Now, in a world where our imperfect thoughts and imperfect compassions cannot escape the most painful truth of the immense suffering of numerous girls and women, this thought seems to be fully justified. This (gender) violence[10] is directed toward all of us and our possible redemption: as a (co)mediatrix between God and ourselves, and being the divine model of Christianity and spiritual ancestor and mother of Jesus,[11] the spiritual/bodily wound of Antigone is thus also reflected in the spiritual/bodily wound of Mary.

But there is a story from the Hebrew Bible we wish to address: this is the story of the Unknown Woman (the Bethlehemite Concubine/daughter/wife) from the *Book of Judges*.[12] Having occupied an identity as concubine of the Levite of Ephraim, she is a double symbol—she is the sacrificial gift for the host and his compassionate hospitality, but she is also the sacrificial victim for the enemies and their hatred; as a woman/daughter she represents the impossible logic of hospitality, its pure excess and collapse into the most horrible tragedy; dwelling at the very threshold of ethics, she is marking the extreme, even deadly, vulnerability and fragility of an existence of a woman.

In Judges 19–21 we can read of a story of the Levite's concubine woman being raped by the mob and left unbreathing in the morning—only because she is a woman.[13] This woman, of course, is more than *just* a victim of a mob of men—she represents ancient sexual genealogies of Israel and its sacrificial religion. Although there are two different possibilities of answering the question of who is sending her to the mob to be raped—the Levite or his host—it is still without any doubt that a woman has been sent *outside* the hospitable place by a man. We know that after this event, it is the Levite of Ephraim who dismembers her and sends her to the twelve tribes of Israel[14]—as a reminder, and to show the magnitude of an act of rape by the Benjamites. Her body has been desecrated, and, it is true, "God's womb is constantly bleeding" with her.[15] We know that there is a similar story of Lot in Genesis 19. Since in the well-known story of Lot, the mob rejects the old man's offer of his two virgin daughters as a substitution for his male guest, and there was no rape as a consequence. In the second story, according to Judith Still, we have a double substitution at work. The Levite offers the concubine for the host as a substitute for his daughter, which, again, has been offered previously as a substitute for the Levite.[16] This double substitution marks the extreme and in a way endless vulnerability of women (and children, we may add) in the Hebrew Bible. The collective and brutal response of the tribes of Israel toward the tribe of Benjamites representing perpetrators, shows "the collective (or divine) punishment for an act that strikes at what is regarded as the heart of civilisation"[17]—now problematically and tragically multiplied to encompass the punishment of an entire community: "Go, put the inhabitants of Jabesh Gilead to the sword, including the women and the little ones."[18] In her exposition of this story, Phyllis Trible relates the problem of female presence in this narrative to the silence of "the woman his concubine" (whereas two nouns in this phrase also indicate her inferior position). The story of Levite's concubine woman, therefore, is the paradigmatic story of "the horrors of male power, brutality, and triumphalism," on one side, and "female helplessness, abuse, and annihilation" on the other.[19] If for these reasons the suffering of this woman (and numerous other unnamed women) is *not* redemptive in any possible way (or, as Trible warns us, no subordination to suffering of the cross is possible in this context), which mode of violence does this violence reveal to us? It could be argued now that this precisely is the wound, committed to the person in her *matrixial* identity,[20] with Trible:

> Woman as object is still captured, betrayed, raped, tortured, murdered, dismembered, and scattered. To take to heart this ancient story, then, is to confess its present reality. The story is alive, and all is not well.[21]

Apart from the Bethlehemite Concubine, we find in the Hebrew Bible two other accounts of the sacrifice of a woman—namely the female sacrifice of Bat-Jephthah's virgin daughter in Judges 11, and the slaughter of a Midian "prostitute" Cozbi in Numbers 25. Cozbi is particularly interesting for our understanding of female sacrifice since she has been stabbed by an Israelite man (son of Aaron the priest) with a spear—precisely "through her belly."[22] This act undoubtedly testifies to the sacrificial/scapegoat logic of the event, marking the antimatrixial theological logic which will be addressed and contested later. They all remind us of war and endless violence—both that we have inherited them in ourselves from the most ancient times and have always already been wounded by them. We all are thus responsible for this, and the more subtle message of Biblical narrative on Levite's concubine—despite its narrative logic—we believe, is directed against revenge and for reconciliation and the redemption of women—both as parts of a difficult and enigmatic process of rupture/disruption within the very kernel of cosmic justice. It is our task to listen to this name of justice and keep in our hearts the memory of this distant event.

But let us for the moment keep the stories from the Hebrew Bible in our hearts, only to be able to return to them upon our exposition of the question of Mary of the New Testament. Ludwig Feuerbach illuminates, in his major and most important work *The Essence of Christianity*, our hearts and souls with the most tender description of the relation between Jesus and Mary, the Son and the Mother. He writes in the chapter "The Mystery of the Trinity and the Mother of God":

> It is true that the Son, as a natural man, dwells only temporarily in the shrine of this body, but the impressions which he here receives are inextinguishable; the Mother is never out of the mind and heart of the son.[23]

According to Feuerbach, Jesus has received his first impressions (this marks the extreme sensitivity, love, and compassion of him) already in his mother's womb. His material (/maternal) body has thus been shaped in the body of his Mother, and Feuerbach will also tell us with a haunting poignancy that "we find in God the beating of a mother's heart."[24] Perhaps, someday in the future, this statement will have a far-reaching meaning for us and indeed inaugurate a new trinitarian epoch in the process of Incarnation of a God/dess into the world. Related to these impressions (later in this chapter we will interpret them as the origin of Jesus's compassion), Mary's womb-matrix (*chóra?*)[25] could thus be understood as a sacred *shrine*, already embracing in itself the pure and holy essence of the Godhead, the first seed of all relationality, and before all and everything, compassion as *agápe* (or, misericord as "emotion of the maternal womb").[26] For a philosopher of Jewish origin, Bracha Ettinger, already Isaac has to be recognized as bearer of this feminine compassion, for being compassionate toward his father in a way of a primeval compassion, his emotion originates from the "Levinasian 'an-archic' and feminine kernel of the ethical sphere."[27] We know that Isaac has been, as it were, *immaculately conceived* and his birth is a miracle for his parents: his feminine compassion upon his father, as indicated by Ettinger, could thus be understood as a gift of God to Sarah, Abraham, and their people, as an an-archic and impossible share of an offspring/child in the ancient generational orders of Israel; an ultimate sign of God's care and mercy for humanity. But also as a sacrifice—and in this Isaac is a part of the same ontological order as the concubine (Unknown Woman) from Judges, as well as children (sons or daughters) being offered in sacrifice in the context of the Hebrew Bible (for example, in Exod. 22 and 2 Kings 3).[28] And we already know that in Hebrew, there is a word for this compassion—and this word is *rakhamim*; *in utero*, then—Sarah and Isaac, Mary and Jesus; these are markers of a paradoxical tension between justice and compassion within God. But how is this tension to be resolved?

Here we wish to return to Mary and develop, in the following section, a theology of incarnation capable of resolving this riddle. According to the corpuses of both medieval mystical literature (Hadewijch of Brabant, Angela of Foligno, Marguerite Porete) as well as contemporary feminist theologians, incarnation firstly takes place in the body of the woman, but Mary has been denied her own incarnation.[29] To be aware of this gesture, according to Irigaray, this now requires

> Mary to have a personal link—unmediated by man—to the divine, and that she remains faithful to this. The event of the Annunciation establishes or celebrates this link between Mary and God—independent of her people, of her genealogy, of her fiancé, and even of her future child.[30]

In the second part of this chapter it will now be our task to address this difficult question by pointing to an inner ontological tension within the triadic concept of the ethico-theological logic of the subtlest of all relations—the relationality of spiritual exchanges between the divine and the human—as understood within the broader trinitarian structures. With this gesture, we intend to introduce a ternary structure into an original constellation, a structure that will enable us to introduce the thinking of a triad into the search for incarnation in the feminine.

The Third Presence

Following our initial constellation, it is now time to focus on Feuerbach's theory of Mary as related to the trinitarian logic. In his main work, Feuerbach has indicated that "we find in God the beating of a mother's heart."[31] Following his own intuitions, Feuerbach is now *logically* led to the following important consequence of his theological analyses:

> And the idea of the Mother of God, which now appears so strange to us, is therefore not really more strange or paradoxical, than the idea of the Son of God, is not more in contradiction with the general, abstract definition of God than the Sonship. On the contrary, the Virgin Mary fits in perfectly with the relations of the Trinity, since she conceives without man the Son whom the Father begets without woman; so that thus the Holy Virgin is a necessary, inherently requisite antithesis to the Father in the bosom of the Trinity.[32]

How do these trinitarian thoughts of Feuerbach speak to us today? His statements are marked by similar (although in Feuerbach they are hidden, or, only "negatively" present through his silence on them) genealogies as we have seen earlier with Irigaray: for both thinkers, the Holy Trinity bears cosmic, sexual, and generational elements in itself. But what is the actual trinity or triad as a concept, and how might it be understood as a form, representing the most perfect model for the divine and for the human Being? How is it related to the thinking of the "Third Presence," the relational link between One and Two as primeval ontological realms? Before we can develop our own attempt at a new matrixial theology of the divine incarnation within the trinitarian logic, let us elaborate on some concepts of triadic thinking and thinking in triads.

We know from the theory of semiotics—especially if we look into Charles S. Peirce's work—that meaning is constructed across the difference and separation between the signifier and the signified, where a basic triadic structure is established (i.e., symbol, sign, and icon).[33] In his *War and Insurance* address from 1914, Josiah Royce has rightly observed that it only within the triadic logic that hostility might be overcome and peace be reestablished.[34] Transposed into a cultural level, Homi Bhabha would now argue—by giving his account on cultural hybridity—that "all forms of culture are continually in a process of hybridity," and thus the essentialism of any prior given culture is denied. As a key concept of nonpolarity or nonbinarism, the third space is here defined by Bhabha as a category, actually *enabling* "other positions to emerge."[35] And to make the third step here—from semiotic theory and cultural hybridity to ternary structure in our intersubjective relations—it is now precisely this dynamization of the third space that leads toward a necessary internalization of the triadic process as such. This process thus finds its own way within our intersubjective relations, as presented by Jay Johnston in her analysis of dual subjectivity. In her analysis of Irigaray's concept of subjectivity, Johnston rightly observes that we need to think beyond the so-called dual subjectivity and its ontologico-epistemological divide. She calls this third element a "ternary structure" and states:

> Irigaray's *To Be Two* is really a *To Be Three*, with the between being ascribed an ontological agency which is both of, and not of, dual subjectivity. It is a shared space of creative and dynamic subtle relation.[36]

Relational ontology now becomes a trinitarian process. It is precisely this ontologico-epistemological interval, or space of ethics, that enables and preserves all intersubjective relations and spiritual/bodily exchanges, including those of cosmological and theological character.

Based on these initial observations and remarks, we can now move into the theological space. In her insightful book on religion and monotheism, Laurel C. Schneider rightly asserts that in order to understand the trinity in our time we have to turn our minds toward "divinity in multiplicity,"[37] which is to be understood as a renewed ontological gesture, disabling the old abstract or numerical (or mathematical/monarchical) modalities and positions of One (and Second), and thus opening for us new possibilities for divine incarnations within the category of the Third(ness). She thus pleads for a new theology of multiplicity, a theology of Many, which, again, works beyond some naive and simple

"God or the gods" thinking or dilemmas (monotheism versus polytheism, or One versus the Many) and leads also toward new trinitarian cosmologico-theological thinking we intend to defend in this book.[38] This indeed is a very important observation and a methodological credo, since throughout the history of religion and theology, triads have been probably the most powerful model for representing spiritual exchanges within the Divine-Circle,[39] or within the divine-human cosmic and ritual circles and spiritual exchanges. Triads, as we have already seen from semiotics and epistemology, represent an effort toward unity in diversity and thus toward mediation, reconciliation, and peace, while the thinking of One and Two (Dyad) is marked by monolithic, static and a(nta) gonistic (relational but dialectical, even to its very borders—violence and war) principles.[40]

Let us now approach the problem of incarnation as related to trinity and multiplicity. Within the early stages of Israelite religion, we slowly trace a monotheistic movement, which reached its first pinnacle in the 640–609 BCE period during the reign of King Joshiah. We also know from historical sources that at latest by the time of Second Isaiah (540–520 BCE) we can define Israel's religion as becoming strongly monotheistic in its "intolerant monolatry" form.[41] We also know, on the other hand, that the efforts of the first Western philosophers (Thales, Pythagoras, and Xenophanes, followed by Socrates, Plato, and Aristotle) were oriented toward shaping stable ontologies of the One (i.e., forming Western ontotheology), which differed from those inherited from earlier cosmological and polytheistic thinking in ancient Greece. But here we do not intend to follow the well-known theological developments from the early Israelite forms of monolatry and monotheism towards the trinitarian theology, as defined by the fourth-century Christian Nicene creed. Instead, let us discuss an alternative model represented by African traditional religion. It will serve as a model for a possible reorientation of our thinking of triads and enable us to reground and, as it were, "materialize" Christian understanding of the Trinity, including the role of cosmic, sexual, and generational differences in this. On this basis we intend to return to the topic of incarnation in the third and concluding part of this chapter.

The first ever account on multiplicity in the vicinity of the Jewish-Christian world can be found within the ancient Egyptian and African traditional religion. In *An African Interpretation of the Trinity*, African theologian A. Okechukwu Ogbonnaya[42] presents us with a fascinating thesis of early African influences on Christian doctrine of trinity (i.e., of Tertullian). Ogbonnaya even claims that African cosmology was actually a background of Tertullian's own concepts of the trinity and trinitarian divinity. For Ogbonnaya, following the communitarian character of African religion,

> mutual relation is far more than a dyadic relation in which two are lost uncritically in each other. The African emphasis on offspring assures that dyadic relation does not lead to egotism can be avoided because there is always the possibility of a "third presence."[43]

What Ogbonnaya is arguing here is very important: first, dyadic relations (known from the old metaphysical and theological models (Heaven and Earth, God and the world, macrocosm and microcosm, but also the *mythos-lógos* dichotomy) *cannot* assure the space in which both ontological or divine realities would exist in a mutual peaceful atmosphere and without an ontological conflict or any other form of appropriation, either by higher or lower vertical realms, or any one of two horizontal sides or realms of the dyad. The third presence is thus necessary for establishing a full relationality without any form of appropriation by any member of the triad. Secondly, still more important, the third presence is related to the offspring/child, and thus marking a communal atmosphere with its cosmic-ontological, sexual and generational aspects included and, most importantly, preserved. Both issues (relationality and idea of an offspring) will be extremely important for our concluding remarks on a matrixial theology. Now, we know from Plato's *Timaeus*, that "a third kind" (*tríton génos*) or "the third type is space,"[44] known enigmatically as *chóra*, is a receptacle of becoming—its wet nurse, as it were; thus, it is an ontological category par excellence—and, perhaps most importantly—*chóra* (already for Plato) always resides in the feminine element.[45] And to add another intercultural comparison: there is a striking similarity between this concept and Daoist philosophy as represented by Kuang-Ming Wu. In his book on material ethics and philosophy of religion, *On Chinese Bodily Thinking*, Wu presents us with two idiosyncratic modes of thinking, called "wombing forth" and "wombing motherliness." "Wombing forth" is based on a concept of the "womb-power" as a feminine ontological presence, which we can find everywhere—"in water, in roots, in valleys," and furthermore, also as a presence in ourselves, which enables us, as human beings, to be humble, compassionate, and devoted to others. Womb-power, according to Wu, is

> the empty room between Heaven and Earth . . . a motherly bellows, vacuous, inexhaustible, continually letting forth [things].

Moreover, Wu continues,

> [e]very human relation worthy of its name is a mothering and wombing—your being vacuous draws me forth, lets me become as I am. . . . The inner personal touch fills the void in me and in you, making us one. Yet we remain two, for two-ness enables touch. We are thus two in one, and one in two, thanks to our personal void and touch inside. All this describes mutual fulfilment. Personal void generates love— inner touch—that *mothers us* to grow into ourselves.[46]

We have thus the third kind/element represented in another intercultural context. Moreover, this element is *apophatic*, for it is necessarily related to my self-annihilation, a void-space in myself, to my absolute giving for the sake of the others. The *womb-power* in Her essential potency—now called "wombing motherliness"—is the ontological space of our mutual becoming, the possibility of an "inner touch"[47] between two realities, firstly between mother and a child (foetus), but ultimately between God/dess and any human being. This would be the place of the ternary structure as mediating principle of all (including human-divine) intersubjective relations. In Christian terms, and radicalized in theological way, we can find Christ in ourselves as inner touch, the subtle, yet powerful spiritual (Holy Spirit; Breath of proximity) presence of love, humility, and absolute self-annihilation qua self-transcendence.

Analogous to Wu's Daoist *womb-power* stands Derrida's *chóra*: it/she also is powerless, but still having had no power at all, it/she itself represented a *womb-power*, an ontological riddle, as it were, the enigmatic and mysterious presence of all things created.[48] Let us then keep in mind this enigmatic and feminine character of *chóra*-(matrixial space?), as a third presence (ternary structure), or a third element of becoming (as wet nurse, she is in the privileged relation to the offspring). We have seen that in African triadic thinking, the idea of the offspring is crucial.

In this sense, we can also understand Jürgen Moltmann's thoughts from his book *The Trinity and the Kingdom,* that, in the light of the Son proceeding from the Father, we can indeed speak of a "motherly Father" and "fatherly Mother"[49]—and this undoubtedly introduces into the concept of the Triune God the renewed dynamics of an ontologically understood sexual difference. We are now close to the initial question of this chapter—How is incarnation in the feminine possible? This brings us to the third part of this chapter.

Toward a New Matrixial Theology of Incarnation

There is one step we have to take before we are able to propose a new matrixial theology of Incarnation. According to Irigaray, as we have seen, it is necessary for Mary to have a personal link to the divine. For being able to connect her thoughts with our previous analyses of the feminine and third presence, we have now to return to Feuerbach and analyze in more detail his statement from *The Essence of Christianity*. For Feuerbach, recall that Mary was "a necessary, inherently requisite antithesis to the Father in the bosom of the Trinity."[50] But how is this to be understood? Also, in this passage Feuerbach is very close to Irigaray: for him, and following his idiosyncratic trinitarian logic, it is very important that also Mary has been accepted into heaven:

> It was therefore quite in order, that to complete the divine family, the bond of love between Father and Son, a third, and that a feminine person, was received into heaven. . . . [I]t is enough that the maternal principle was associated with the Father and Son. It is in fact difficult to perceive why the Mother should be something unholy, i.e., unworthy of God, when once God is Father and Son.[51]

This statement is very profound: according to Feuerbach, Mary is worthy of her own access to the divine and thus also to her own ontological dispositive. But how? According to Irigaray, in the analyses from "The Redemption of Women" there are only a few instances showing us the full spiritual identity and divinity of Mary—and these are Annunciation, Assumption, and Coronation: among them the Assumption plays perhaps the most prominent and perhaps even decisive role.

Irigaray hints at the possibility for Mary to rise to heaven "without any death or resurrection similar to those of her son."[52] We know from the 1950 dogma on the Virgin's Assumption that the question of whether Mary actually died before departing this world has remained open.[53] After a time of striking silence about the end of Mary's life in the New Testament and in the first centuries of the Church, we have various apocryphal texts from around the fifth century which deal with Mary's Dormition and Assumption and are now mainly part of the later Byzantine tradition. These narratives explain the last days of Mary in this world. In one of them, called *Narrative of St. John*,[54] we find a striking description of the moment of Mary's Dormition and Assumption: Jesus comes from heaven to take her with him. This passage goes as follows:

> The Lord embraced her, and he took her holy soul and placed it in Michael's hands, wrapping it in indescribably splendid skins. And we, the apostles, beheld the soul of Mary as it was given into Michael's hands: it was perfect in every human form, except for the shape of male or female, with nothing being in it, except for a likeness of the complete body and a sevenfold whiteness.[55]

Jesus Christ, the Son of Mary, arrives with a company of angels and receives/takes her soul, "which appears as an infant clothed in white"[56]; this astounding testimony ("except for the shape of male or female") shows both positively as well as *per negationem* the centrality of fundamental generational and sexual genealogies and relations in the cosmico-theological sense, and opens the possibility of interpreting the Dormition and Assumption of Mary in a completely new ontological way. Put in a theological language of hospitality—if Mary has been Christ's *host* and protector (mother-parent) during the time of her pregnancy and the early childhood of Jesus, the Son is now *her* host and, as it were, protector *and* mother-parent—on her way to heaven through Dormition and Assumption. This perfect reciprocal relation between Mary and Jesus thus marks one of the rare, if not (perhaps) the only perfect presence of the relation/exchange of pure hospitality, in its impossible limit at the very threshold of life and death, and resurrection . . .

Now, let us finally try to approach what it could be titled a new matrixial theology of Incarnation, based on these beautiful narratives as well as Feuerbach's statements of the Trinity. We have already seen that even for Moltmann, there was a need to revive our understanding of the Holy Trinity. For Moltmann, the problem lies in the historical patriarchal tradition of theology, within which the so-called patriarchal hierarchies includes "Father" in one of his many varieties.[57] But on the contrary, and quite in line with our thinking of the sexual difference within the Trinity, for Moltmann this "Father" instead is "two-gendered or trans-gendered"[58] in itself/himself/herself. God is now both "motherly Father" and "fatherly Mother,"[59] and this now opens an entirely new question of the immanent sexual relationality within the Holy Trinity. We know that after the Eleventh Council of Toledo in 675 CE, we can believe that Son has been conceived and born *de Patris utero*: "We must believe that the Son is begotten or born not from nothing or from any other substance, but from the womb of the Father, that is from His substance."[60] For us this now marks the possibility of introducing the logic of womb-matrix into the Trinity. Moreover, it could be asserted that the famous statue of *Vierge ouvrante* (from cca. 1400) shows precisely the idea of Mary the cosmic Mother, "as containing the entire Trinity and cosmos."[61] Related to the ideas as we can find already in the apocryphal *Gospel of Bartholomew*,[62] this statue shows the perfect, but also enigmatic cosmic Trinitarian constellation we are getting at here. It is enigmatic, because with this constellation, Mary, as it were, could now be understood in a double role: firstly, as earthly Mother of Jesus, and secondly, as a mysterious Matrix (*chóra*, or trace) of the entire cosmos. *De Patris utero* now means that Son is begotten from the womb-matrix *of* the Father—in a double meaning (*genitivus absolutus*) yet to be fully revealed to us in its cosmico-ontologico-sexual sense.

In the beginning of this chapter, we already defended the idea that the thinking of a new embodiment of the divine needs to be invented, indeed, a new theology being able globally and dialogically to respond to some of the most pressing socioethical issues. Among them, the first and foremost issue to be addressed and supplied with theological discourse was the ignorance or dismissal of the notion of sexual difference—as present in various antimatrixial forms of violence. According to Irigaray, the task of our age is "to respect the life of the other, in maternity and in love itself."[63] For Irigaray, women are called upon to fulfill the spiritual task of our time, for because of their matrixial genealogies, they have the privileged access to the *life*. But this also, and equally, opens ethical spaces for men in their "mothering" identities, as we have seen from Christ's, as it were, wombing motherliness gesture towards Mary upon her Assumption. For Irigaray, this marks the opening of the third age (called in her writings *the age of the Spirit*), when the humanity does not remain enclosed in a masculine world (as also criticized by Moltmann) anymore. We, both as men and as women, also in a way of reuniting us with other religious traditions, have to become more linked with the life of the universe, its immanence/interiority (womb-matrix, *chóra*) its cosmico-theological pulsation and spiritual becoming. On this basis, and by recalling the triadic principle, we now wish to propose the following triadic model for Christianity, positioning the (in)visible trace (^{T}) of *chóra* into the very bosom of the Trinity:

God-Father
(T)

chóra
womb-matrix

Jesus-Son **Holy Spirit**

Here, *chóra* as a trace$^{(T)}$ in its/her femininity is precisely what Feuerbach wanted to propose in his trinitarian analysis—namely, as a "necessary, inherently requisite antithesis to the Father in the bosom of the Trinity."[64] Moreover, in a beautiful passage on The Holy Trinity Icon painted in 1411 by Andrei Rublev, Richard Kearney argues that the empty chalice appearing in the center of the icon actually represents the "womb-heart" of Mary itself (as *chóra*).[65] This beautiful anatheistic thought thus fully supports our thesis on a possibility of an own ontological dispositive of Mary.

But *chóra* is powerless, we have seen. It/she cannot operate within any model or existing logic we know. It/she is the primordial and thus an anarchic pulsation of Life, the ontological relationality in its cosmic (i.e., sexual and generational) sense. But again, how is *chóra* as womb-matrix related to the third presence, or third element? Already for Plato in *Timaeus*, we have seen, the third type was defined as space, a receptacle of all becoming. But it is also something more: we would define womb-matrix (having its divine incarnation in Mary) as a third presence at the very bosom of the Trinity, an ontological dispositive related to the immanent idea of the offspring/child, and thus to the compassionate pulsation of a primordial wombing motherliness,[66] the presence of all things created in the very heart of the Trinity, the absolute or pure gesture of giving—the mark of pure hospitality. *Chóra*, in its/

her ontological passivity and futurity (the inherent idea of offspring as related to her maternal role as well as her Dormition and Assumption) is what could on a basis of a possible reading of The Book of Revelation 12:1–6[67] be described as a mysterious and "an anonymous Mary whose true nature and function has not yet been revealed."[68]

But there is a final question to be answered: How is *chóra* as *womb-matrix* related to the Bethlehemite Concubine *and* Mary, and their distinctive feminine presence? In her *God and the Rhetoric of Sexuality*, Phyllis Trible argues that "[i]n the Hebrew scriptures, wombs of women belong to God."[69] Apart from this, and even more importantly, *womb* (*rehem*; we know that this noun in its plural form *rakhamim* means "compassion" in Hebrew) in Job 31:13–15 is described by Trible as "the place of human equality."[70] This is now our concluding argument: what has been attacked, brutally annihilated, and sexually violated in the story of the Bethlehemite Concubine and all related stories and tragic events is precisely this primeval ethico-theologico-ontological space of equality (*chóra*), and it is again this space that is now restored in Mary's womb—with the Christ as a promise of a new life, and restoration of equality. Christ's compassion is of a matrixial origin. This is now the full spiritual and theological meaning of Mary's virginity, as also explained by Irigaray[71]—quite opposite from what we could infer from the patriarchal versions of Mary's virginity *as* submission and dependence, the virginity of Mary should finally be understood as a *trace of chóra*, which is the name of justice and equality.

To conclude—we do not know if there is *chóra* in the bosom of the Trinity, or whence it/she dwells. We cannot affirm nor attest its/her ontological status, nor its/her sexual identity. But it is now perhaps possible to affirm that Mary, Mother of Jesus, in her radical and absolute hospitality can lead us toward a possible place in the future, when we will be awaiting and rejoicing the event of an Incarnation in the feminine in its most powerful, yet absolutely powerless and peaceful presence of the eternal cosmic pregnancies and plentiful springs of eternal life, we need to respect, fully protect, and nurture.

(Sophia)

In the Old Testament book of Proverbs we encounter the following passage, just as celebrated as it is enigmatic, which has inspired numerous philosophers and mystics, as well as feminist theologians:

> The LORD possessed me in the beginnings of his way,
> Before his works of old.
> I was set up from everlasting,
> From the beginning, or ever the earth was.
> When *there were* no depths, I was brought forth;
> When *there were* no fountains abounding with water.
> (. . .)
> Rejoicing in the habitable part of his earth;
> And my delights *were* with the sons of men.
> (Prov. 8: 22–24; 31)

How should we interpret these words about the primordial creation of Wisdom and its relationship to the idea of the child (is Wisdom itself a paradigm or the idea of the child, inherent in the idea of God?)—particularly in the perspective of reflection of the internal dynamics of the Trinitarian mystery and its relation to the feminine principle? Among the thinkers to whom we should dedicate attention here are Russian philosophers Vladimir Solovyov, Sergei Bulgakov, and Pavel Florensky, on the one hand, and Teilhard de Chardin, on the other, who experienced and articulated, each in his own way, this enigmatic presence and mutual connectedness of the feminine principle of love in the very core of the Holy Trinity. And according to C. G. Jung, Sophia is the forgotten feminine aspect of God.[72]

Now, let us approach Teilhard de Chardin and his sophiology. Teilhard wrote his hymn *The Eternal Feminine* (*Eternel Féminin*) between 1916 and 1918.[73] In his work *The Future of Man*, he referred to the cosmic Mary with several glorifying epithets, among which the association to the great Greek goddess of fertility, Persephone's mother, stands out: to him, Mary is "the Pearl of the Cosmos, and the link with the incarnate personal Absolute—the Blessed Virgin Mary, Queen and Mother of all things, the true Demeter."[74] Even for the Slovene interpreters of Teilhard's cosmic Mary, the latter is "internally linked with the universal and personal action of the Son."[75] And this is how Teilhard's hymnal poem itself reads:

> When the world was born, I came into being. Before the centuries were made, I issued from the hand of God. . . . In me is seen that side of beings by which they are joined as one . . . I am the eternal Feminine.[76]

Teilhard does not put into the forefront the matter of its beginning, which in this hymn remains subject to the Lord's (masculine) creational moment. But as a unifying principle, Teilhard's cosmic Mary is connected with the nascent principle of love, which emerges from the very foundation of the *eternal* Feminine. How should this seemingly insoluble duality or enigma be understood? The interpreter of this hymn, Henri de Lubac, believes its Christological dimension is important here: "For Teilhard, the feminine is not an abstract principle since its perfection is realized in a personal being—the Virgin Mary"[77]—and Lubac links this thought to the very idea of cosmic Mary. With this, the question of her cosmic/theological mission opens even more radically and it appears that Teilhard was unable to provide a complete answer to it. In his comments, Henri de Lubac clearly and quite predictably writes that we should not search for "any analogies with the sophiological theories of Bulgakov" here and that "Wisdom is not a hypostasis which, in its created aspect, is realized in the Virgin."[78] Once more, this strips the eternal feminine of its ontological edifice. But Henri de Lubac was unwilling to think deeper into the mysterious nature of Wisdom within Sophiology. Teilhard, however, left us a hint that is worth being read into more carefully: it relates to the principle of desire/love and the processual nature of the Divine self-revelation itself. Within this frame of reference, we can sense the exuberance of love reaching as far as the very core of the divine self-revelation. In the second part of the hymn we thus meet with the following words describing the key moment in the process of revelation as the *dis-uniting* (i.e., processual oneness and co-integration of revelation-unfolding-birth) of God and his/her departure into creation:

> Only love has the power to move being.
> If God, then, was to be able to emerge from himself, he had first to lay a pathway of desire before his feet, he had to spread before him a sweet savour of beauty.[79]

Now the introductory words from the Book of Proverbs (*ab initio creata sum*) acquire a clear processual meaning and we have to try follow in this very path and the traces of ontological *différance* (source or matrix of love) contained in it, a path that let itself be revealed to a select few, which include Vladimir Solovyov, Sergei Bulgakov, and Pavel Florensky, and their Sophiology.

Since childhood, Solovyov (1853–1900) had a series of mystical visions (the first one as early as at the age of nine, at the chapel of the

University of Moscow) in which divine or eternal Sophia (Rus. *premudrost*) or "the Eternal Feminine" revealed herself to him in the way of *all-oneness*. Solovyov was of course aware that he would have to link this thought, which incorporated an enigmatic duality (cosmic-universal versus Christological-ecclesiastical), to the difficult question of its relation to the Trinitarian precept, which in the 1930s culminated in Bulgakov's, in the opinion of many, heretic doctrine of Sophia as the alleged *fourth hypostasis of God*.[80] Solovyov stands at the end of a long history of celebrating Wisdom in the framework of Byzantine and later Russian Orthodox spirituality, which can be marked off by its beginning in the early fourth century (Constantine's Hagia Sophia, the Council of Ephesus in 431, and the investment of Mary with the title of *Theotokos*). After a period of slow decline of early "Sophiology" at the time of a gradual westernization of Russia, it was precisely this Solovyov who revived the movement, conferring on it new theological-cosmic and philosophical meanings. To Solovyov, the eternal or divine Sophia (i.e., Wisdom in the aspect of its eternity) was now the inner essence of the very God within the mystery of the Trinity.[81] Solovyov sees Sophia as a revealing or unfolding substance of God in cosmic history. In a neo-Platonic way, and beyond the simple dualisms of the male and the female, he thinks about Wisdom in a processual manner, by seeing it as a "latent potentiality . . . of all things"—and as the principle of all humanity: Wisdom is "the eternal body of God and the eternal soul of the world."[82]

Hence, Bulgakov, who in a way followed Solovyov's doctrine, already had in his works before him a double nature of Sophia, which can be designated by the difference between the divine (cosmic) and the created. This is what Sládek says about Bulgakov and his theology (now quoted in its entirety):

> Bulgakov had to deal with the concept of eternal Wisdom of God from the theological perspective. Above all, it was necessary to clearly define the relationship of Divine Sophia to three persons (Hypostasis) of the Holy Trinity. Should Sophia be a living creature in God, as everything conceivable—then one has to establish the relation to the Hypostases of Father, Son and the Holy Spirit—or what is Sophia's existence in the Trinity. Bulgakov solved the problem by distinguishing between "hypostasis" on the one hand and "hypostaticity" on the other. Hence, for Bulgakov, Divine Sophia is not "hypostasis, but hypostaticity: it is included in the personal

life of hypostasis and thanks to that, it itself is a living being. The Divine Sophia is self-manifestation of divinity of the life of the Holy Trinity and as such, it is both pre-eternal and it is created; it is a Trinitarian act of self-realization.[83]

To Bulgakov, the Divine Sophia is thus the very essence or *ousia* of the Trinity:

> That *ousia*, that substance of God, is not an abstract principle, but a living one, Sophia. In the divine *perichoresis*, or co-inherence, the persons of the Trinity are seen to be united not only by their single nature, but also, hypostatically, each in relation to each. Sophia is the mutual love of the persons of the Trinity for each other, their mutual co-inherence in each other, their distinctiveness in relation: "the tri-hypostatic God possesses, indeed, but one godhead, Sophia . . . *Ousia*-Sophia is distinct from the hypostases, though it cannot exist apart from them, and is eternally hypostasized in them. Sophia is not a fourth hypostatis, or a second God, but "the nature of God . . . a living and, therefore, loving substance, ground and 'principle.' "[84]

Even in the interpretation of Bulgakov by John O'Donnell, Sophia is understood as a *tertium datur* in an essentially dually understood relationality within the Trinity, as

> the revelation of the depth of the divine being. The Abyss of God's reality is revealed in the divine Wisdom. Hence Wisdom belongs to all three hypostases but is not itself a hypostasis. The Divine wisdom is both uncreated and eternal. It belongs to God's own life.[85]

In his work *The Pillar and Ground of the Truth*, Bulgakov's contemporary and friend the great Russian philosopher Pavel Florensky also thematizes the still-unanswered question of the pre-eternal nature of Sophia. To Florensky, Sophia now "participates in the inner life of the Trinity, but not as Hypostasis, but as an eternal creature."[86] Thus, in the theological sense, Sophia is not the fourth hypostasis, but the inner essence (*Ousia-Sophia*)[87] of three hypostases, or the three Divine Persons, the life of God himself/herself in love, the source of its exuberance, which flows into the world of the created through the life of Christ and the action of the Holy Spirit.

Here, it is necessary to Thomas Merton's awakening to the feminine divine, or Wisdom-Sophia.[88] Merton was highly indebted to Russian Orthodox thinkers of Sophia, but, of course, "the breakthrough of Sophia into Merton's consciousness did not simply 'happen' . . . but was the flowering within him of years of study and meditation on the Hebrew Scriptures, patristic and Russian theology, Zen, [and] Eastern iconography."[89] In a letter from May 14, 1959 he writes the following:

> The first thing to be said, of course, is that Hagia Sophia is God Himself.[90]

But for Merton, now in a more emphatic and ontologically radicalized manner (within the same letter), Sophia is "'the dark, nameless *Ousia* [Being]' of God, not one of the Three Divine Persons, but each 'at the same time, are Sophia and manifest her.'"[91] We can now sum this thought up in our final model of love originating from a matrixial principle, interpreted theologically in a Mertonian sense like this:

God
Wisdom
Sophia-Love
(Mary's) Matrix
Jesus   **Holy Spirit**
The matrixial *ousia-arché-chóra* of God: Wisdom-Sophia.

first announcing

INTERLUDE

mirroring ethics

Interval / Time of Love

Yet, as Aristotle shows, the interval is never abolished, only forgotten. There always remains an intervening body between our flesh and what it touches, a three-dimensional layer of air or water.

—Jean-Louis Chrétien

This interval—and this medium—is first of all nature, as it remains left to itself: air, water, earth, and sun, as fire and light. Being par excellence—matter of the transcendental.

—Luce Irigaray, "Ethical Gestures toward the Other"

Introduction

As a preparation toward an analysis of interval of ethics, it is necessary to look into Schopenhauer's pioneering contribution toward the opening of a new ethics, as based on the immediacy of bodily experiences. In *On the Basis of Morality*, Schopenhauer writes the following:

> With these allusions to the metaphysics of ethics I must rest content, although an important step remains to be taken. But this presupposes that a further step be taken in *ethics* itself, which I could not do, because the highest aim of ethics is limited to jurisprudence and moral philosophy in Europe, and here no one knows, or indeed will admit, what is beyond these.[1]

Usually, we think that for Schopenhauer, the ethics of compassion and sympathy (and thus, a kind of precritical intersubjective ethics) can only be affirmed metaphysically by acknowledging the Will in the world and its total denial in ourselves through ascetic practice (i.e., quietening of the will, which means surpassing the ego(t)istic will in ourselves). As a result, I realize that others are actually the same as I and thus feel compassion with their suffering. But in this metaphysical model (designed in a clear anti-Kantian manner) there is a lacuna, namely, that the body felt in its immediacy is for Schopenhauer the first object in the epistemological constitution of the self as will. My body is to me, paradoxically, the first external object. This is clearly traceable in the fourth book of *The World as Will and Representation*, where we are faced with the following ethical paradox: in the moment before we feel that the other has been wronged or before we act compassionately toward the other (i.e., "see" or "recognize" their pain) we always already feel the "secret presentiment" (*geheime Ahndung*; §65) inside (our body)—as a "sting of conscience" (*Gewissensbiß*). When I realize that the others are the same as I, I already share in their pain. This suffering is "wholly direct and even instinctive [*instinktartig*]."[2] And ultimately, this is to Schopenhauer the exact essence of freedom, which is again understood as grace.

Some recent developments in scholarship devoted to G. H. Mead's philosophy have raised his thought to an equal standing in relation to other key philosophers, not only in American pragmatism but also in the context of the Western philosophical tradition. Besides the undisputed role that Mead's thought has played in the social sciences, it is clear that his philosophy has much to offer with regard to some key contemporary epistemological and ethical problems. Erkki Kilpinen, for example, has recently convincingly argued that Mead would need to be recognized as the forerunner of Lakoff and Johnson's philosophical project,[3] calling Mead an empirically responsible philosopher. With his and other similar attempts, Mead's philosophy has become a part of the epistemological tradition dealing with the embodied mind. Others still have read Mead in an intercultural key or discussed some interesting comparative possibilities concerning the attunement of the body or the mind-body problem (e.g., Steve Odin in his paper[4] on Mead in *Philosophy of East and West* [1992] or philosophers using Shigenori Nagatomo's thought for his philosophy). But Mead's most important contribution to philosophy is undoubtedly his theory of intersubjectivity.

Much as Mead's role used to be underemphasized by the tradition of philosophy, Ludwig Feuerbach, too, was long considered a transitional philosopher to whom many authors ascribed significance for the later development of certain philosophical topics, such as criticism of religion, materialism, sensibility, etc., but to whom the Western tradition, nevertheless, did not wish to award a place of honor among the other philosophical giants of the West. However, with the epistemological preeminence of *skin* and *touch* and his original philosophy of sensibility, Feuerbach paved the way toward the first Western theory of intersubjectivity. The epistemological space of sensitivity in Feuerbach can be compared to Mead's genesis of an intersubjective self—in terms of gestures and as based on the primacy of "contact experience" in Mead. In his "phenomenology" of gesture, Mead ascribes great importance to the hand, which also opens interesting possibilities of interpreting him as a "haptic philosopher" (a remark made by his student David L. Miller; note also an elaboration of "hand" in Heidegger—as a gesture, carrying out the bodily/felt dimensions of meaning, as David Kleinberg-Levin asserts).

On the other side, there is Jean-Louis Chrétien, who in his *The Call and the Response*[5] deals precisely with the bodily scheme as proposed by some interpreters of Mead. Chrétien's epistemological credo ("I never start by saying 'I,' I start by being 'thou-ed' by the world"), together with his rehabilitation of touch (and space), is what we find to be a most interesting possibility today for extending both Feuerbachian and Meadian concepts of self to the contemporary philosophy of intersubjectivity. But Chrétien, in the ethical line of his argument, also mentions a related "nothingness" of self as a possibility for negating the old Biblical saying, "I am, and there is no one besides me" (Isa. 47:10). While here, both in his concept of touch as well as the nothingness of the self, interesting intercultural possibilities open, and it is through Watsuji Tetsurō's thought that we intend to eventually show the importance of the concept of *aidagara* ("relatedness," "betweenness") and climate, interpreted as both space *and* touch/contact, for the understanding of Mead's philosophy.

Coming to the Stage of Ethics

Let us begin our reflection with a highly interesting citation from *Kakyō*, Zeami's most important work on Japanese aesthetics. Zeami Motokiyo (1363–1443) was a Japanese aesthetician, actor, and playwright, influenced by Zen. *Kakyō* is his important work on the essence of Noh theatre. Symbolically, a reflection on theatre can, in our opinion, represent the essence of our intersubjective relations. The citation reads as follows:

> When [the actor] enters stage in a *sarugaku* [performance] and begins the [opening] speech or *issei* [passage], there will

be a peak for that moment. [Too] early is wrong. [Too] late will also be wrong.

To being with, [the actor] leaves the greenroom, walks onto the *hashigakari* [the bridge connecting the backstage to the main stage], and stops; he [then] takes in all directions, and he should speak just when the audience holds with anticipation the thought, "There, he's going to speak!" This is "the opportune moment [that] corresponds to the feeling [of the audience]," whereat [the actor] speaks after having caught the spirit of the audience. If this opportune moment is even a little bit late, the spirit of the audience will once again relax, and when he begins to recite after that, it will not correspond to everyone's feeling. This opportune moment is, simply, [a reflection of] the [receptive] *ch'i* of the spectators. What is called "the opportune moment that is the *ch'i* of the spectators" is a peak that the actor perceives by his intuition. This is the critical moment when [the actor] draws everyone's rapt attention just to this state of concentration. It is one of the [most] important moments of a given day['s performance].⁶

This paragraph by Zeami is extraordinary: it brings to the fore the most important elements of the intersubjective and gestural conversation we wish to analyze here: the threshold between the Noh actor and audience (me and other[s], in Meadian terms), indicating the conversational (breath-) space (*aidagara* in Watsuji, *air* and *water* in Aristotle's *On the Soul* 423a22,⁷ and, as we will see, in Chrétien) between them, and, importantly—in tune with Zen philosophy—the role of breath in this process. For a Noh actor it is decisive to appear on stage precisely at the moment when his audience would expect him to appear—and raise his voice. He has to come to the stage and raise his voice accordingly to the "spirit of the audience" (German *Gemeingefühl*). This points at the temporal as well as spatial problems of all intersubjective relations: if he is too late, even only by a moment, the common atmosphere/collective mood is lost. If he is there too early, again, the link with the audience is interrupted or broken. The actor must be a master of this *threshold*: he must know/sense intuitively, in his interiority and from the *breaths* and *hearts* of the audience, the exact time-space of his vocal appearance—a vocal gesture that, of course, is always an intersubjective or social act already.

Now, these short paragraphs by Zeami show the essence of what we understand as a fundamental layer of all intersubjective relations and especially ethics: the threshold (in theological-ethical terms, it will later be related to grace) as our time-space-between, as based on bodily signs in the course of our contact experience. We know that in Mead's philosophy in *Mind, Self and Society*, our body is itself a bridge to the other. We are also "reading the meaning of the conduct of other people, when, perhaps, they are not aware of it . . . just the glance of an eye, the attitude of the body."[8] But the bridge is always already a threshold that we need to address, both by intuition and cognition. Mead himself points to the first (precognitive) layer in his *1914 Lectures in Social Psychology*, in the chapter "Imitation and Imagination," when he states that we can discern various bodily signs in ourselves/our self, which can help us first establish the threshold or difference between the ego and the *alteri*, and then also bridge the gap to the other—such as an "organic sensation, cyclopean eye, feeling in the throat that accompanies articulation, kinaesthetic and visceral ideas."[9] All these elements are in the closest proximity to similar empirico-organic or process philosophies and theologies of our age. But their first predecessor was Feuerbach. Let us first take a closer look into his philosophy.

Constitution of the Other in Feuerbach, Chrétien, and Watsuji

Now, through some recent scholarship on Mead it has become clear that his philosophy is complementary to the field of embodied cognition or embodied mind. Moreover, in the "Introduction" to his already mentioned 1914 and 1927 class lectures, D. L. Miller calls Mead both a process philosopher and, even more importantly, a haptic philosopher.[10] In relation to the concept of the so-called contact experience in Mead, this is of great importance for this analysis. Namely, in this line of reasoning we can easily think Mead's original constitution of the conversation of gestures in the language of the philosophy of skin (Feuerbach), touch (Chrétien), and the betweenness of persons (Watsuji; also a climate or *fūdo*). But even more importantly, all these reflections inaugurate a completely different layer in the relation between the "I" and the "me," between my self and the selves of the others, which now constitutes my social self. As K. J. Booth[11] argues, in this process "there must be a basic level of consciousness that is developmentally prior to taking the attitude of the other and that develops into self-consciousness." He refers to Shigenori Nagatomi's well-known distinction between the subject-body and the object-body, where the former is the body in the sense of the epistemic center of our consciousness. We can acknowledge this as a basic postulate for securing the place of interiority in our social selves. But what kind of logic constitutes this interiority? At this point, one step farther has to be taken. We know that for Mead both attitude and gesture are fully embodied. But how does Mead, being a haptic philosopher, understand our intersubjective relations between embodied individuals or bodies that touch one another? Let us now take a detour through three other philosophers and present three meditations on a Meadian theme, only to be able to return to Mead and try to offer some answers to this question.

According to Hans Joas,[12] Mead is "the most important theorist of intersubjectivity between Feuerbach and Habermas." But is there an even more substantive link between Feuerbach and Mead? Feuerbach's theory of intersubjectivity is not defined in "Meadian" terms, of course. But there are two important facts to be discussed: the very constitution of the other, on the one side, and the role of the body/skin, on the other. Analogous to Mead's constitution of the intersubjective/social self via "I" and "me," is Feuerbach's statement, at the end of *Principles of Philosophy of Future*, that the true dialectic is posited not as a monologue of a solitary thinker to himself, but as a continuous dialogue between "I" and "Thou." Moreover, Feuerbach bases his philosophy of sensibility on the elements of Nature. To these he adjoins the human being as another element of Nature, along with organs or body parts (eyes, head, heart, stomach, sexual organs) among which, in its preeminent position as the fundamental organ of perception, appears none other than the *skin*. Feuerbach as a haptic philosopher? Perhaps—for the philosophy of sensibility (or rather sensitivity) begins in the body, especially in the skin/touch. In an exceptional passage from his 1841 work entitled *Some Comments on the "Beginning of Philosophy" of Dr J. F. Reiff*, Feuerbach states the following:

> Through the body, the Self is not the Self, but rather an object. Being-in-the-body means being-in-the-world. So many senses— so many pores. The self is nothing other than the *porous* self.[13]

The porous nature of our self now indicates something extremely important: our self (which is basically understood as the sentient being) is only constituted objectively or socially through its fundamental intersubjective act; just as we depend epistemologically on Nature (the role of elements and sensitivity), we depend ethically/socially on others. Feuerbach adds something else to this constellation: it is precisely and only through our intersubjective and social acts that we experience something infinitely bigger than we and our finite selves are, which is love (or grace).[14] This *excess of love* in Feuerbach is precisely the missing link of all previous ethics: the interval of love/grace—as already shown by Schopenhauer and now posited by Feuerbach for the first time in the history of philosophy—as an intersubjective act. Löwith reminds us that even before I am aware, "I have already left *Nature,* the *unconscious,* founded on the *Dasein* of the Other."[15] Another step needs to be taken—toward the reflection on touch in the philosophy of Jean-Louis Chrétien.

If we insist on the significance of contact experience in Mead, and put Feuerbach's theory of sensibility (skin, sense organs, and nature) qua intersubjectivity into an *epoché* for a moment, then Chrétien's philosophy of contact/touch as a key novelty in recent phenomenology (and philosophy in general) is of great importance for any constitution of intersubjective relations. Firstly, for Chrétien, we only live to respond—to the other, to our closest environment, and to God. In this, for him, the body is the highest representation of the spirit. But the most important of all experiences is the tactile/haptic experience, or touch. In this constellation, the call, our voice, our conscious response and act, always comes too late, or in Chrétien's words:

> Does the call, upon which we have meditated at such length in our preceding chapters, not indeed always come too late, if it finds us already constituted without it, before it, in the silence of a sensing that is originally turned toward the self, even when the self is affected by another?[16]

The priority of our self-constitution is based on the self-receptivity of touch. Translated into Meadian terms, our desire to emit any kind of vocal gesture is already constituted prior to any reflexivity, in a milieu of touch. In Chrétien, touch exceeds tact, since it is not limited to a mere contact. In the paragraph by Aristotle, we have seen that no animal is deprived of touch and that "the sense of touch is inseparable from life itself."[17] Through touch we enter into relationships with others, since the experience of touch is a basic experience of contact (or, its precondition and milieu) that we all have in our life affairs. But it is important to acknowledge, as also Aristotle would already know, that the interval between us and others is never abolished, that our touch, paradoxically, never touches and thus, as it were, safeguards the difference and autonomy of the other person. The touch is, of course, present in a manner by which we generally address (same as in Feuerbach) our sensitivity. But there is another paradoxical element in the touch: as a sense organ (i.e., skin) it is oriented toward the outer world, for, as an organ, it "cannot be nor become an object to itself."[18] Here, the intersubjective process begins (structurally, this is analogous to both Feuerbach and Mead):

> I feel myself only by favor of the other. It is the other who gives me to myself insofar as the return to myself and to my own actions or affections always supposes this other. The most intimate sensation, the sensation of my own sensitive life in act, is also the most open, and its intimacy is deployed only through its openness. To feel oneself is not a beginning, but a response to the appeal made by a sensible that is other than myself and that elicits the exercise of my acts. I never start by saying "I," I start by being "thou-ed" by the world.[19]

This statement, written in the phenomenological language, is very close to Mead's constitution of gesture as a social act. But perhaps it is only in its excess that the logic of touch can really be understood. In his final words in the chapter "Body and Touch," Chrétien goes so far as to refer to the *touch* of God: Saint John of the Cross, namely, speaks of "God's touch" and interprets it as the "'merciful hand of the Father' with which he touches the Son."[20] This is a caress, an ethical gesture of sympathy and compassion. And it is Aquinas who understands this touching as grace, an excess we cannot understand or—properly speaking—condition. Isn't Mead's elaboration of sympathetic gesture in the closest proximity to this mystical constellation? He states: "The other is a different person and, being different, his suffering is different from mine, but he is a suffering being to whom I react immediately."[21] It is now time to address our third example, Watsuji Tetsurō's philosophy of *aidagara*.

In his excellent study of Mead's and Watsuji Tetsurō's (1889–1960) philosophy and communitarian ethics, Steve Odin[22] points to a deep structural proximity between both thinkers.[23] For Watsuji, the main problem in philosophy is related to the question of personhood (*ningen*) and betweenness (or, relatedness; *aidagara*)—as our social self. For him the substance is multiple, not solitary. Influenced by Heidegger, Watsuji's philosophy aims at addressing the neglected problem of spatiality (as we know, temporality was in the forefront of Heidegger's analyses). As Odin[24] states, "The notion of self as a substance with a fixed essence is abandoned for a relationally defined self which is fluid, shifting, open, decentred, multiple, and social in nature." Since Watsuji's philosophy is closely linked to Japanese aesthetics, it is of no coincidence, of course, that there is a close analogy between the constellations of Zeami's *Kakyō* on the one hand and Watsuji's on the other. Watsuji (as a Confucian and a Buddhist) has devoted his entire thought to the communitarian problem in ethics: being-with-others in community is now the basic mode of our self-constitution. In his analysis, Odin shows this in a convincing manner, also by addressing all of the most important elements of Mead's philosophy.[25] It is also important to acknowledge—as Odin[26] presents to us in his paper—various analyses on the topic of Buddhist emptiness (*shunyata*) and the interrelated existence as an organismic process in Whitehead and American pragmatism.

But to be able to go one step farther and prepare the ground for an analysis of Feuerbach, Chrétien, and Watsuji *with* Mead, let us take a closer look at Watsuji's work *Climate* (*Fūdo*), which gathers all of the most important themes of his philosophy and relates them to a unique cosmological constellation, which is nevertheless similar to our pragmatist process-oriented thinking in Whitehead, Dewey, or Mead. For Watsuji, climate "includes both society and living nature,"[27] and *aidagara* as an interval (and the main "function" of climate) is structured on the basis of the Buddhist ontological mode of emptiness—which thus "empties" our self and establishes a new *space* of interrelatedness or betweenness of persons. Some critics saw this as a weakness of Watsuji's theory, possibly leading to fascism or strong communitarianism as compared to Mead and his model, based on communicative or symbolic interaction. But in a more positive reading, the climate as an interspace can be of great value for our intersubjective relations. It can become the matrix of a new ethics, based on touch, sympathy, and humility. Norman Wirzba[28] addresses humility as a key consequence of Chrétien's philosophy of touch: we have to empty ourselves of our egotistic nature of the mode *I am and there is no one besides me* and enter ethical relations with the other based on humility, and thus reciprocity and responsiveness: "I feel myself only by the favor of the other,"[29] and, even more importantly, "We need the space between self and other, so that we can learn to act on another's behalf."[30] This space is the *climate* of our intersubjective relations, based on contact experience and touch. For Watsuji,[31] climate is what constitutes and underpins our self-understanding. We can never begin with a Cartesian or even Kantian gesture since we are always situated in an interspace—i.e., climate. Here we must return to Feuerbach: his philosophy of the elements as natural habitats of our body-self (especially water and air) and also the related echo of Aristotle in Chrétien—as an insistence on a medium (also consisting of water or air) between our "touch" and its "object" is now the main argument for a new understanding of an ethical constellation of gestures in Mead, as well. There is an analogy with our example from the Japanese Noh theatre—as in art and our conversational processes, so in atmospheric phenomena: according to Watsuji, we cannot feel the cold of the outer world or exist in it without always already being exposed. Analogically, we live in a social climate with its rituals. But the question still remains: Which impulse in *ourselves* enables us to enter intersubjective relations, or, how is it possible to move our hand toward the other within the betweenness, time-space (*aidagara*, climate) of an ethical gesture?

An Interval of Grace

> For there to be gift event (we say event and not act), something must come about or happen, in an instant, in an instant that no doubt does not belong to the economy of time, in a time without time, in such a way that the forgetting forgets, that it forgets *itself*, but also in such a way that this forgetting without being something present, presentable, determinable, sensible, or meaningful, is not nothing.
>
> —Jacques Derrida, "Given Time: The Time of the King"

We have seen that in Chrétien's phenomenology the basic intersubjective constellation ("I start by being 'thou-ed' by the world") is accompanied by the notion of humility (emptying of our self), in a space that we both/all share. In the final part of this presentation we intend to argue that behind the scenes, as it were, there appears a possibility in Mead for an inauguration of a space of interiority where our "social" time (communication as a mode of reciprocity or reflection of the reactions of others in me based on one-dimensional or successive time) similarly reverses into an ethical time—as an impossible time of grace as gift and hospitality. This grace, or this absolute and impossible gift, as Derrida[32] observes, "interrupts economy" and thus does not permit us to lean on any vulgar form of the economy of exchange and reciprocity. Economy is circular, says Derrida. Intersubjectivity based on economy and exchange is also circular. But the gift of an ethical gesture in us is an interruption, an impossible act that inaugurates the time and space of interiority.[33] Only within the atmosphere of this interruption is an ethical act possible.

From Schopenhauer we know that there is a gap between our conscious (in ethical terms *egoistic*) act, which follows my will (and is, in turn, part of the metaphysical Will), and our pure altruistic action (such as sympathy, compassion, *agápe*, or *caritas*), which is based on the denial of the Will. This gap cannot be explained in logical terms, and is only possible when the very rational (volitional) logic is reverted: in order to be able to act ethically, we have to deny our will. It is precisely in this act of the denial of the Will that Schopenhauer[34] discloses freedom qua grace.[35] Translated into the ethics of intersubjectivity, and in relation to our constellation above (with Feuerbach, Chrétien, and Watsuji as three peaks in our new interpretative space), all this means that there is a shared ethical space in our interiority or within our ethical core that we can call the atmosphere of ethics. Beyond the more common inside-outside divide where dualistic logic leads us toward old dualisms, we rather seek for a processual ethics of reciprocity (call, response, anticipation, common climate), but with one important feature: that ultimately, our ethical act and our touching of the other (with the touch/direct/contact experience understood more broadly and not merely in the sense of "tact" and tactile experience) is always already situated within an ethical interval or gap in a time-space.

Let us remind ourselves once more of our example from *Kakyō*: we think that Mead is actually very close to this constellation: our act is always attuned to the very response of the other. Mead does not use words such as the *ch'i* of the audience (society), but from his thought it is evident that he knows perfectly well that we have to secure our inner space or interiority (embodied mind, embodied cognition) to be able to enter, as it were, the stage of epistemology or ethics. Upon discussing sympathy, in his 1914 class lectures Mead gives an interesting passage:

> The idea of looking into the eyes of one who is suffering involves an inner idea. . . . The other is a different person and, being different, his suffering is different from mine, but he is a suffering being to whom I react immediately. Other individuals exist for us as having inner ideas, which in a certain sense we can never penetrate. . . . It is because the material is the same that other persons have an inner idea of us. . . . The child is conscious of the hard floor long before

he is aware of the introdermal self that is injured by the hard floor.[36]

There is a further need to explore this secret and paradoxical time-space of ethics, and here we have only taken the first step in that direction. We can never become other persons, and this fact secures their and our autonomy and freedom. There always exists an interval between us, one that Aristotle mentioned in his *On the Soul*. But there is another gap or interval, one that cannot be observed epistemologically since it evades its very logic: it is best visible in a caress, and the *behind the scenes* logic, as it were. Like the actor from *Kakyō*, who must know, even before coming on stage, what he is to expect from the audience, we too, precognitively know well before his appearance how we would act. But the mystery of all ethics that we wanted to point out here lies precisely in this infinitely short moment before our ethical act: this moment is called an *interval of grace*, or the *excess of love*.

meeting interval

PART II

PHILOSOPHY / ONTOLOGY OF LOVE

clearing love

4

CLARA / THE MATRIX

In *The Erotic Phenomenon*, Jean-Luc Marion[1] puts forth a hypothesis on the forgetting of love in the history of "philosophy" and wants to reconstruct an inquiry on love—only to be able to give (erotic) love the proper place and attention that it deserves. As a phenomenologist, Marion is primarily concerned with the erotic phenomenon and with its various philosophical forms, such as erotic reduction and related phenomena accompanying its incarnations in our lifeworlds (for example, the lover and desire, the body *as* flesh, but also the child as the "third party"; *The Erotic*). Various accounts of the topic of love can be found throughout the history of philosophy and theology; they generally focus on either its *erotic* or *agapistic* character. From Plato to Maximus the Confessor on the one hand or, for another example, from Kierkegaard to Lacan on the other, love has too often been philosophically and theologically appropriated, even metaphysically abused. Love could not become a way of cultivating our Being as self-transcendence and was too often guided and appropriated by a preestablished idea of the divine/God—a God being generally a monarchic Lord, predominantly male, and existing for us in one of its metaphysically stable forms. In this attempt, we wish to analyze the primordial and immanent nature of love in its ontological temporality and show that it is only through this ontological preeminence of love that the divine can be revealed to us. This revelation is a mystery; a gesture *of* and *for* our soul, a gesture that is even stronger than death. We are thinking of a gesture, beautifully described by Irigaray with the following words:

> Philosophy and theology will find in this wisdom of love a possible reconciliation. The divine there assumes an important

place as the becoming of the human itself which, through love, transubstantiates body and spirit.[2]

By reading Schelling and Irigaray, we will show here that their original attempts toward (re)grounding a new ontology of love were needed in order to fill the lacuna in the very heart of the history of our philosophical (and theological) thought. This regrounding is the meaning of the term *reconciliation,* as used by Irigaray in the above passage from *The Way of Love.* It seems too obvious that love (mainly of wisdom, sometimes of a fellow human being, or even nonhuman animals) has been the fuel of philosophical activity since the most ancient times. In theology, love—self-evidently—was even one of the cardinal theological virtues. However, there is another remark, again from Irigaray and similar to Marion's observation on the forgetting of love, a remark that questions this self-evident nature of love in philosophy (and, by addition, in theology): it is the question of why "philosophy" (like theology, a "discourse about God") could not have become the wisdom of love and has, instead, always been understood in a reverse sense as the love of wisdom? And, analogously perhaps, why theology was not first a narrative of love in its earthly incarnations—love as a scent of proximity—and has instead become a sterile and odorless scholastic discipline, dealing with various metaphysically underpinned categories and "proofs" of God. Perhaps this statement cannot be properly linguistically or semantically justified, but without doubt this rule of wisdom over love is still one of the most significant features of Western philosophical history.

Toward Schelling's *Clara*

Schelling's *Clara* (written in 1810)[3] is without doubt one of the rarest and most precious events in the history of philosophy since its inception in the ancient Greek world. Having Clara as its main character—in the very center of the German Idealism period and, for instance, being written only eighteen years after Mary Wollstonecraft's *A Vindication of the Rights of Woman*—it is without doubt philosophical prose worthy of our most careful reading. In relative proximity to Schelling's feminine gesture, only Ludwig Feuerbach, in his essay "On Spiritualism and Materialism,"[4] invokes sexual difference as a key ontological feature of our Being.[5] Schelling's *Clara* is situated in his so-called middle period with, in our opinion, three of the most important works written at all by Schelling: *Philosophical Inquiries into the Nature of Human Freedom* (1809), *Clara* (probably written in 1810 and first published as a fragment only in 1861 by his son), and, finally, *The Ages of the World* (the 1813 and subsequent drafts). These works fall into a very difficult period, following the illness and death of Schelling's beloved wife Caroline in 1809. Jason Wirth rightly states in his "Introduction" to *Schelling Now* that, with his middle works, Schelling is "better construed not as the already sublimated objective counterpart to Fichte . . . but rather as the belated contemporary of thinkers like Heidegger, Derrida, Bataille, Irigaray, Foucault, Deleuze, Levinas, and many others."[6] Wirth also nicely captures the topics, defining this uncanniness of Schelling for his own age: the ontological difference, the primacy of the Good (or *love*, as we will see), the irreducible remainder in his thought, the self-overcoming of dialectical thinking, and nonduality, among other features of his work.[7]

The main theme of *Clara* is death. *Clara* is also a dialogue on the ontology of mourning, though. The dialogue begins on All Souls' Day, with Clara, the Priest, and the Doctor discussing the special setting of the festival of the dead, with its inherent scent of the autumnal transition into winter. Clara, remembering and mourning the loss of her husband Albert (i.e., Schelling, mourning his loss of Caroline—one of her middle names was "Albertine"), argues that there must be a link, or a communication between this world and the next world—the spiritual world of the dead. This ontological temporality of Clara's main question and concern emerge from her devotion to her late husband, and from her love for him. Clara's question leads us to the very un-Kantian line of argument that, somehow, and in a way still to be revealed to us, a spiritual world (of deceased others) lives in us and is thus accessible to us. Clearly, and this is Schelling's idea, this thesis *cannot* be represented or even analyzed by means of our inherited philosophical or theological vocabularies but, rather, is an expression of our inner world, a world of ethical anatomy, and its materiality—for which we still need to invent the language, as well as ethical gestures. Let us approach Schelling's narrative as a proof of this movement. At the very beginning of the text, we find these tender words of a young mother, mourning the loss of her children:

> [T]here at the grave of her children lost so young, a mother stood in silence, with no need for consecrated water to represent her tears, for tears sanctified by sweet melancholy flowed gently down to freshen the mounds.[8]

These words are not only a literary expression, or a metaphorical tool; important material and ethical signifiers are encapsulated in this short paragraph: *elemental waters, sanctity and materiality of tears, feminine presence, silence,* and *melancholy (or mourning)*. Tears, as emerging/materializing from our bodies—literally from nowhere, transgress the invisible border between the body and the soul/spirit and represent our forgotten or hidden memory of primeval cosmic waters and the feminine divine. The tears of this silent or discrete mourning are a powerful symbol of a hidden cosmico-spiritual connection we still need to conceptualize. Already, in *The Gift of Death*, Derrida argued that we would need "to make new inroads into thinking concerning the body . . . in order to come closer one day to what makes us tremble or what makes us cry."[9] This primordial setting is followed by a gentle eschatological hint from Schelling; namely, that on All Souls' Day, "brothers came again to brothers, and children to parents; at this moment all were one family again," and with the question of how meaningful and fitting it might be that "these autumn flowers should be consecrated to the dead, who hand us cheerful flowers from their dark chambers in spring as the eternal witness to the continuation of life and eternal resurrection."[10]

Clara is a text on life worth mourning, and, in our opinion, the first philosophical text in the history of Western thought entirely dedicated to the forgotten ontology of love. Contrary to our expectations, the ontology of love could not appear within a dialectical/phenomenological or theological relationality and its inherent intersubjective or human-divine logic. The ontological setting Schelling is getting at here is of another order. Let us first listen to Clara's words on life, its grievability, and death, in order to be able to see this ontologically invoked inception of proximity in ourselves:

> Thousands of relationships may break apart in this life, perhaps they only ever affected our inner being in a hostile or at least disturbing way, but the tie of a truly divine love is as unbreakable as the essence of the soul in which it is founded and is as eternal as a word of a God. If children had been given to me and then they were all taken away, I could never consider it as chance or a temporary fortune to have been the mother of these souls; I would feel—yes, I would know—that they belong to me eternally and I to them and that no power on Earth or in heaven could take them from me or me from them.[11]

These are clearly words on the preeminence of love, and its inseparable part is the maternal-feminine genealogy, as put into the very core of her thinking of *a soul* as an inner controller (i.e., a subject in her self-affection), and not as an object of God. Paradoxically, only with this ontological reduction into the logic of the feminine-maternal-matrixial subject, are we able to approach the plane of immanence (Deleuze), where material communication or a link with our most dear will be able to appear. With this reflection of Clara, we are thus abandoning heteronomous logic or appropriation of love. Now, let us return to our text: on Clara's exposition of the eternal nature of our attachment and love, the Doctor raised an objection, that it is in fact our subjective feeling that makes these attitudes of ours and relationships eternal, to which Clara answers one more time:

> Don't you believe, Clara interrupted, that other higher relationships, such as love and friendship, are also of a divine nature; that a quiet, unconscious, but thereby all the more compelling, necessity draws one soul to another?[12]

What is it, then, again, that draws one soul to another? In Clara, we have three realities: body, soul, and spirit. While the Doctor represents the bodily aspect, and the Priest our spiritual existence, Clara is attached to the soul and its mysterious role of uniting both bodily and spiritual aspects of the human being. The soul, understood in this way, is the link between the two realities and it is only in this sense that it is also "the logical foundation of consciousness and basis of existential individuality."[13] Moreover, Clara contends that even after death there exists a continuation of an "uncorrupted communication of souls."[14] If this connection is not based on our bodily or spiritual awareness, what kind of link connects the living with the departed? What then, is a soul?

In his interpretation of *Clara*, Alexander Grau points to the Catholic and, more specifically, Franciscan context of this dialogue: in his opinion the answer to the question of soul lies in Schelling's "efforts to reground the relationship between a human being and Nature."[15] Schelling argues in his *Stuttgart Seminars* from 1810 (they therefore also belong to the middle period of his writings) that a human being is a link between Spirit and Nature. Moreover, it is the destiny of a human being to elevate Nature to its higher rank: but wasn't it precisely Christ who was first able to elevate Nature toward its (pen)ultimate spiritual rank or, to put it more emphatically, to enliven nature with a breath coming out of his Soul? We want to approach this most difficult of all questions, posited by Schelling, by quoting another passage from *Clara*:

> Yes, isn't it conceivable that the more the spiritual breaks through in this external life, the less the underworld has power over the dead; or shall we consider even those words carried down from Christ about victory over the ancient kingdom of the dead as completely empty, general figures of speech?[16]

In his recent theological narrative (*The Insistence of God*), Caputo deals with the problem of us, human beings, facing death: he states, not without a slightly ironical note, "When faced with death, resurrection is always the issue."[17] To take this seriously, though, the possibility of the impossible, from radical resurrection theology, as Caputo puts it (we will be able to detect in these phenomena the mystery of love, but only later), this event of life in the midst of death, is what might help us to understand the rather obscure scenery of Schelling's *Clara*. Caputo elaborates on this in his three examples of resurrection theology (one of them is the raising of Lazarus, the second is Deleuze's pure immanence of *a* life and, obviously, the third is the very resurrection of Christ's body). It is important for us which word (it is *love*) Caputo uses at the most decisive place of his argument: on facing death, and hoping for more life to be able to spend with our beloved or with our friends (we would be grateful even for a moment, or a day more to be with someone we love), we live in faith that this miracle can happen: this faith, for Caputo, is precisely believing in life *as* love, whence "belief" must be understood in its archaic English/Germanic sense from the root *lief* (*lieben*)—to love:

> To believe is to be-love, to love what we believe, to believe what we love, and what we love is life, more life, and a chance for a new being.[18]

This is what the New Testament authors wanted to tell us from the highest time of their first-century faith, and this is why they decided to include the rather impossible story of the death and raising of Lazarus (impossible even in the context of New Testament miracles) in the *Gospel of John*. There is more to this story, though: we learn from this story that Lazarus had already been in the tomb for four days. However, two sisters, Martha and Mary, who believe in resurrection on the last day, still cannot accept the death of their beloved brother: it is mourning and love for their dead brother that we experience in this story. When he comes to Martha and Mary's home, the two sisters tell Jesus that if he had been there earlier, their beloved brother would not have died. Jesus consoles the sisters and starts to weep. Caputo, in his radical hermeneutical manner, now says that these were obviously crocodile tears, since Jesus evidently knew that Lazarus was dying and had still decided not to come to Bethany before Lazarus had actually died. We would like to interpret the story of Lazarus in a slightly less hermeneutical manner, though, and instead offer a cosmical reading of this parable: according to us, this story recounts in its idiosyncratic manner what was already stated by Irigaray in her reading of Antigone: according to her, what Antigone wanted to protect with her act was respect for life and the cosmic order, respect for generational order, and respect for sexuate differentiation—after all three orders were brutally attacked and annihilated by Creon. New masculine genealogies were installed in their place. Antigone wanted to protect the *singularity* of her dead brother—in his unique and irreplaceable generational role (since both parents are dead)—with a proper burial. Jesus's act of raising Lazarus to life is of a similar order but, if Antigone's logic is of a cosmic character, Jesus operates on an eschatological plane. Antigone's and Jesus's acts are both of the highest ethical order: both operate at the supreme level of the ontology of love, love being belief in the impossible in life, love thus being stronger even than death. This belief and this love means, if we recall Butler here, that life is grievable. For both Martha and Mary, the loss of their brother is irreplaceable. All three have shared the same motherly womb, and the tears of both women express the maternal-feminine genealogy already mentioned above. This is why Jesus weeps on seeing the two women in their mourning—as stated by many feminist theologians, there are many signs pointing to the fact that he belongs ontologically to the same maternal-feminine genealogy.[19] Nevertheless, why was it necessary to raise Lazarus from the reign of dead? Why were this impossible story and this impossible act necessary for early Christians and their faith? The answer might be surprising: the reign of love, and the related ontology of mourning, are of a higher, or better, a more primordial order than *both* life and death. Christ was thus both incarnated as Jesus and—as many theologians since Teilhard de Chardin have described—also in the cosmos.[20] This is what Schelling was attempting to prove in his *Clara* (but even more in his major writings from the middle period: we will have to return to Schelling's ontology for this purpose). It is because, according to Butler, "there is no life and no death without a relation to some frame."[21] This frame is now beautifully described by Caputo, who leaves aside completely his earlier hermeneutical irony and speaks with the words of a theologian. By returning one more time to Lazarus in the final chapter of his book on cosmopoetics, Yeshua, as he is now called by Caputo,

> had come to mediate between the sisters and the stars, to let the cosmic graces of the earth and sky, the cosmic gifts of bread and wine, of airy laughter and moist tears, pass back and forth between his grieving flesh and theirs. . . . Yeshua gave them back their lives. He gave them more life. Yeshua fulfills the promise of the world. When people meet him, they are reborn.[22]

This is our "truth" now, but still not without a cosmico-ontological mystery, or mediation of *a* difference: the world we inhabit is more than just a world; its "truth" is related to what Clara asks—and we need to return to Schelling here—namely, within her final meditation on elements when she raises the following question: "Where does that deep devotion to Earth come from?"—a question immediately following the astonishing observation of hers:

> Shouldn't we generally more often observe the same sensitivity to the departed that we believe we owe to the living? Who knows whether they partake more deeply with us than we think; whether the pain we feel so intensely, the excess of tears we weep for them, isn't capable of unsettling them?[23]

This observation by Clara might illuminate what we might call the mysterious remainder that still persists in the story of Lazarus, namely: From whence did the sisters' mourning come?

We now wish to wind up this meditation with the words of absence and presence, of tears, sorrow and mourning, written by Jeff Stewart.

> You have kept count of my tossings: put my tears in your bottle. Are they not in your record?
>
> —Ps. 56:8

A vase for tears. That bottle. Each tear drop caught, safe in a slender long necked phial held against someone's cheek, just below the tear duct. The clear, or perhaps blue, or even gold filigreed lachrymal cold against your face, warming infinitesimally with each freshly caught drop. He thought, I wish for its glass lip to touch my cheek, catching the flowers of those memories of our son. Holding again, first as tear drop, second within the phial, what the man knew to be still alive refusing all counselling to die.

This is him. In his clothes, in his shoes we bought especially for the day. This is him. Yet not. He is present, but not here, simultaneously. If this is not him, how could that be? If we were to continue saying that this person is somehow not him, would we be saying that he is no longer a person at all? But how could that be? And if we did continue to speak of him as no longer being present, we could, or would have just, contributed to his further vanishing. Yet, looking into the coffin, into his face, at his shut eyes, and at his large folded hands, there is confusion, and we ask again, is this still him? Yes. But then, no. How could it be? Looking through grief with a friend who in tears has come to see him, consoling her, together we know this is him, but also in our sorrows are aware of his true absence, which is why we grieve. Jostling forward and back between absence and presence, never understanding. To kiss his face is to touch his once complete aliveness masked by the brutal and cold passivity of a preserved no longer flesh. Is that rouge? Are those really still his hands? To her standing close: I will help hold you up, if you could please help hold me? Even if it's impossible? Facing him, how could he be both absent and present? How could this body laid out so neatly still be he who has gone from us, he who was never so still? Even in sleep. How could this body be him, when it will be ashes in a grey neat box resting on top of a bookcase, a box always near, surrounded by sentimental ornaments with a card sent by him one Christmas open on top of the box's closed lid. While this, in this open box, is this still him? He, who will never call again, who will never again respond to any of our reachings out. As he will never be able to speak—to us, to anybody. To himself. And we, we three, will never be able to resolve what we feel so desperately needs to be resolved. Never again to witness his continued becoming. He will remain, as he is in the photo taken shortly before he died, laughing, and as he said in his Christmas card, feeling like it was going to be a good year. And here, now, in this casket, is this the one who wrote to us? Or is that person gone? And if neither absent or present, how? Where? As this strange body? As this photo, these ashes? This memory? Not merely memory surely? Not memory but something far more substantial, more alive, yet so frail. How is that so? This more than memory that comes to us from within our body, and from him, and from his mother, felt here, and here. From where his touch, our living arises.

The mother tells her dearest friend:

Not long after we returned home from the mountains where we celebrated our son's birthday, the first after his death, a young woman, with her two and half year-old son, knocked on our front door. I didn't recognise her, but she said she was an old school friend of our boy's, and because it had recently been his birthday, she thought she would like to say hello. After talking for a while I recalled who she was. She spoke of her love for our son, even though he had robbed her, and lied to her. These were not the stories I was hoping to hear, the woman said. But the young woman also told us of how much she loved our son, how he had helped her. Helped her become the woman she was today; still studying, trying to do well in her life, with her own son. And our son, the old woman continued, had also been this young woman's first true love. And, she still loved him. My husband and I took it in turns playing with her child while the other talked with her. And playing with the boy, for us, said the woman smiling, was as important as talking with her, an old friend of our son, who had taken time to visit.[24]

Schelling with Böhme: The Matrix

The sublime presence of love in this world, our mourning for the departed and our mysterious connection to the abyssal ground of our existence—they all point to the surplus of love we still need to conceptualize. This mystery of our being within the paradoxical and tragic temporality of love—first as evaporating and disappearing minute after minute with the passing of a dear person, and radicalizing through the very last gestures of intersubjectivity toward the closing in death—but then, again, also as a mysterious and discrete remainder, or surplus of love that cannot be taken away from us even with the death of a beloved person. . . . All this is presented in the painting "The Sick Child" by Edvard Munch from 1886. Munch painted in this artwork his beloved sister Sophie, a sixteen-year-old child on her deathbed (at that time Edvard was fifteen years old; he painted it when he was twenty-three). Now, in his essay on "The Sick Child," Hans Henrik Grelland writes the following:

> The painting depicts Sophie Munch at her deathbed, on the edge of dying of tuberculosis. At the bedside, we see the head of Aunt Karen, her deceased mother's sister, who had taken over the role of a mother in the Munch family. . . . I imagine the shocking experience this incidence must have been for the young sensitive boy. Not only is Sophie ill, she is really ill, it cannot be dreamt away or wiped out, it is real, intensively and cruelly real, it is really her, and what he sees it is really happening. For Munch, making a painting is not about dreams or images, it about real experiences, it is a way of confronting what is there, what is, being.[25]

In Munch's painting, the grieving aunt sitting at Sophie's bed represents an existentially radicalized intersubjective moment of two women—Edvard's sister Sophie, suffering from tuberculosis, and dead from the same illness Munch's mother's sister—aunt Karen. Within the framework of our matrixial theory of love, the painting represents the dying daughter and the desperately sad mother (here replaced by the aunt) in an impossibly sad moment, observed by the painter itself: the mother knows that the daughter is dying. Edvard observes this moment with the eye of a younger brother, and transfigures it into the extreme melancholic expression of the painting. The roughness and darkness of the bed, women's clothes, and all the surrounding environment represent the waning of the strongest tie—love of a mother for her child. Motherly care for the child retreats slowly, but unreturnably, into grief and mourning. But the clearing in front of Sophie's gaze—an unhomely horizon of pale brightness and enigmatic light offered to her—is it there for her eyes, to console her, or is it there for us, silent bystanders of this drama?

In this world, we have an excess, or a mystery of love: love of the living—being even perhaps able to unsettle the dead, and our mourning for *a* life being lost, our tears and sorrows coming from the hidden memory of—what exactly? From whence precisely does this sorrow come? In his interpretation of *Clara*, Jason Wirth approaches this problem from the point of view of the Ground or, in a still more radical manner, its inherent (self-)intrusion into an abyss (*Ab-grund, Ungrund*). Schelling elaborates on this mysterious relationality within the Ground as follows:

> The essence of the basis, or of existence, can only be precedent to all bases, that is, the absolute viewed directly, the groundless. . . . But the groundless divides itself into two equally eternal beginnings only in order that the two which could not be in it as groundless at the same time, or there be one, should become one through love.[26]

The secret of love, as we will see, is *abyssal*; and it is love that unites all beings—beings that would otherwise be separated and exist each only for itself. However, the nature of this unification or cosmic connection is what we would like to tackle in our reading of Schelling's *Clara* with his *Freedom* essay and *Ages of the World*. For Schelling, it is necessary that God also has in itself a source of sadness—it is "the veil of sadness that is spread over all nature."[27] This is why it is necessary for Schelling to have a concept of God, who suffers as a human being (Jesus Christ) and shares sorrow and tears with us human beings. Jesus's nature is one of a nexus between two ontological realms, as we will see (i.e., between the matrix and the soul). Now, according to Schelling, the procession of things from God is a mark of the self-revelation of God. In Christ, as the paramount stage of the self-revelation of God, are revealed both our past and our future—Christ must rule until all enemies are defeated—and, he adds, until "[t]he last enemy that is transcended is death." It is this sentence on the preeminence of love that enables the ontological circle within the Ground of all Being to be closed again:

> But if all will have become subject to him, then the Son himself shall also be subjected to him that did subject all things unto him, that God may be all in all. For not even spirit itself is supreme; it is but spirit, or the breath of love. But love is supreme. It is that which was before there were the depths and before existence (as separate entities), but it was not there as love, rather—how shall we designate it?[28]

For Schelling, in the groundless realm of the first Being there exist neither good nor evil. This ontological realm is beyond all duality. The most important gesture of Schelling comes now, though, when he states (and now we read his perhaps most important paragraph in its entirety):

> But the groundless divides itself into two equally eternal beginnings only in order that the two which could not be in it as groundless at the same time, or there be one, should become one through love; that is, it divides itself only that there may be life and love and personal existence. For there is love neither in indifference nor where antitheses are combined which require the combination in order to be; but rather (to repeat a word which has already been spoken) this is the secret of love, that it unites such beings as could each exist in itself, and nonetheless neither is nor can be without the other.[29]

We have two beginnings, and they are posited within the Groundless (*Ungrund*), and they can only be conjoined by love (and not by spirit); this abyss, or Groundless, is beyond all identity and difference. But we still cannot give a proper answer to this "great riddle of all times"[30] of love and God without reading another paragraph from *Ages of the World* here:

> And just as the will that wills nothing is Highest in man, so too in God himself—this very will is above God. For under God we can only think of the highest good, which is an already determined will. But in the will that wills nothing there is neither this nor that, neither good nor evil, neither what-is nor being, neither affection nor aversion, neither love nor wrath, and yet the strength to be all of them.[31]

There is love or, better, primordial (abyssal) immovable will (primordial love) that precedes God and his unfolding. This will is absolute peace—which cannot be thought of in a dialectical or temporal manner. It is love in God, as it itself develops in time, as an archaic and impossible *event* of peace, reconciliation of all beings (singularities) within eternally evolving Nature. This Nature, clearly, encapsulates spiritual and material realms and, by extension, in ways still to be explained, links the soul to both realms as their obscure (perhaps even "abyssal" in its most fundamental ontological sense) nexus. Surprisingly, perhaps, one of the possible answers to the related question of love as relation between the living and the dead—as also already posited by *Clara*—now lies precisely in the notion of *matter*. For Schelling, matter, as in itself, is "spiritual and incorporeal."[32] Although we still cannot answer Schelling's cosmogonical riddle, the possibility of an answer lies in the triadic dynamism of potencies, or the phenomenon of the synchronicity of Schelling. It is a composition of the three potencies of the will—namely A^1, A^2, and A^3 from *Ages of the World*. There always *was* life, in all its singularity. The secret of love therefore is abyssal (one of its names could be *chóra*, as a name for a primordial cosmic-ontological womb-matrix), as we have seen in our reading of *Clara*. This reign, or regime, of love is higher than both life and death proper. In the beginning (A^1), as it were, the abyssal will—as primordial (subtle) nature—was not yet divided or unfolded (A^2 and A^3, being signs of its spiritual and material unfolding toward greater love, or full divinity) and we can neither speak of its existence nor of its nonexistence.[33] This primordial potency (A^1) is also neither God itself nor is it human life in its individual material-spiritual dimension: "And just as the will that wills nothing is Highest in man, so too in God himself—this very will is above God."[34] We thus have the following constellation: unfolding of the three potencies is both joy and mourning, the sign of life evolving in Nature, as well as its decay with death. Time and eternity, then, or life and death—as evolving of divinity, or with Schelling:

> We thus recognize the will that wills nothing as the expressing, the I of the eternal, unbeginning divinity itself, which can say of itself: I am the alpha and the omega, the beginning and the end.[35]

The bond of love, or its secret, lies precisely in this triadic processual unfolding of God qua love: this is why Jesus himself *is* the final unification of primordial Nature with the Spirit: his appearance is an appearance of subtle or spiritual matter itself. The parable about Lazarus showed us that Jesus is the only person capable of transcending both life and death; even "God" cannot be thought of in this manner: moreover, after his death on a cross, Jesus appears first to Mary Magdalene (as a woman) and only then to his male disciples. Jesus is "dead" but his spiritual presence still remains emphatically located in this world. We know from *Clara* that the notions of ghosts (*Gespenster*) and (higher) spirits (*Geister*) are of the highest importance in discussing and searching the place of the dead. Now, like Jesus, Clara also "is a kind of living ghost, already departed from quotidian concerns."[36] Her presence in the dialogue, as compared to the Priest and Doctor, has a character of an ontologico-eschatological nexus, for she, also in her feminine identity, represents a soul, being perhaps even closer to the dead than to the living. Soul is a promise and hope, directed toward the past as well as toward the future.

Love is the highest, though. To achieve peace and tranquility always already means to be haunted by the secret of the past—i.e., the secret remainder in ourselves, which reminds us of an abyssal womb-matrix, as an eternal germ of Being, before even the division of being and nonbeing, or before all things were ontologically divided. It is no coincidence that Schelling—precisely at the point in *Ages of the World* at which he needs to find an answer to the riddle of creation—invokes none other than Jakob Böhme's mystical concept of the abyssal divine feminine—*Sophia*. It is perhaps not a coincidence, then, that for both Schelling and Feuerbach, Böhme's influence was of the most exclusive or preeminent character.[37] In a paragraph, the inclusion of which in his work clearly must have been influenced by Jakob Böhme's thought, Schelling implicitly explains the relation of Wisdom to the notion of the Abyss:

> Language in a book that is rightly considered divine drifts over us like a fresh morning breeze from the holy dawn of the world, language that introduces Wisdom in speech. The Lord possessed me in the beginning of his way, before he did anything. I was set up from eternity, from the beginning, or ever the earth was. When there were no depths, I was brought forth; where there were no fountains abounding water. Before the mountains were settled, before the hills am I brought forth. When he prepared the heavens above, I was there: when he set a compass upon the face of the depth; when he

appointed the foundations [*Grund*] of the earth, then I was by him, (as one brought up with him): and I was daily his pleasure, playing always (by) him.³⁸

Schelling then explains in a more explicit manner the following distinction:

With these words, Wisdom is sharply distinguished from *Lord*. The Lord possessed Wisdom, but she was not herself the Lord. She was with him (before the) beginning, before he did anything. (We say) that a man does nothing if he is sleeping, or dead, or enraptured—if, in short, he does not manifest himself as a thing-that-is. Wisdom is compared to a child: a child can be called self-less when, in the earliest time, all of its inner forces work with each other, but without a will having come forth to hold them together and make itself their collective force and unity. (Wisdom, together with the first corporeality in which she is clad, is like a tranquil, passive unity that cannot lift itself up from a merely germinal state into a state of activity.)³⁹

What can be inferred from this? Firstly, that having Clara as the main character in his dialogue is not a coincidence. Secondly, on an ontological level, Schelling is fully aware of another riddle at the very beginning, or better, at the most distant age of the world: Wisdom was with God, but She was not (yet) God. Wisdom, for sure, is here characterized with a certain sense of passivity, but this passivity is of an archaic cosmic character and points to the subtle prematerial (i.e., not matter, not spirit) character of *Sophia*. Schelling invokes the idea both of a child and of death as nonbeing in this passage. To understand Schelling, though, we need to seek help in Jakob Böhme's own thoughts. According to Böhme—in Her subtle meaning, Sophia is precisely the place of the abyss (*Ungrund*)⁴⁰ or of the revelation and/or birth of the most primordial abyssal powers (will, desire, power) from the primordial cosmic feminine. She is now is eternal cosmic Mother of beings or, as Böhme claims, gives birth to all things in her virginity (for Irigaray, the virginity of Mary, mother of Jesus is to be taken in a spiritual and not natural sense).⁴¹ The most important of all concepts of Böhme for us, though, is his concept of the matrix. We have seen in cosmic Jesus the paramount stage of the self-revelation of God, where both our past and our future are revealed. Now, Böhme radicalizes this by pointing to the body (*Leib*) of Sophia *as* Virgin Mary and calls it the cosmic/heavenly matrix.[42] In an even more radical sense, and this brings us back to *Clara*, Böhme now states: "It is for this reason that Christ took his soul from the feminine as from the virgin, and became a man."[43] This feminine genealogy, or its inception within the primordial matrix, is the first cosmic cloth, in which the first Being is mysteriously enveloped by an abyssal shrine, or primordial frame, which precedes all being and nonbeing; as such, the feminine matrix is the paradigm of all life (but also a precursor of death):

> This is the blessing of Mary among all women, / that she was the first from Adam / in which this heavenly matrix was disclosed.[44]

For Böhme, the revelation of this heavenly matrix testifies to the preeminence of love within Sophia, or both Her incarnations—Virgin Mary, mother of Jesus, and Jesus himself. It is for this reason that Jesus took his soul from woman in her full spiritual virginity—which, with the help of Irigaray, would mean in the full autonomy of this preontological root as a matrixial principle. This also unifies—in a limited and still obscure sense (this relation has not yet been revealed to us, since we do not yet possess a proper cosmic-ontological genealogy for this ultimate gesture of love)—Jesus *with* Antigone. Jesus as Antigone's sister: this unfolding of Christ's essence from the Matrix is therefore of greatest importance for us. It enables us to understand the soul as nexus, as already stated by Schelling in his *Clara*. It also enables us to understand and interpret his rather obscure thoughts on the mystery in the abyssal or groundless (*Ungrund*) bosom of all existence, where the secret of love is also hidden. Again, though, from whence does this love come?

We have already seen that it is only through Christ's cosmic presence that humanity can (spiritually-eschatologically) transcend both life and death and return, as it were, to the state of the absolute peace/indifference of the primal ground,[45] i.e., being beyond life and death proper. The secret of love is that it unites beings, as already stated by our philosopher: "But the groundless divides itself into the two equally eternal beginnings only in order that the two that could not be in it as groundless at the same time, or there would be one, should become one through love."⁴⁶ Let us now recall one more time this most important passage of all passages of Schelling's *Freedom* essay:

> For not even spirit itself is supreme; it is but spirit, or the breath of love. But love is supreme. It is that which was before there were the depths and before existence (as separate entities), but it was not there as love, rather—how shall we designate it?⁴⁷

It is only with Böhme that we can answer this great cosmic-ontological riddle of Schelling: it was with the notion of matrix, as a primordial envelope of Being, that we can approach the secret of love.

Back to Schelling's *Clara*

After this detour we can now finally return to *Clara*. The question that still remains unanswered is, What relation does the notion of matrix, or the preontological envelope of Being, have to the main questions of Clara: about death, the ontology of mourning, and the related preeminence of love? As we have already seen in the earlier part of this chapter, Clara claims that "the tie of a truly divine love is as unbreakable as the essence of the soul in which it is founded and is as eternal as the word of God."⁴⁸ We have already pointed out that these were words on radical proximity, as one, being even stronger than death. For Clara, this is closely tied to the very essence of soul in its feminine-maternal (womb-matrix) genealogy, on the one hand, and to the radical and, as it were, "maternal subjectivity" of Christ on the other. The secret of love lies in the—for us, still mysterious or obscure—relationality of both to the abyssal, or groundless matrix. Sorrow, as depicted in Jesus's tears for Lazarus, or the sadnesss that is in God—this is what unites the living with the departed—and this also is represented in Clara's emotions for her late husband. What unites all Being (even beyond life and death), though, is this matrixial atmosphere of love, or primeval peace of the first potency (A^1), which even precedes God. It is the evolving and unfolding (*breathing?*) of God, as remembrance of matrixial Being—even to the point of death.⁴⁹

This peaceful atmosphere of love, which reigns above life and death proper, is a progression toward ideal communication among mortals, and a sign of divine exuberance. *Clara* is all about communication—between mortals as living beings, but also living ghosts and the departed, a search for pure relationality beyond any material/spiritual divide. This ideal and unobscured communication would—according to Grau's interpretation,[50] and this is not good news—be possible only in death; but there is a *soul*, which already enables us to grasp the first clear hint of this pure intersubjectivity.

(Sister Angelica)

Puccini's opera *Suor Angelica* is an exceptionally sensitive account of a young mother and the immense love she has for her child. The opera, first performed on December 14, 1918, is set in the seventeenth century in an Italian convent in which Sister Angelica lives with her fellow nuns. Her monastic life is pervaded by a secret, a sin kept hidden from the other nuns, the reason Angelica was sent to live in the convent. There, Angelica, the most mysterious of the nuns, lives surrounded only by flowers and medicinal herbs with which she alleviates the suffering of her female companions. Angelica has been living there for seven years, when an unexpected visit by her aunt (both of her parents have already died) reveals that Angelica had an illegitimate child who was taken from her at birth, while she was sent to the convent. Despite the strict monastic requirement to renounce all desires and thereby suffer imposition of utter penance, Angelica has, in some anti-Abrahamic and, as such, fundamentally matrixial gesture, never been able to completely renounce the love for her son. Her delicate words speak to this:

> But there's an offer I can never make!
> To that Mother, the sweetest of all Mothers
> I cannot offer to forget . . . My son.
> My son! . . . My darling son!
> The sweet, dear baby torn away from me
> Whom I have seen and kissed but once!
> My darling child! My darling child so distant![51]

It turns out that these past seven years, Angelica has lived in the convent in complete misery—as she has received no news from her relatives about her child—but has never given up hope of seeing him at least one more time. Upon the unanticipated visit by her aunt, her only living relative, Angelica learns that her son died two years before from a sudden illness, at the tender age of five. Hearing this news, she finally breaks down and at that very moment she expresses, in her own words, the mysterious reciprocity in the relationship between the parent and the child, the mother and the son:

> Without thy mother,
> Dearest, thou didst die!
> Thy sweet lips
> Without my fond kisses
> Grew white and
> Cold as snow!
> And thine eyes
> Thou didst close, my darling!
> Then, unable
> To caress me,
> Thy tiny hands
> Were crossed on thy chest!

Angelica cannot reconcile herself to the fact that she will never see her son again, and all she wants now is to die—so that she may be united with him in heaven. She decides to kill herself; the flowers, who used to be her only friends, are now her final patrons: Angelica picks toxic herbs and drinks the poison. But only while she is drinking it, does she realize that by committing suicide she is also committing the sin that will forever prevent her from seeing her son. Hence, she turns to Mary, imploring her as she would her own mother, to help her and save her. Mary, appearing graciously, surrounded by angels, comes to her in a soul-stirring way—with Angelica's son, dressed in white, in front of her. The Mother of God brings the dying woman her son, who takes three steps and reaches his mother. Angelica lays eyes on him for the last time in her life, and dies.

Standing at the horizon of the stories of Antigone, Savitri, the concubine of a Levite, Fair Vida and Clara, Sister Angelica's is a story about the highest exuberance of love, illustrated by the miracle that takes place on stage in this touching opera. The story of Angelica shows that love is stronger than anything—for, as we have seen in the cases of all of the mentioned figures, it is able to cross the invisible divide between life and death.

the inverse fourfold

5

Beyng / Sister

The woman you call the mother of the child
is not the parent, just a nurse to the seed,
the new-sown seed that grows and swells inside her.
The *man* is the source of life—the one who mounts.
She, like a stranger for a stranger, keeps
the shoot alive unless god hurts the roots.
I give you proof that all I say is true.
The father can father forth without a mother.

—Aeschylus, *The Eumenides*[1]

Toward the Ontology of Love: Ludwig Binswanger

In the previous chapter about Schelling's *Clara*, we touched upon two of the most challenging issues in philosophy and ethics—the questions of the relationship between life and death, and the link between love and mourning. Reading Schelling's *Clara* we saw that love is stronger than living and being themselves. Love dwells in the mysterious silence that cannot be broken, perhaps even by breath (see "atemlose *Stille*" in Binswanger).[2] At this point, it is still too soon to talk about the relationship between love and being/Being, of course, but we would like to build on the previous chapter, which already hinted at the elemental or material signifiers of the action of love, such as its primordial traces—primeval waters, the sanctity and materiality of tears, the feminine presence, silence and melancholy (or mourning)—and therewith suggest the elemental or material phenomenology that we wish to develop further. In the analysis of this mysterious and abysmal nature of love we have already highlighted an important passage by Schelling that we would like to repropose here:

> But if all will have become subject to him, then the Son himself shall also be subjected to him that did subject all things unto him, that God may be all in all. For not even spirit itself is supreme; it is but spirit, or the breath of love. But love is supreme. It is that which was before there were the depths and before existence (as separate entities), but it was not there as love, rather—how shall we designate it?[3]

In his work, Binswanger draws on the legacies of Buber, Löwith, as well as on the philosophy of his namesake Ludwig Feuerbach. Levinas and Jean-Luc Nancy, too, are thinkers operating in the range of the foundational conceptions of Binswanger's thought. A peculiarity of Binswanger's analysis of love is that, at first glance, it appears to be an anthropological and ontic correction of Heidegger, but at the very moment we take all of its outsets seriously it transforms, almost imperceptibly, into a new ontology of love. If we now set out into the realm of love, one of the most neglected questions in ethics is the question of ontology, and therewith the genealogy of love and its link to the field of its ontic actualization, including in relation to the idea of sexual difference. While Schelling's works only dealt with the ontological (and thus philosophical-cosmological) aspect of love, phenomenology—if we take a closer look at two key figures alone, Heidegger and Levinas (and, of course, Marion in his *Erotic Phenomenon*)—assigned love and other phenomenological topics of being-with-others their ontic places, as well. But ever since Levinas's well-known remark about the ontic nature of *Dasein* (when it seems that *Dasein* is never hungry),[4] we have also known that the world that Heidegger populated with his *Dasein* is robbed of many a genuine gesture of interpersonal love. Let us now take a step back to Binswanger, and thus return once more to the dialogue with Heidegger and the question of the *possibility* of an ontology of love at the heart of his thought after the so-called turn (i.e., after the works from the 1936–38 period, beginning with his *Contributions to Philosophy [Of the Event]*). The other topic to be linked to a reflection about the role of love in Heidegger's philosophy in the conclusion of this chapter will be the possibility of a more radical feminist (re)interpretation of Heidegger, as suggested by the title of this chapter, foreshadowing this aspect along with the rehabilitation of love in his thought.

Ludwig Binswanger (1881–1966) was a German psychologist, psychiatrist, and phenomenologist who worked at the Bellevue Sanatorium in Switzerland.[5] In 1942, he published his major philosophical work *Basic Forms and the Realization of Human Dasein* (*Grundformen und Erkenntnis menschlichen Daseins*), in which he tried, in an idiosyncratic, in philosophy virtually unknown manner, and in the midst of the horrors of World War II at that, to counter the spirit of the times, as well as one of the greatest philosophical works in general, Heidegger's *Being and Time*—by writing about *love*. In many ways, Binswanger echoes another "solitary traveller," Arthur Schopenhauer. It is well known that Heidegger in his *Being and Time* simply does not speak about love or the material proximity of the other, there is just one (!) mention of that in his entire work, in a footnote about Saint Augustine. As Schrijvers points out, the problem lies in that the phenomenon of love, essentially, shows more "the facticity of the 'all with all,' the basic phenomenon of togetherness, rather than the 'all against all,' which transpires through Heidegger's analysis of anxiety and the *Jemeinigkeit* of one's death."[6] Binswanger's principal work about love is divided into two parts: in the first part, love is understood and discussed as the intimacy of two—as "love"—while in the second, the author talks about love in terms of "friendship."[7] My analysis will focus on the first part of his explication of love. Any approach to the question of love can, of course, proceed from the naive and quite empirical evidence of its omnipresence in the lives of male and female "*Daseins*." It is, therefore, curious not to find a more extensive phenomenological explanation of this "phenomenon" in Heidegger. This is the essence of Binswanger's philosophical intervention. Farther on, we wish to provide an analysis of Binswanger's philosophy of love and use it to shed light on Heidegger's philosophy from another, less common viewpoint.

To Binswanger, the fundamental gesture in introducing love into philosophy or phenomenology is precisely its relationship toward *violent* modes of dwelling and "making room" (*Ein-Räumung*), which is also crucial to our later transition into the possibility of explicating love within the context of Heidegger's *History of Beyng* (at the time, this and other works by Heidegger following his "turn" were not available to Binswanger, of course; but then Binswanger only referred to *Being and Time*). To him, the underlying or foundational gesture of love is in the (peaceable or nonviolent) "gesture of surrender" (*die Gebärde der Überlassung*), which takes place between two subjects and denotes the fundamental admittance of the other's being next to mine. It is a gesture beautifully conveyed by Irigaray through her admonition that hospitality is *not* contained in giving up what we already have or possess (to put it in vulgar/ontic terms, in giving up what we do not need [anymore]), but takes place at the level of surrendering something of value and of the logic of a certain surplus or exuberance in the very act of giving that justifies every intersubjective economy (in that respect, this logic is nicely inscribed into the very logic of the Marxist critique of capitalist economy). The same can apply to the voice in Binswanger—when I lower my voice while speaking and let the other enter into communication with me, or when with a glance or some other bodily gesture we indicate subtly, but perceptibly, that we are willing to forsake a part of the space-time that would otherwise continue to belong to us. Behind the surplus that we forsake for the benefit of the other is, for Binswanger, the foundational gesture of love, the gesture that works in such a way that through the very forsaking and giving away of what is mine I gain more love. Binswanger refers to this relationship with the term "loving togetherness/loving Being-with-one-another" (*das liebende Miteinandersein*).[8] It is clear that in doing so, Binswanger, right from the start, radically breaks with the explication of authenticity and ever-mineness (*Jemeinigkeit*) of Heidegger's *Dasein*, for in him the subject is based in this very ontological-ethical renouncement (although we are getting a little ahead of ourselves with ontology here, this excerpt already anticipates its advent). At the same time, this serves as an original outset for his theory of love as a fundamental intersubjective mode of coexistence. But Binswanger goes farther, and may hold in this the greatest advantage over the philosophers of his time: he strongly rejects any activity based on the struggle for recognition (*Kampf um Anerkennung*); in a radicalized sense, to him, "the embrace is the ownmost gesture of love," which through its break with the logic of possession, violence, control, desire for self-being (*conatus essendi* of the modern thought) becomes the fundamental mode of togetherness—denoted by the syntagma "the 'we' of love" (*Wir der Liebe*; or perhaps "the 'ourness' of love").[9]

At this point we need to step back to Feuerbach. In *The Essence of Christianity*, Feuerbach clearly states: "I differ *toto coelo* from those philosophers who pluck out their eyes that they may see better; for my thought I require the senses, especially sight; I found my ideas on materials which can be appropriated only through the activity of the senses."[10] Besides the eyes, Feuerbach ascribed special importance to skin as, of course, the medium through which contact takes place, in the ethical sense primarily in the form of feeling, touch, or affectionate or sensual embrace. In his work *Some Comments on the "Beginning of Philosophy" of Dr J. F. Reiff* from 1841, he writes about skin as follows:

> It is through the body that ego is not just an ego but also an object. To be embodied is to be in the world; it means to have so many senses, i.e., so many pores and naked surfaces. The body is nothing but the porous ego.[11]

This places us in the field of material intersubjectivity and the related epistemology, which Feuerbach did not yet think in the fashion of the philosophy of the second half of the twentieth century, yet which should most certainly be considered as its principal predecessor. Binswanger (while often citing Feuerbach) fits into this logic due to his manifestly Nancyan intention regarding the fundamental plurality of our being.[12] How do we get to the constitution of love, then, in this interspace of proximity? Love is "the unfolding or openness of *Dasein* towards its oneness or, if you will, integrity in a primordial form of 'we' (or 'ourness') (*Wirheit*)."[13] With respect to spatiality, love is the provider of a place of residence/home (like *Ort* or *Heimat* in Binswanger, who states: "Only where you *are, there is* a place for me"), which we are going to analyze in more detail in relation to Heidegger. The ingression of temporality into the relationship between two subjects is seemingly surprising; whenever the moment occurs during speech that I let the other tell me something or surrender my space to the other with some other gesture, this very interval or gesture of silence/pause envelops the meaning and the paradox of ethical or intersubjective time (cf. Levinas), which Binswanger here introduces less subtly, although the sense of his thought is nevertheless clear: the dual may be an adequate linguistic expression of a loving encounter only when you and I are able to speak in it at the same time, in some impossible modus of a perfect match of loving affection or love, which, however, is unachievable due to the very nature of speech and conversation:

> Therefore the true expression of love is not (the verbal) language at all; it is the "silent" gaze and kiss, a "silent" embrace (*Umarmung*) of love.[14]

This logic of encounter incorporates the boundlessness or the surplus (we will call it exuberance or excess; Binswanger uses the term *der Überschwang*) of love . . . to be dealt with a little later on. Although it may seem that Binswanger's embrace refers to the ontic phenomenon of love, the term disguises an ontology of love that no one before him had ever developed.

Love is thus situated or oscillating between the ontological and ontic areas of our dwelling. The evidence of the ingression of ontological problems lies in Binswanger's derivations that follow the above mentioned phenomenology of embrace or proximity of love; its mystery (*das Mysterium der Liebe*) lies in that, as he claims, a love or affectionate relationship would not be possible "were not *Dasein* in its essence already a loving encounter."[15] Binswanger explicitly links this trait of *Dasein* to the phenomenological/ontological field—in his particular "empirical" and idiosyncratic way—by drawing in a longer Thoreauvian passage by Hugo von Hofmannsthal about the logic of encounter in general. As the artist says:

> It is certain that going, searching and meeting are somehow part of the mysteries of the eros. It is certain that on our tortuous path we are not merely pushed forward by our actions, but are always attracted by something that is ostensibly always waiting for us somewhere and is always veiled. There is something of a love lust, a love curiosity in our progression, even when we are searching for sylvan solitude or for the silence of the mountains or for a deserted beach, on which the sea, softly murmuring, disperses like in a silver fringe.[16]

And then, in this immediate and, in appearance, conceptually emptied environment, something happens—an encounter. Whether we come across a lone tree or a forest creature stopping in its tracks for a moment and throwing us a glance from behind a bush, or we hear a distant bird singing that echoes through the valley—in such cases, which Binswanger quotes after Hofmannsthal, one finds one's self in the space-time of an encounter, which lets them know they are not alone in the world. With these examples drawn directly from nature, Binswanger further radicalizes Feuerbach's conception of the ethics of intersubjectivity and places man into the realm of their ownmost dwelling. So even before or alongside the Fourfold (if we have in mind, for instance, Heidegger's Fourfold from his essay *Building Dwelling Thinking*, written in 1951), Binswanger put man in the midst of a cosmological/ethical space, which we still have to thematize more thoroughly. For Binswanger, love is grounded in the silence and in the original peace of an encounter—in the foundations of the "primeval possibility of a loving encounter in general"[17]—itself a search, expectation, and promise of togetherness. Here, Binswanger's ethical cardiology is revealed (similar to the one that Caputo mentioned and missed when reading Heidegger), pointing out directly his fundamental correction of Heidegger:

> In the loving togetherness, *Dasein* (Being-there) is therefore to be understood as "having a heart" or, more precisely, *Dasein* reveals itself as a heart and the "there" of this *Dasein* reveals itself as the home of the heart.[18]

Furthermore, only because *Dasein* is disclosed in such a way—i.e., as love—is it now possible to think Christian religiosity and the Christian philosophy of religion in the first place; moreover, adds Binswanger, this is the reason why "God can reveal himself to the human beings in the world as the God of love."[19] This certainly resonates with Feuerbach's philosophical thought in all its momentousness and at the same time its misinterpretation by his contemporaries and successors.

On the horizon of this thought, we would now like to move to the central part of Binswanger's explanation of *Dasein* as love and its exuberance, which provides entirely new possibilities of ontological interpretation of this basic phenomenon of loving and affectionate coexistence, even with respect to death and dying. To care, as the principal existential of *Dasein*, Binswanger now counterpoises love. Care (concern) exists in a world ruled by the active modes of human performance, grounded in various potencies of power (*Mächtigkeit*), which are always definite and understandable in terms of historical logic; love, on the contrary, stems from an opposing motion based on the modes of gift, giving, and grace, which unfold into the area of boundless, extrahistorical, eternal even (as will be evident from the thematization of love that conquers even death). Here is revealed what Binswanger calls exuberance of love (*Überschwang der Liebe*) or exuberance of *Dasein*, with the term *exuberance* suggesting a transcendence in love that can overcome its otherwise invariably ontic temporality; an encounter is thus something that does not take place in the realm of care in any of its forms. In this respect, Binswanger is close to Irigaray, who finds the transcendent in the relationship with the other. If in Heidegger's *Being and Time* the existence of *Dasein* unfolds from an anxiety initially exposing our Being-in-the-world to an inauthentic, uncanny existence, and allows one to become, by assimilating this anxiety through care, "what one can be in being free for one's ownmost possibilities" (including Death as "the *ownmost* possibility of

Dasein"),[20] it is clear that Binswanger is, in essence, no longer concerned with the care for *Dasein*, which despite being integral to various shared/communal modes of Being-with or Being-with-others within its world in Heidegger remains in ontological terms essentially confined to the modus of ever-mineness (*Jemeinigkeit*)—all through its (brave or even heroic) death. But what could be the purpose of Binswanger introducing here into the logic of *Dasein* and intersubjective encounter the seemingly nonphilosophical topic of grace? As we could see in the *Interlude*, Schopenhauer, too, had understood human freedom—albeit in his own (essentially metaphysical) way—as grace: when will turns away from life, away from the constant validation of itself and assertion of its own authenticity, a so-called catholic, transcendental change takes place, about which, in §70 of his seminal work, Schopenhauer says it is the effect of divine grace or an expression of the ultimate freedom of a man ethically awoken to *caritas* or compassion.[21] Binswanger understands grace as "a gift from *Dasein* to itself,"[22] as its willingness for a loving, affectionate coexistence that is in its core—although it may sound coarse (but was, nevertheless, present on the horizon of Heidegger's thought about the mortals and their Being-towards-death)—nonhistorical. This paves the way to the issue of death, the topic through which the transcendence of love can finally be revealed in its full sense.

Thus, in his ontological basis, man is a relational being or a being of twoness. Ontic forms of love, therefore, cannot deplete its essence. Love is only complete when we consider its transcendence, love as exuberance elevated above life and death. In this, we are revisited by Schelling's Clara and his/her sensitive ontology of love and mourning. Let us take a look at an important quote from Binswanger's work introducing an ontological turn into our line of reasoning:

> Just as we speak of the love immanence of death in life, we have to speak of the love immanence of life in death. The former is called loneliness (*Einsamkeit*), the latter "twogetherness" (*Zweisamkeit*).[23]

At this point, Binswanger makes his own distinction between love and care—love is elevated above care, placed beyond life and death. But how? What phenomenality of death opens with this gesture? The place that you and I inhabited with our encounter, and which exists between us, is also the dwelling place of our thought of death. We will see that the mourning that Schelling speaks of in his *Clara* is in phenomenological terms related to precisely this feeling. Just as I know, says Binswanger, that with every goodbye I live on in you, I know that I will live on *in* you and in a way also *with* you even after my death. However, Binswanger does not associate such knowing with some thesis about the hereafter or about a reunion in the afterworld; he wants to think it in the perspective of phenomenology. Its basic character is thus not "hope" or "faith" (although, of course, it is always that, too), rather—here perhaps somewhat unexpectedly, yet emphatically—this way of being-with-death is expressed through "silence:"

> That knowledge is absolute silence. Therefore, true love is only the love which still "in life" hears the "silence of death."[24]

Speaking of death on the horizon of love is impossible; just as the heart stands above reason, silence stands above the language of love. In this consists its transcendence. Love is the fulfilment of *Dasein*, but here as transcendent of all ontic phenomena of language (in its everyday expressions, in more or less felicitously chosen words, in more or less affectionate speech gestures, etc.): love is exuberance, "holy peace and quiet around and within us," profound silence (*atemlose Stille*).[25] Schelling already knew that the bond of true or indestructible love between two individuals is connected to the essence of the soul, in which this love is based. Moreover—we have seen "that a quiet, unconscious, but thereby all the more compelling, necessity draws one soul to another."[26] With his phenomenology of love, Binswanger, just like Schelling, reached the end of the path: if we take a step farther (into the field of the ontological), as the two of them did, it means we will be treading a field that we philosophers have not yet negotiated. It may seem that Schelling is navigating the field of the spiritual (the "spirits" of the dead) and thus immaterial, and that Binswanger, on the other hand, wants to reach the immanence of life in death through phenomenology, but in both precisely the contrary is true: in the key parts of his interpretation, Schelling, as we have seen, relies on subtle material signifiers, such as tears and mourning, feminine presence, and a melancholy feeling (broken heart), while Binswanger passes from material phenomenology (touch, embrace, language of intimacy, gestures of loving affection) into a silent completion of *Dasein* in pure exuberance of love.[27] When Binswanger speaks of love, it is clear that in him the latter is first or most easily understood as an erotic relationship, but such logic of Eros—which we intend to show farther on and in this sense reach across Binswanger—should here be interpreted outside the purely sexualized mode of this relationship; love should be regarded in the sense of transcendent love desire/longing on which all types of love relationships are based (and not only the friendly ones, which Binswanger, however, treats with the same earnestness later on)—between partners and lovers, but also between brothers and sisters (the story of Lazarus, or Antigone's love) and between parents and children, who are linked by the closest of love bonds, as testified by Clara in one of the most delicate passages in Schelling's homonymous treatise. Love in Binswanger is based on the logic of "encounter." Its primary place, therefore, is not in the mentioned family relationships. But when we have before us the immortal bond of pure partner love and the equally immortal bond between the mother or father and the son or daughter, are we not talking about one and the same love, one and the same longing, an encounter that may be of another kind, but still belongs to the same order of proximity? Our treatise on love must touch on this question, possibly the most difficult one, that reaches beyond the phenomenal and may even substantiate the primordial encounter (*Ur-Begegnung*) itself, and which Binswanger, nevertheless (and perhaps to the reader's astonishment), chooses not to thematize. It is, of course, possible to think the encounter on the horizon of the being of *Dasein*, which Binswanger sets into the realm of dwelling, while failing to thematize its ontological origin with adequate precision. In this, we see the task of the next chapter, in which we intend to prepare the terrain for a return to the second Heidegger, outlining in that way the origins of the ontology of love.

Forms of Pure Love: Parents and Children

> I was already signed with the sign of the cross and seasoned with salt from the time I came from my mother's womb.
>
> —Saint Augustine

From the horizon of Binswanger's phenomenology of love we would now like to approach the question of love through a gradual return to Heidegger's philosophy. We want to investigate the remainder that slipped away from both Heidegger and Binswanger, alluded to by Irigaray's late thought (after her work *The Way of Love*)[28] and, before that, by Heidegger's philosophy after the turn, even though the issue did not appear in his work in this precise form. Let us, by way of introduction to our reasoning, first link up to Euripides's lesser-known, yet perhaps most sensitive Greek work of all—*The Suppliants*. In it, we will find that sign and trace of a relationship of love and affectionate regard that was severed by Plato and remained hidden in the history of philosophy up until Saint Augustine; with that, we will return into the realm of the issue that at the beginning of this chapter shed light on that wound of malice in the very Being of Heidegger, and led us into a new phenomenology of love.

Euripides's drama is set in the proximity of Sophocles's *Antigone* and therefore of particular interest to us. By presenting the events of the so-called Theban Cycle it transports us into the very center of ethical premises that is being thematized in this book. The events, just as in Sophocles, are laid out in light of Creon's ban on the burial of Polyneices, the difference being that in this case the latter appears as one of the seven army leaders whom the sovereign of Thebes denies the ancient right granted to us by unwritten law. The Athenians, headed by Theseus, are faced with a dilemma: whether to allow Creon to assert his political will over his opponents and the defeated, or arm an attack on behalf of the allied cities (Athens and Argos) to bring home the dead sons, fathers, and husbands and allow them to be buried in accordance with ancient laws. *The Suppliants* is shocking for the language used by its characters—the mothers and children of the sons and fathers killed. The text falls within the genre of the philosophy of mourning, in which it is akin to the mentioned *Confessions* by Saint Augustine and Derrida's masterpiece *Circumfession*. *The Suppliants* is a text about the pure love that surpasses death, about the immanence of life in death, a text about desire and sorrow springing from the same origin, about the Being that bestows tears on mothers, so that they may purge the evil of the humankind.[29] The work is a lament pervaded by compassion, and the following passage displays that in all its might (these are supplications uttered by the mothers of the deceased Argolid army leaders and directed to the mother of Theseus, the Athenian Aethra):

> Beholding the bitter tears which spring to my eyes and my old wrinkled skin torn by my hands; for what can I do else? who never laid out my children dead within my halls, nor now behold their tombs heaped up with earth.

[. . .]

> Thou too, honoured lady, once a son didst bear, crowning thy lord's marriage with fond joy; then share, O share with me thy mother's feelings, in such measure as my sad heart grieves for my own dead sons; and persuade thy son, whose aid we implore, to go unto the river Ismenus, there to place within my hapless arms the bodies of my children, slain in their prime and left without a tomb.[30]

This ethical/cardiologic constellation conceals the meaning of the ontology of love. We have seen in Binswanger that love is based on an encounter (or more precisely, on the primordial encounter; *Ur-Begegnung*), which bestows on two individuals a dwelling place for their loving togetherness. This togetherness, which does not end with death, requires the rituals of burial and last goodbye for its preservation. But the death of a child transcends any death; it is a disruption and overturning of the genealogical order, an ingression of the bad straight into the logic of love. And denying a child the right to a tomb hurts the very core of Being itself. But the principal question arising here is whether the love of children, the love that brings on the mourning of the mothers from *The Suppliants*, is of the same ontological order as erotic love. The answer to that is twofold: it relates to the logic of eros, and to the idea of the child. In his *In Praise of Love*, Badiou—whom we mention because he wants to deliberate on love from a strictly philosophical (and at the same time atheist) position—circumscribes the issue of child to the objective of love, to a point or a specific event in a love relationship.[31] Luce Irigaray, on the contrary, in her work *To Be Born*, deals precisely with the idea of the child. We believe that in her thoughts about the link between love and desire the key to the riddle of all riddles is hidden: Where does love come from? As witnessed in the previous chapter, Schelling placing in Clara's mouth the following delicate words:

> [T]here at the grave of her children lost so young a mother stood in silence with no need for consecrated water to represent her tears, for tears sanctified by sweet melancholy flowed gently down to freshen the mounds.
>   If children had been given to me and then they were all taken away, I could never consider it as chance or a tempo-

rary fortune to have been the mother of these souls; I would feel—yes, I would know—that they belong to me eternally and I to them and that no power on Earth or in heaven could take them from me or me from them.[32]

With these two excerpts about the immanence of life in death, we now approach the heart of our issue of the ontology of love. Irigaray's *To Be Born*, which introduces us to this chapter, is in our opinion the only philosophical work in the Western philosophical canon to be entirely dedicated to the idea of the child and the related ethics of intersubjectivity. Written from the point of view of a female philosopher and a philosopher of sexual difference, it opens up questions that Binswanger, being male and thus less inclined to the philosophy of sexual difference, did not perceive or tackle yet. For Irigaray, the fundamental question of the entire *To Be Born* is the question of origin. This is what she says: "Unveiling the mystery of our origin is probably the thing that most motivates our quests and plans."[33] The question of origin can refer to two possible paths: first, to the ontological thesis about the origin of our Being, and second, but by no means less important, to the question that is most closely connected with the idea of the child. We come into this world from our mothers' wombs as a gift of Being, as we have seen Tine Hribar write in his work *The Gift of Being*—and our Being is to him a gift from the Being itself. This thought bears within a question addressing us as thinkers of love. But in what relation does this Being stand to love? Is love a part of Being or does it perhaps—as Schelling implies in one of the key passages of his entire opus—in some mysterious and not yet entirely thought way even precede Being itself as the ground(less)?[34] There is no easy answer to this question.

Irigaray introduces her explication of the idea of the child in *To Be Born* in an idiosyncratic and, at first, recondite manner: she argues the thesis that whatever the factors of our conception or creation as individuals coming to this world, we have wanted to be born—our will to live manifesting itself already at the moment of our birth.[35] This, naturally, leads to a break with the established perception of the child as the third one in relation to its parents, one who *is born* and thus does not *give birth* to oneself. But if the original idea of the child is related to its explicit singularity (which assures the child its autonomy),[36] it means that the birth is at the same time a transition into a different world of dwelling, which nevertheless preserves the memory of the original dwelling in the other (the mother; cf. our term *matrixiality* from previous chapters and the related original *mater-ial* hospitality). We thus speak of two separate yet closely connected origins of dwelling, and the understanding of their interconnection, so it seems, is where the secret of love now lies. Irigaray is aware of the trap that such a position presents: the family in which the child grows is the primary as well as supreme symbol of care for the child, but at the same time, it does not necessarily ensure autonomy and freedom in itself. Achieving that requires a transition from the so-called spiritual transcendence (based in some heteronomous source of authority—such as family, state, or some other community—and preserving the mode of power in all these contexts) to a horizontal transcendence of love as a space of peace, the only space with the capacity of recognizing the other in their otherness and, at the same time, singularity. This is the transcendence of love reflected in the (eternal, archaic) longing/desire for the other and for a mutual surrendering of two individuals. Horizontal transcendence is dynamic and processual by nature. Let us take a look at the extraordinarily complex and perhaps even key passage associating love with the longing for the other, in its entirety:

> Love brings space and time to the other outside of us but also within us in order that what this other entrusts of his or her being to us can live, grow, blossom—which cannot occur with the immediacy and impetuosity of desire. Love grants a silent peace which enables the lightning announcing desire to become an enchantment which no longer attracts outside of oneself, but invites to dwell in oneself, to cultivate what has been perceived, received and let it develop up to, but also thanks to, the word that it will generate. Love gives word to what desire has drawn, opened up, cleared, caused. It is love which can give to desire the power to say, to tell itself, while preserving a source of word which, itself, never comes up directly to language. Love watches out for the hardly born, which needs to be safeguarded and assisted in growing and blooming until it appears, dares to manifest itself, and so becomes sign.[37]

In this passage, Irigaray articulates all that Binswanger intimated (love as "profound silence;" *atemlose Stille*) and what we suspected he had left unsaid, especially with regard to the idea of the child or unborn creature. In reference to Heidegger ("A Dialogue on Language"), Irigaray succeeded in unfolding the space of the language of love (i.e., of love in one of its gestures), which she describes here as the most intimate time of exchange, a carnal dialogue, to which she also links the idea of the child as "a third being," but now as "the most unsayable source of the gathering which rules over the unfolding of the word."[38] That is why Irigaray relates to numerous religious traditions, which often chose to illustrate this source with a divine couple in all the sacredness of this relationship. Nevertheless, Irigaray stops here and does not thematize the love of children beyond the language of longing and desire. Next to the idea of the divine couple, religions also feature a theological idea of parenthood, which is, given the subsequent patriarchal detritus, more often expressed through the father-son relationship (Father and Son in the Holy Trinity), though in ancient Greek theology or mythology also at the mother-daughter level (e.g., the relationship between Demeter and Kore/Persephone, thoroughly thematized precisely by Irigaray in many of her works). In philosophy, on the other hand, the idea of the intergenerational mother-daughter relationship has sometimes been conceived as an ontological and ethical expression of the foundation of our existence, and as such taking precedence over the father-son relationship (for example, in Irigaray and her philosophy of sexual difference, and in Levinas). But what do ideas about the immanence of death in life and of life in death have in common with such thinking? How should these thoughts be read together with Schelling and Binswanger? What role does love have in all this, particularly if we think it in the sense of pure (erotic) love and of (ontologically higher or even primordial?) love for the child?[39] To find the answers to these questions we need to enter the thinking of Being in its three most archetypal—theological, mythological, and philosophical—senses and unfold this most important field of love with a phenomenologically radicalized approach.

One of the subtlest treatments of Trinitarian theology in general, by Jürgen Moltmann, reveals a paradigm of love that may be of key importance for our reflection. In Moltmann's work *The Trinity and the Kingdom of God*, we can find an exceptional study of relationships within the Trinity. As we have seen, we should think love—insofar as we consider it in its transcendental sense—as a way of sharing, giving, of desire for the other as the other, as a gift of coexistence. At one point, which is perhaps crucial for us, Moltmann states the following about the logic and motion of love within the mystery of the Trinity:

> *Love is the self-communication of the good.* It is the power of good to go out of itself, to enter into other being, to participate in other being, and to give itself for other being.... Love wants to live and to give life.... The loving person enters entirely into the other whom he loves, but in that other he is entirely himself. The unselfishness of love lies in the loving person's communication of himself, not in his self-destruction.
>
> [...]
>
> The theology of love is a theology of the Shekinah, a theology of the Holy Spirit. This means that it is not patriarchal, but rather feministic. For the Shekinah and the Holy Spirit are "the feminine principle of the Godhead."[40]

It derives even from the Trinitarian theology of Thomas Aquinas that love in the Trinity is conceived as *amor unitivus*; that is, as a reciprocal connection and relationality of the three divine persons. Their relationship is based on reciprocal self-giving:

> Gift is not only a personal name but also a proper name of the Holy Spirit. A gift in the proper sense is something gratuitously given without the expectation of a return. The reason for gratuitous donation is love whereby we wish the recipient well. All true gifts are possible only through love, which therefore constitutes the first or primordial gift as condition of all genuine giving.[41]

This logic of gratuitous giving is the fundamental logic of love as the primordial gift. In the continuation of this chapter, while reading Heidegger, we will have to interrogate ourselves about the grammatical structure of this absolute genitive case: love as the gift of Being—which even in its grammatical name refers to the logic of a certain procreation of thoughts. Although the roles within the Trinity are distributed among the three persons according to their original functions (initially, the Father is not the Son, and the Son is not the Father), in their interlinking (*perichoresis*) they are construed in their synchronous sense as the supreme form of a special exchange of energies. Moltmann now understands this constellation as follows:

> An eternal life process takes place in the triune God through the exchange of energies. The Father exists in the Son, the Son in the Father, and both of them in the Spirit, just as the Spirit exists in both the Father and the Son. By virtue of their eternal love they live in one another to such an extent, and dwell in one another to such an extent, that they are one. It is a process of most perfect and intense empathy.... In the *perichoresis*, the very thing that divides them become that which binds them together.[42]

In this process, love is the original name and motion of the feminine Holy Spirit, whose other name is also Gift. Any selfless love of parents (mother, father, caretaker) toward their child is enveloped in this Trinitarian paradigm of love and precedes any of its other forms (agapeic, erotic, platonic or romantic, friendly; even cross-species love toward other creatures or toward nature). When a father or a mother love their son or daughter in this Trinitarian way, they are, in their love, fully devoted to their child. But this relationship is not hierarchical, as their complete and unconditional love is fed precisely by what they themselves and each on their own *had never possessed or been* and by what they in equal perfection receive from their child; this is what horizontal transcendence of the relationship and exchange of love consists in—a process of reciprocal giving and thus of the gift of mutual love among them all (as a third thing).[43] This (proto-)form of love could also be termed *genealogical love*. The Trinitarian movement of love also reaches into the ontology of death and thereby into the immanence of life in death. The ultimate symbol of this immanence is the resurrection of Jesus, while in the analysis of Schelling's *Clara* we have seen how, as in Antigone, as well as in Jesus, of course, love conquers death: there we pointed out that compared to life or death, love is of a higher or even primordial order (even in Schelling we said that the bond of love lies precisely in the triadic-processual revealing of God as love). In Clara we thus recognized one of the genealogical sisters of Antigone.[44] *But where in this genealogy does love as the gift of Being (or Beyng as Seyn) have its place?* To understand the comprehensive ontological structure of this question and perhaps provide an answer to it, we have to finally return to the philosophy of Heidegger.

Love as Beyng's Sister

O sister of the spirit which lives and sways in us with fiery power, O holy air!

—Hölderlin, *Hyperion*

Come to me even now, and free me from harsh
anxieties, and however many things
my spirit yearns to get done, *you* do for me. *You*
become my ally in war.

—Sappho

In his *One Is Fury* Tine Hribar notes the following about Antigone:

> Antigone acts as she does out of love, and not out of ordinary love, such as sexual or family love, not even out of the love that can develop in other relationships between living people, but from the love that binds the living and the dead.... The love that establishes a communion of the living and the dead may not be an active love in itself, but it is the purest love-for-nothing. Antigone is not bound to *conatus essendi*, the desire for Being as a will to be from Spinoza's ethics, or to *Anerkennung*, the struggle for recognition from Hegel's *Phenomenology of Spirit*; for this reason she disregards the death penalty threat and is indifferent to whether people agree with her or not.[45]

To further a return to Heidegger, we intend to treat in this part those works that most authentically address the issue of being and to confront them later with certain feminist readings of this philosopher. These include, in particular, his works *Contributions to Philosophy (Of the Event)*, *Mindfulness*, *The History of Beyng*, and some lectures from this period (*Building Dwelling Thinking*). But first, we have to recover the context of Binswanger's phenomenology of love, which allowed us to think love in the mode of its exuberance. To Binswanger, love would not be possible "were not *Dasein* in its essence already a loving encounter."[46] It thus turns out that *Dasein* in the mode of nonviolent surrender or encounter is linked to that archaic (perhaps cosmological/ontological/ theological in nature) phenomenon that Binswanger calls primordial encounter (*Ur-Begegnung*) as mysteriously silent places of the lovingly affectionate dwelling of *Dasein*. How to connect this constellation of love to Heidegger's ontology? The best starting point for that is precisely *The History of Beyng* (1938–40). Heidegger does not speak of love in it, but still, this love as gentleness is present as a latent possibility of a different history of being. This is what Heidegger says:

> The history of beyng, as soon as this history brings itself into its essential grounding, is the axial site in whose field the priority of beings and the power of correctness shatter in favour of the mildness of beyng [*der Milde des Seyns*] from out of the essential unfolding of the clearing [*Lichtung*] of sustainment.
>
> [. . .]
>
> Thinking is "of" beyng, and thus attuned opens, in its saying, the truth of beyng as sustainment into the simplicity of the word that keeps silent.
>
> [. . .]
>
> Propriation and the gentleness of supreme sovereignty, which does not require power or "struggle," but originary critical setting apart. Power-less holding sway.[47]

The favor of the mildness of beyng is an expression of nonviolent dwelling in stillness and in the commencement of beyng, which is also the place of divine dwelling[48] or the way of dwelling of god(s), who also need(s) beyng. Beyng is thus the "abyssal ground of the in-between,"[49] which in its way of event of appropriation (*Ereignis*) and mildness delivers everything that we possess and in which we dwell to their ownmost, most intimate, and quietest. In the work *Building Dwelling Thinking* this way of being was termed "sparing." Heidegger says: "To spare and preserve means to take under our care, to look after the fourfold in its essence."[50] Heidegger thus undoubtedly sees the most important trait of beyng in its complete and final renouncement of machination as a way of dwelling out of subjectivity—of its will to power as violence, force, etc. If indeed Heidegger thinks beyng out of its complete and final renunciation of the logic of machination and any kind of violence, we have before us a unique ontological constellation that requires reflection, particularly if we consider the following sentence:

> Only when power runs into the nothing, when it can no longer even "make" an opposition for itself, does it collapse within itself and its essence.[51]

According to Heidegger, power always needs power as its own means.[52] Love, on the other hand, does not need power: we have seen in Binswanger that love is based on the gesture of surrender (*die Gebärde der Überlassung*; cf. Heidegger's "sparing"), which occurs between two subjects and thus entails the admittance of the being of the other in the space next to me. So what does this encounter feed on if not on power? But at this point, Binswager, as we have seen, does not further ponder the origin of this encounter. He sets it into a place of *dwelling* that is characterized by profound silence (*atemlose Stille*), speechlessness. And yet: How can this gesture come to be in the very being, in its silence? Can beyng be love in the way of this dwelling in mildness without us asking ourselves about what within this beyng represents primal memory or the immanence of "we (ourness)" (*Wirheit*; perhaps in the form of sexual difference), the primordial encounter outside life and death, in a place of dwelling that still needs to be thought out, perhaps, if we risk transition into a sphere that we still must reach and cannot describe (yet)—even some remnant of experience that refuses to lend itself to ontological analysis? Or does beyng, contrariwise, refer to a certain nature of *cháris* (in the sense of gratitude and reciprocation; love) in itself, as writes W. F. Otto on the question in regard to the divine essence of the Greek Aphrodite? To him, Aphrodite is—in the passage that also follows the mission of Heidegger's history of beyng as mildness—the one who "causes human hearts to beat for one another and who produces perfect harmony and unity in great world-periods."[53] In her divine typology, Aphrodite is fundamentally distinct from Eros, her son: Eros is associated with the energy for reproduction (and thereby subject to the primary mode of machination as multiplication of this, in essence, erotic power), while "Aphrodite's realm is of another sort and much more comprehensive," and proceeds "not from the desiring subject, but from the beloved object."[54] And this is the sphere of genealogical love. We know that, for Derrida, Heidegger's archetypal indifference both toward sexual difference and toward the ontological dual in the *Dasein* from *Being and Time* is an indication of his utmost caution lest he should slip into a sexualizing nature of *Dasein*. Binswanger already found this a challenge to his own thought.[55] But on the horizon of the triadic-processual unfolding of God *as* love, both in Schelling and Moltmann and, ultimately, in the framework of the Greek culture, as we have now seen, this process incorporates a certain archaic (preontological?) gesture of the feminine, which we would like to investigate in more detail farther on and link to *chóra*, as revealed to us through our study of God, incarnation of the feminine, and Mary.

Ecofeminist theologian Trish Glazenbrook believes that "an alternative conception of nature, and ecofeminism can recognize in Heidegger a gynocentric epistemology,"[56] such that it can replace the phallogocentric logic within the thinking itself and can think being on its behalf—i.e., in the name of love. In the logic of the Fourfold and mutual affection, as well as sparing, is where contemporary feminist philosophers and interpreters of Heidegger discovered a superior or more primeval motion of love between mortals and gods that refers to the reciprocity of love within the Fourfold (man and divinity) as well as on its margin, in the meeting space between the immanence of life in death and that of death in life. In her presentation of possibilities of the late Heidegger and her, as she says in the introduction,[57] Carol Bigwood opens the question of the origin of mildness and love in the dialogue with the divine figure of Aphrodite or her earthly deputy or herald Sappho or the so-called Tenth Muse, a question that may prove of crucial importance for us. Bigwood strongly emphasizes that her words—on the very verges between *mythos* and *logos*—are essentially always words of mildness, reciprocity, love. This is what she says:

Her description of love, however, is not simply between mortals but also expresses a reciprocal divine love between mortals and immortals since love for Sappho always brings us in contact with Aphrodite. Her poetry offers premetaphysical understanding of the ontological difference. In some sense, All is Love for Sappho, where Love is not simply intersubjective human love, but is already in some way inclusive of All, or "Being" (a concept that was non-existent in her day).[58]

Love—so, which is closer to it, Aphrodite (as a woman) or Nietzsche's Dionysius (as a man)?—wonders Bigwood. Aphrodite, who is gentle and loves children, who protects and preserves—could the path toward the plane of the being of love (beyng) be foreshadowed in that? Heidegger himself is perhaps closest to feminist epistemologies in his interpretation of Antigone. The latter seems not to belong to the genealogical order of love that fills Sappho's poetic realm; rather, at first glance, it radically opposes it in her "determination" and ascribed "masculinity." But only at first glance: Antigone's dwelling place is still close to ancient pre-Olympian and chthonic goddesses, protectresses of the spheres of birth, life, and death and, especially, of the matrixial orders of being—particularly in the way it is reflected in care for girls and sisters, women and mothers (Metis, the Earth goddess, Erinyes, Demeter, Kore/Persephone; also Aphrodite as Erinyes's sister):

> Thus in the maternal deities of the earth we see the guardians and representatives of those revered ordinances which constitute a bond between parents, children, and siblings. The various birth-rights of children are also hallowed in them.[59]

And this is the world of Antigone. According to Heidegger, Antigone is the uncanniest (*das Unheimlichste*) of the uncanny.[60] Her essence, however, does not lie in remoteness, but contrariwise, in the nearest of the near: i.e., in sisterly love, which Tine Hribar, when interpreting Antigone's famous line on love ("My nature is for mutual love, not hate"),[61] places inside the following framework:

> What is the relationship between Antigone's love and the unwritten law on the sacredness of the deceased? Antigone is autonomous in her decision. She is law to herself when

out of love (for the dead brother) she decides to undertake a sacred act. Sisterly love is not, as Hegel thought, the point of departure, rather the peak of a love that takes no adjective and is without cause. In the cited Antigone's thought about love, Sophocles uses the word *sym-philio*, which means I join in love, I love with another. Like *sym-patheo* means I join in another's feeling, I feel with them. But sympathy originates in symphilia. From the love for nothing, but for everything.

This love is Antigone's point of departure. To love, that is all. Joining in love is what makes people want to be in this world. Without that there would be no relations or fellow men or neighbours. If we didn't love our nearest, the pain of remembering after their passing could not touch us.[62]

Antigone's sisterly love is the love dwelling at the heart of beyng. But it would seem that only Luce Irigaray in her reading of *Antigone* noticed the discreet, yet crucial presence of Aphrodite. Near the end of the third choral ode, which speaks about Eros and his power, appears this goddess of love, set in the very proximity of the sacred or unwritten laws. This is what Irigaray says in a somewhat longer passage related to the scene in which Creon decides to wall Antigone up in a tomb:

> Thus, at the moment when the Greek culture lays the foundations of the western socio-political order, King Creon—according to Sophocles' tragedy *Antigone*—establishes a tyrannical power at the expense of the family and inheritance law, forbidding Antigone to perform the last rites for her brother Polyneices, who died in a fratricidal battle while attempting to take control over the city. These rites are necessary for the preservation of the cosmological order in accordance with the matriarchal law that Creon wants to supersede. A dead man left without burial will not only be condemned to eternal wandering and never finding his peace, but will also sully and disrupt the whole balance of the universe: the air, the sun and the world of the living beings, the animal world in particular. Creon no longer wants to respect such laws, neither those concerning the whole of universe nor those existing among the humans themselves. He establishes authority that

defies the cosmic balance and challenges the right to a love respectful of the natural affiliation of humans, be it Antigone's respect of her maternal genealogy or of her love for her fiancé Haemon, son of King Creon himself. Despite the intervention by Aphrodite, the goddess of love—another feminine figure of the period in which natural order regulated the relationships between the world and the humans and among the humans themselves—Creon condemns Antigone to being buried alive in a rock cavern, deprived of air, sunlight and the possibility of experiencing love and motherhood.[63]

The third choral ode about Eros is not easy to interpret. It follows the most critical moment in the entire play, when Creon announces he will have Antigone walled up into her rocky tomb. In his thorough reading of Sophocles's play, Seth Benardete wonders about the nature of this Greek deity and Antigone's relationship to it. In Benardete's opinion, the Chorus in this ode—and this is now crucial—*does not* establish a link between Antigone and Eros.[64] In this choral ode, Eros is indeed characterized as the most violent of gods, whom no mortal or immortal can escape; he is a god who leads people into deception and madness; a god who puts people up to committing injustices and causing disagreements. In this sense, Eros is the reason for the dispute between the two brothers, which lies at the basis of Sophocles's *Antigone*. This is how this constellation is defined in an important passage from Benardete's work:

> But the Chorus understand Eros as primarily sexual, and Antigone's denial of sexual generation, which the Olympian gods share with men, sets her above Eros. Antigone seems to overstep the limit that limits the gods.[65]

This is now of critical importance: in his relation to gods and mortals, Eros may be the most violent of gods. As already mentioned, the love that we can associate with Antigone is situated at the margin of the Fourfold, in the sphere where the love between the mortals and the immortals meets the sphere of the dual immanence of life in death and death in life—beyond the sheer dichotomies of being and nonbeing; in a place where Eros's tremendous power, if we may borrow Heidegger's words, "runs into nothing" and "collapses within itself and its essence."[66]

It is difficult to locate Aphrodite's exact place in this framework as she is summoned into the choral ode. But undoubtedly Aphrodite, in a well-chosen manner (and the goddess is evoked in the very conclusion of this ode about Eros) is placed close to the unwritten laws of beyng—in fact, the text in the coda says: "It is power enthroned in sway beside the eternal laws; for there the goddess Aphrodite is working her unconquerable will."[67] We will to return to this goddess of Love, or Beyng's sister, in the closing of this chapter and in the Postlude.

This is now the area in which a select few can move (perhaps only Antigone, Savitri, Clara, and, of male figures, only Jesus). If Eros is the god who provides and multiplies lives, this energy is nevertheless grounded in something more than primordial—now primordial more so than life itself. Antigone does not walk into death to dissolve into the shadows and night in some mad or pathological desire, nor does she search for this dwelling propelled by some pathological death drive. Antigone's gesture is what reveals and brings to all of us, to mortals and gods in the Fourfold, the feminine *matrix* of Love as the sister of beyng. Antigone, who has no home with the living or with the dead (v. 852), with her passage across the margin of the Fourfold only makes it possible for us to see ourselves as dwelling in the affiliation to this sisterly ontology of Love, the primal Matrix of all dwelling. Antigone's hardly comprehensible thought that she would not risk the same ethical gesture either for children or a husband (vv. 906–909)—if she had any—can thus only be understood on the horizon of the logic of this absolute matrix, that is, of the more primordial ontology or proto-genealogy to which all subsequent genealogical orders belong—and this thought is, in terms of cosmic order, cognate to Abraham's dilemma in the Old Testament. Here, Irigaray correctly establishes that only with this turnaround can Antigone become divine, through her protecting life as such; primarily, we can see an interruption and presence of the immanence of death in life—both in the unborn and in the unburied—in the sense of a violent and essentially antimatrixial disruption of family genealogies. To Antigone, life has supreme value. And, equally importantly, if she is trying to protect the dead brother, it is not because of any sexual impulses (incest) or "because she takes a particular interest in the dead, as has often been said. She wants to preserve life."[68] In this lies the exuberance of her love and, at the same time, her closest proximity to Christ. Antigone is Christ's genealogical sister.

We have reached now another important dimension to which we would like to dedicate special attention: Antigone's relationship to the previously described maternal genealogies. As Irigaray ultimately says:

> The maternal genealogy favours the values of life, of generation, of growth. It is based on unwritten laws that do not clearly distinguish civil order from religious order. It does not attach an absolute importance to family as such, as patriarchy does. It privileges daughters and, later, the youngest son as heirs.[69]

The pre-Olympian genealogies respected this cosmic order. As Gail Schwab finds in her interpretation of Greek genealogies in the works by Irigaray, it is precisely the *vertical* and *a*sexual love in the mother-daughter relationship—as in the case of the myth of Demeter and Persephone/Kore—that contains or preserves that primary cosmological/ontological matrix of the relationship that precedes all other relationships, among mortals and gods alike: "When the link between mother and daughter—the intergenerational link between women—is lost, life does not flourish."[70] Like Antigone, the goddess Persephone had been sent away or banished into the realm of death intended to interrupt forever her matrixial bond with the orders of being and deliver her body to the order of violence and thereby Death. That is why Vrasidas Karalis could make the bold remark at the margin of the even more primordial Greek genealogy (i.e., the first generation of gods/goddesses) that it is in the beginning of Greek genealogies—in Metis as the first goddess of this proto-genealogy—where the hidden continuity between the origin of everything and the germ of the first being is comprised: this is the mythological place of the prime plane of love/Love—which now unfolds in this context through genealogy, conveyed by a wonderful phrase: "*Mother/Daughter/holy spirit*—the primeval Trinitarian doxology."[71] Where is this matrix of Love to be found?

Beyond the Margin: Beyng as a Plane of Love

Finally, let us make an attempt at answering the question into what dwelling we are invited when interpreting love as a gift of being (in its already suggested double meaning) in the above described original or proto-matrixial genealogy. Binswanger emphasized that the exuberance of love is comprehended in the peacefulness of the primordial encounter, in profound silence (*atemlose Stille*) or speechlessness, in a place of dwelling that we as the ones inhabiting this stillness of beyng (event of appropriation or *Ereignis*) give to ourselves.[72] But what does this *Ereignis* come from? In this concluding part of the chapter, we would like to return one last time to Heidegger and try to provide an answer to this query by reiterating the link with the cosmological/ontological/ethical genealogy of love.

In one of the previous chapters we saw how Derrida characterized *chóra* as dwelling without any power, nevertheless active through the presence of all things created. We have seen in the previous treatment of Mary that the universe pulsates in the space of the matrix of interiority (or primeval uterus) in the manner of archaic pulsation of love in the very core of the primordial ontological model (in theology, the model for this motion was expressed by the Trinitarian co-existence in perichoresis). What could be the ontological signification of this matrix of interiority? We know from Plato's *Timaeus* that the so-called third kind,[73] known enigmatically as *chóra*, is a receptacle of all becoming (perhaps dwelling?) described as some kind of wet nurse. This *tríton génos* is an ontological category par excellence and, perhaps most importantly, *chóra* (even in Plato) always resides in the feminine element.[74] There is a similarity between this concept and the Daoist philosophy as represented by Kuang-Ming Wu. His work on cosmic/material ethics and religion (*On Chinese Body Thinking*), as we have seen in our previous treatments, puts forth two notions, namely, "wombing forth" and "wombing motherliness." The wombing forth is based on the concept of "womb-power" as a feminine ontological presence that can be found everywhere: "in water, in roots, in valleys," even as a presence in ourselves that enables us, as human beings, to be humble, compassionate, and devoted to others. Womb-power, according to Wu, is "the empty room between Heaven and Earth . . . a motherly bellows, vacuous, inexhaustible, continually letting forth [things]." Wu continues with the following words:

> Every human relation worthy of its name is a mothering and wombing—your being vacuous draws me forth, lets me become as I am. . . . The inner personal touch fills the void in me and in you, making us one. Yet we remain two, for

two-ness enables touch. We are thus two in one, and one in two, thanks to our personal void and touch inside. All this describes mutual fulfilment. Personal void generates love—inner touch—that *mothers us* to grow into ourselves.[75]

We have thus the third kind/element, presented in a Daoist context. Moreover, this element is related to the primordial vacuity and silence in myself, to my giving it all away for the sake of the other (person or thing) in their reciprocal and again complete giving it all away to me. This is a plane of horizontal transcendence, a bellows of proximity and *différance* of dwelling. The womb-power in Her essential potency—wombing motherliness—is thus an ontological space of our mutual becoming, of possibilities of an "inner touch"[76] between two realities, first between the mother and the child (foetus), and ultimately between God/Goddess and the human being. In Christian terms, we might say that we find Christ in ourselves as an inner touch, a subtle, yet powerful spiritual (breath of love) and maternal presence of love and humility and acceptance in ourselves. This is now the realm of beyng. We know that from his *Contributions to Philosophy (Of the Event)* onward, Heidegger suggested and searched for a shift into a different mode of being (*Gelassenheit*), which—as Caputo establishes in his insightful and at the same time feminist reading of Heidegger—reveals to a philosopher a "more welcoming and receptive, more prayerful and less warrior-like relation to the world."[77] Heidegger is now able to thank being for affection, even hope that a future god will save us, but he still cannot, as Caputo correctly points out, shed a single tear at the immense suffering of people in the world, thus remaining cold and distanced and, apparently, without an ounce of compassion in his heart, or, to put it even more bluntly:

> When a prominent Heideggerian wrote a book called *Stone*, he said it all. Dasein has stones, not flesh. . . . Everything in the later thought of the worlding of the world has to do with the splendor of Being, the shine of *Sein*, the shining *Schönheit* of *Sein*. Everything takes its measure from the fouring of the Fourfold, which leaves no room for the immeasurable misery of the masses, the suffering of the oppressed, the countless, untold tears of those who neither think nor poetize.[78]

Does Heidegger's being in this *phainaesthetic* event then completely oppose tears, compassion, with the suffering and, ultimately, the exuberance of love? His beyng can only be thought out of the horizon of its matrixial co-essence, ontological (co)sisterhood in the area of the plane of beyng. At the margin of the Fourfold, as we have seen, mortals do not appropriate death as the acceptor of the essence of the Being of being in its—and to Heidegger, most authentic—dwelling. When in *The Forgetting of Air in Martin Heidegger* Luce Irigaray meditated about the air, breath, and atmosphere of freedom, she knew that there is not enough fluidity or openness beyond the *logos* in Heidegger's Being that can within the range of its topology of Being and its own ontological self-limitation provide or give to the human being a space for its most authentic proximity, beyond the gathering or in some sort of dwelling in life that gathers in being. "When life still was . . ." says Irigaray in her work *In the Beginning, She Was*—but here we are faced with another kind of life.[79] A contemplation about Empedocles and the meaning of his relationship between Love (Aphrodite) and Hate (Neikos) raises a similar doubt as that which she expresses through criticism of Heidegger. Aphrodite, who "is perceived by no mortal man as she circles among them"[80]—and who as a non-name of love dwells in the mode of the immanence of life in death, and of death in life, as a dual motion of Love—is the one to allow all things and all beings of this world who long for and love one another, to gather into One(ness). The exuberance of love coming from Aphrodite is not generated from its own opposite (or with regard to forever the *same*),[81] as in Empedocles, but is born and preserved in ever-new nearness that represents an ontologically pre-original promise of pulsation or exuberance of Love within the very interior of Beyng. The structure of this relationship—in the *différance* prior to (but also simultaneously with) the sexual difference[82]—enables us to recognize in it the possibility of what Binswanger named with the syntagma "the we of love" (*Wir der Liebe*)—which to us who dwell in its proximity finally unfolds as "a primordial form of 'we' (or 'ourness') or 'embrace of love.'"[83]

(Orin)

> I also want to come to the summit. I don't want to die in my bed and be buried near there. The result is the same. All our souls will come to the summit in the end. All of us will meet at the summit together.
>
> —*The Ballad of Narayama*

There may not be a more soul-stirring cinematographic image of a death of a mother nor a more aesthetically consummate depiction of the life-and-death process than that presented in the Japanese movie *The Ballad of Narayama* (*Narayamabushi-ko*) from 1958 in the original version by the director Keisuke Kinoshita. In the movie, based on the homonymous novel by Shichiro Fukuzawa, Kinoshita adopted elements of the classic Japanese *kabuki* and *bunraku* theatre. Through their idiosyncratic use he drew near to the mysterious central point of the Fourfold from Heidegger's constellation of Beyng, as well as to the enigmatic outer limit of the marrow of Binswanger's thought—that the exuberance of love is encompassed in the holy peace and quiet of the primordial encounter, in profound silence, in a space of dwelling that we as dwellers in this silence of beyng (appropriative event) bestow on ourselves—and, also, on one another. The impossible and radical boundary of this peace of encounter is—and precisely in this consists the tragedy of the story of Narayama and the tragedy of life itself—unattainable in the sense of merely mortal being. It reminds us of the story of Lazarus and of Caputo's concise remark about it (also supplemented with a note about Derrida's mortal illness and his friends' wish to have him at least for another day, one *more* day . . .) that perhaps the one thing that we really desire in life is merely to live one more moment of love—to hope for such closeness and preserve its time of love, to hope for its future, the evermore. This is why *The Ballad of Narayama* is an articulation and enactment of this radical constellation, as well as a demonstration of a gesture that pushes this boundary into the sphere of death and dying.

The Ballad of Narayama is based on an old Japanese legend about a remote village in Nagano Prefecture, where, according to tradition, men and women, when they turn seventy, must leave for Mount Narayama to meet their death. The mount's other name is Ubasute, literally "the mountain of abandoned old people."[84] The movie, which imitates the traditional manners of *kabuki* theatre, in the very first scene connects the viewer to the world of the elements, of being between heaven and earth, of the significance of the natural cycles, of fertility, pregnancy, harvest, and, especially, food, creating thereby an exceptionally subtle and at the same time extraordinarily vulnerable environment of the world of people and gods and nature into which the main protagonists of the story are set.

The movie narrates the tale of Tatsuhei, a middle-aged man with three children. After losing his wife, he lives as a widower with his mother Orin, who is herself widowed. His children are still fostering a close connection with their dead mother, as is evident from a scene at the cemetery, which suggests the mother's mysterious presence in this world. The family, living in dire shortage of food, are swept by the inquietude of an incipient crisis, for Tatsuhei has met a woman and intends to remarry, while one of his sons is expecting a child with his pregnant companion. Hence, the family will soon grow by two members and there will not be enough food to go round. Contrary to the tradition that the elderly depart for Mount Ubasute at the age of seventy, Tatsuhei's mother Orin decides, by herself and for the sake of the family, to leave this world one year sooner than expected. As a widow, she has preserved her health and nice teeth—which the fellow villagers see as a sign of living in plenty. Being ridiculed for that (taunted that her poverty is not real), in a harrowing scene, Orin breaks her front teeth on a grindstone: she is now ready to leave for Mount Narayama. From this moment onward, the story about poverty and family life merges with the legend. Since the film was created in harmony with the classic *bunraku* theatre, it features the narrator, who makes sure that the viewer does not mistake the development of the plot with scenes from real life: it is thus clear that events are staged to conjure up the old legend of Mount Narayama, with a narrator, a theatre bell ringing, a backdrop reminiscent of the stage of life and death. When the moment of departure comes, the narrator announces it with the following ritual words:

> "Abandon the aged on Mount Narayama." The village custom is an ancient one. Even the Narayama Festival song reminds you of your age, as if urging you to depart on time. The early autumn wind is merciless this morning.[85]

The events in the movie are closely intertwined with a game of the elements—wind, earth, fire, water, and food.[86] In the scene where the family shares lunch together for the last time, the viewer can recognize the connection between food, water (rain), and tears, which are part of an elementary constellation now inhabited by sadness:

Inside, the family eats a meagre supper. Outside a drizzling rain. Inside, Tatsuhei's heart is drenched in sorrow, even as night draws on the time of dreaming.[87]

In an intimate scene between Tatsuhei's son and his pregnant lover Matsu, hunger is again in the foreground and thereby food—as an element of growth, pulsation of new life, hope, love, and, through lack thereof, fear. The element of fire, burning in the hearth, is a symbol of life. When Orin reaches the decision to leave for the sacred Mount Ubasute, the flame in the hearth suddenly dies. The very ritual of the journey to the mountain is the key part of the movie: the son takes his mother on his back and carries her up the arduous path on the mountain. The narrator accompanies him with the following words:

> Many years have passed and now this one when son must bear mother on his back. He is in agony, inseparable from his mother. The wind blows over Mount Narayama.[88]

One could hardly portray the genealogical and life bond between the child (son) and the parent (mother) in a more explicit and tragic way. The ancient ritual now forbids the mother to speak. Her silence is an expression of approaching the threshold of life and death, the passage into the sphere of the sacred, as announced by the Shinto *torii* gate, though which the son walks with his mother on his back. When they reach the summit, a fearful view opens before us, of mummified bodies and bones of people who died on the mountain. The son lowers the mother to the ground, and she chooses her final resting place. Tatsuhei places his mother's final rations before her, which she refuses. He embraces her one last time, weeping, and takes leave. The gift of food thus turns into the son's gift to the god of the mountain, and the mother departs this world in a meditative posture, reciting Buddhist prayers. In her yoga position she evokes the god Shiva on top of the snow-capped Mount Kailash. It may be impossible to imagine a closer link between the realms of mortals and immortals, between heavens and earth, than we witness in the scene.

The Ballad of Narayama is thus a story of the power of love and care in this world, of the hope that faith in these two will never forsake us. Although the story is staged and narrated in a tragic way, and although the legend of Mount Ubasute and the entire movie, at first glance, mercilessly indicate the dominance of death and suffering over life, the point of this narration is concealed precisely in love and care of life, in closeness and family as the place of our *dwelling*, in gestures of reciprocity that we demonstrate in this world and at its margins.

feeding diaphragm

6

Irigaray / Breath

Something has happened—an event, or an advent—an encounter between humans. A breath or soul has been born, brought forth by two others. There are now living beings for whom we lack the ways of approaching, the gestures and words for drawing nearer to one another, for exchanging.

—Luce Irigaray, *Sharing the World*

Before Breath Is Born

The question of the epistemological foundations of our religious and theological thinking is perhaps one of the most difficult questions in philosophy: it deals with both theoretical as well as practical layers of our being-in-the-world; moreover, it is also related to the most intimate layers of our personal and social life (questions of life and death, family and kin, our values in social and political environments, our ethical attitudes) that we possess and inhabit. Moreover, for philosophy of religion, today the question would be how to relate our self-transcendence to the transcendence of the irreducible otherness of the other, in other words, how to relate in a new way our most intimate (also sexed) ontological layers with the other, and ultimately God/dess still to come. But it seems that we do not yet have the dialectics to enable this encounter. We pray for this *event* (Caputo),[1] which resides in a yet unknown place and time, as our longing, but also as our forgetting.

Traditionally, Western metaphysics has armed the male (and, mostly, not female) philosopher with the knowledge he needed for this encounter with the unknown or dangerous, and at the same moment has given him permission to safeguard the place he occupied only for himself and which he firmly held only for sustaining and perpetuating this powerful self-affection. With Feuerbach's philosophy of sensibility[2] and Nietzsche's revaluation of all values,[3] for the first time in the history of Western thought the existing topologies of this kind of selfhood (soul, spirit, subjectivity) have been radically undermined—from both the theoretical as well from the practical sense (self-affection as both natural affection in Feuerbach as well as an artistic practice in Nietzsche). With Feuerbach and Nietzsche, the philosopher, a man, is now put into an entirely new relational space that he never before occupied: he is now close to the primordial (macrocosmic) constellation of the elements of nature (water, air, earth, and fire) and to the pulsation of his body (the microcosm)—as radically exposed by Nietzsche; he is also reminded of his sex (Feuerbach being first philosopher to address this new dialectics of intersubjectivity)[4] and thus exposed in an entirely new way to sexual difference; finally, with both Feuerbach and Nietzsche, for the first time the philosopher was faced with the death of the God that he had known and worshipped for centuries. In this, both thinkers (and, as we'll see, also Irigaray) are close to Presocratic thought. Additionally, Nietzsche reminds us in his *Antichrist*[5] that we need to search for truth also in the traditions of the East (i.e., within ancient Indo-Iranian civilizational circle), as in his invocation of Zararthustra and his high praise of Buddha (in this, Nietzsche remained Schopenhauer's best successor; we may also add the Upanishadic thought).[6] Sadly, Feuerbach's philosophy soon faded into oblivion, being, allegedly, superseded by Marxist thought and only resuscitated after more than a century by Irigaray's philosophical project.

Maybe phenomenology was the first to learn this lesson in its entirety; Husserl and Heidegger have each in his own way decided to brush away all of the old philosophical sediments from our spiritual legacies.[7] Husserl's phenomenological reduction in his *Ideen* and Heidegger's in *Being and Time* are without doubt two of the key events in the history of Western thinking. Following them, phenomenology has enabled philosophers to dwell closer to the body, closer to our senses (of ethical/bodily proximity, hearing, caress, and touch—as in Merleau-Ponty and Levinas, but also in Nancy, Henry, Marion, and especially Chrétien; but, with one exception[8]—but still not yet being close to breath—as our "ontological" sense), and later, also in an intercultural sense, to interpret our various lifeworlds only as parts of a pluriform world culture, which is hermeneutically open, eventual, and never enclosed into the one interpretative framework, or the one Truth. But, according to Irigaray, cultivating oneself requires a different kind of self-affection, which still "seems to be lacking for us Westerners."[9] The self-affection, which already was a part of classical philosophical training from Parmenides to Hegel, but which also extended to Husserl and Heidegger, did not cultivate relationality as a way of our individual becoming—i.e., self-affection toward the other was not defined in a proper dialectical way—in a way that would safeguard both my subjectivity and the other's transcendence in his/her difference and full autonomy. Of course, philosophy always was relational in the sense of some temporality of me and the other, the Real, or, ultimately, a God, but not in the sense of an "ecstasy of an encounter"[10]—in an ethically radicalized mode of between-two, based on the ontology of self-affection, sexual difference, and our mutual mesocosmic breathing.[11] In the way of an interaction, this very encounter inaugurates and at the same moment safeguards the new radicalized ontology (at first as *a*theology) of the two, which in its essence is both religious (cf. Irigaray's sensible transcendental) and ethical. What is the ontology of self-affection, then?

In her more recent works, Luce Irigaray works on what we might call "the sexuate ontology of radical subjectivity."[12] Her thinking is based on the notion of auto- or self-affection. In order to be able to get to the ontological layer of her teachings on the sensible transcendental and the breath, it is first necessary to understand this notion she holds as proposed in some of her later writings. We find it for the first time in *The Way of Love* from 2002, in the Introduction:

> An encounter between two different subjects implies that each one attends to remaining itself. And that cannot amount to a simple voluntarist gesture but depends on our ability for *"auto-affection"*—another word that I did not find in the dictionary. Without this, we cannot respect the other as other, and he, or she, cannot respect us. It is not a question, to be sure, of extrapolating into some essence—mine or that of the other—but of a critical gesture for a return to oneself which does not stay in suspension in immutable truths or essences but which provides a faithfulness to oneself in becoming.[13]

Later known as self-affection, this is a key to understanding of her philosophical teaching on sexual difference and our ethical becoming. Irigaray's greatest invention in philosophy is without doubt the introduction of an idiosyncratic dialectical dyad into the very core of our ontology and epistemology. This dyad is always formed by two, who are different (sexual difference is here understood as an ontological paradigm, and clearly not as a call to heteronormativity), and "not united by genealogy or hierarchy."[14] Self-affection thus teaches us to become two, without appropriating or annihilating the other as other, or without being alienated from our own becoming in subjectivity. The becoming of subjectivity also refers to an idiosyncratic logic of a difference between masculine and feminine world(s), since men and women have different accesses to maternal genealogies, to the rhythms of nature, and to sexual becoming and belonging through mutual desire and love. We breathe the same air, but we breathe it differently. We all want to achieve our humanity, but we can only achieve it dialectically—by respecting our differences in an intersubjective and intercultural sense. Irigaray concludes her *In the Beginning, She Was* with the following thoughts:

> Self-affection is neither secondary nor unnecessary. Self-affection—which once more does not amount to a mere auto-eroticism—is as much necessary for being human as bread is. Self-affection is the basis and the first condition of human dignity. There is no culture, no democracy, without the preservation of self-affection for each one.
>
> Self-affection today needs a return to our own body, our own breath, a care about our life in order not to become subjected to technologies, to money, to power, to neutralization in a universal "someone," to assimilation into an anonymous world, to the solitude of individualism.
>
> Self-affection needs faithfulness to oneself, respect for the other in their singularity, reciprocity in desire and love—more generally, in humanity. We have to rediscover and cultivate self-affection starting, at each time and in every situation, from two, two who respect their difference, in order to preserve the survival and the becoming of humanity, for each one and for all of us.[15]

But still, what does self-affection bring us that is not available to us in Western philosophical history? Here we need to return to Feuerbach and

Nietzsche (and their appeal to the body and its practices of self-affection), and also to introduce Eastern teachings (Yoga and Buddha, silence as a mode of our self-affection, and related appeal to the practice of meditation), which all are Irigaray's strongest influences. They all form the fertile ground for her thinking. With Feuerbach, we are witnessing the first philosophical elaboration of intersubjectivity in the entire Western history of philosophy; according to the German thinker, a man and a woman are two beings, fully dependent on Nature (via food, water, air, etc.), but thus also fully dependent on each other. They are sharing each other's finite lifeworlds with the interchange of breathing, touching, and various gestures (such as language), which form a dialectical encounter between any pair of two sensible subjectivities. But in this relational process, my and your finitude also confront the limit—an infinite transcendence of the other, which is ontologically unsurmountable. For Feuerbach, this is the true and first meaning of any religion and love. Nietzsche clearly radicalized this constellation with his appeal to the body and its immanent life and thus with his absolute rejection of any kind of subjectivity having soul or spirit as its immaterial cause, even hypostasized as a God. It seems that Irigaray translates and develops both concepts—Feuerbach's sensitivity and Nietzsche's will—to her idiosyncratic notion of self-affection. There is no logical procedure nor moralistic rule (or religious authority) that could guide us in this dynamic and dialectic of self-affection: and this is where Eastern teachings (Yoga, meditation, Buddha's teachings) enter into the very core of Irigaray's thought. In Yoga and Buddhism, the predominance of vital and spiritual breath is clearly represented in meditational and practical methods, where emptying out our ordinary modes of selfhood is a key to attentiveness (or mindfulness) of ourselves. Now, in order to secure a future world for us, we need to reorient toward dwelling first in our interiority, with self-affection guiding us—in order to inaugurate and enable silence and listening. But to which ontological layer, or reality, will this silence refer? To whom are we first destined to listen? This still is a mystery. We first need to create a sanctuary in ourselves—a place for the advent of *pure breath*, which will be the first sign of compassion and love. As stated in *Una nuova cultura dell'energia*, "thanks to a practice of self-affection"[16] we have become settled in ourselves, protecting life as such—in order to be able to share it with others. Silence and listening (first to ourselves: meditation, Yoga, other spiritual practices) are therefore signs of our affection—first toward ourselves and then toward others (from nature and animals, to human beings and gods, or vice versa). Silence and listening are two modes of our attentiveness, which first is an ontological, and later, as developed in an intersubjective way, also a moral disposition of ourselves, a genuine and ontological dyadic mode of relationality. As argued in one of our previous essays on Irigaray's notion of attentiveness,

> Being attentive to the needs of others is not a simple act or a moral disposition but something more: it is the ideal—but as a certain passivity, an emptying of ourselves, a labelling with "nothingness" of our everyday aims and goals." In a theological language, all of this would be very close to a state of grace. Irigaray devoted much of her later work to the new culture of proximity and intersubjectivity, based on the elements that may, in our opinion, enable us to construct new ethical spaces in ourselves for the welcome of the other. But attentiveness is first of all related to our self-affection. . . . Attentiveness is a relational virtue, but of a pre-reflective character: it shows us that we, as individuals, have sociality (and God) already in ourselves. Attentiveness thus opens an ethical space of transcendence of the other—of his or her irreducible difference to me, or my subjectivity. Only on this ground an ethical gesture, fully respectful of the other and of the needs of others, can emerge. The intersubjective space has thus been revealed and opened to us in a new way.[17]

In this sense, we first need to respect ourselves, being attentive to our inner breath, which always already pulsates in us (although we might not always sense its weak pulsation and it might be obstructed by various obstacles) and enables us to share it with the others, in a respectful, nondiscriminating, and nonpossessing way.

The Love of Breath

> To stand in the shadow
> of the scar up in the air.
> To stand-for-no-one-and-nothing.
> Unrecognized,
> for you
> alone.

With all there is room for in that,
even without
language.
—Paul Celan[18]

Now it is time to proceed to the ontology of breath. In *Una nuova cultura dell'energia* we read:

> If we are conscious of a fact that our life exists only because of our breathing, it is necessary to become autonomous beings. This is why we cannot remain alive on the elementary level of life of a newborn at the beginning of his existence. We need to accept the responsibility for our life and transform it to human existence. This is why we need to safeguard and develop our breathing but also to teach to create the reserve of disposable breath [*una riserva di soffio disponibile*]: a soul, which allows us, that our breath is not dependent only to some necessities we are facing. This, in fact, is the first meaning of the word soul.[19]

According to Irigaray, breath must be a path of our spiritual becoming. When we are born, we breathe autonomously for the first time, but our breath still depends on others who give us food, shelter, and love. In the beginning of our spiritual life, breath is never uninterrupted, never pure, and we do not yet possess the energy by ourselves to bring our breath into an equilibrium and peace. We are born with the body and with the soul (our senses, language), but spiritually we firstly depend on others and thus do not yet breathe in an autonomous way. We do not yet have the reserve of breath at our disposal. In almost all religions of the world we find a cosmological myth or narrative related to breath energy or breathing, giving us the spiritual guidance and, as it were, the reserve of breath we first need for keeping and maintaining ourselves in our self-affection, and then for having its share for the others in our compassion. In the form of "wind," "air," "cosmic breath," or "spirit" (*lil, ruah, aer, pneuma, spiritus, anima, prana, qi, ki, mana* . . .), this substance is the essential link between microcosmic and macrocosmic realities, between immanence (our body) and transcendence (the other), enabling finite human beings to access other spiritual beings, cosmos and its gods, ultimately to become spiritual and express in themselves the infinite. This is the path of divinization and this is what we understand by freedom in a truly ontological way. But Schelling (in his *Philosophical Inquiries into the Nature of Human Freedom*) went even deeper with his elaborations on the primordial breath: for him, the breath of love (*der Hauch der Liebe*) is the very foundation of God/Ground—which existed even before there was a foundation. He argued that in the beginning (ontologically) there is an original gesture of "co-breathing" (*Konspiration;* or *conspiratio*)[20] that, once it is inflamed with the inner fever, becomes fractured and inflamed with evil, and the core of our being is wounded. Schelling's contemporary Franz von Baader gives us a beautiful explanation for co-breathing as breathing-together in his work "The Realm of Love." For Baader, discussing the primordial state of humanity in Eden, "the *Paradisiacal Humanity* could have been able to digest with the mouth and procreate itself from the heart through a kiss" (this is the so called "breath-kiss or spirit-embrace," as further also explained with "hearts or spirits embracing or breathing-together").[21] If we return to Schelling now: a human being is born from the wound of the world and is essentially and ontologically vulnerable (in Christianity this is then expressed in the doctrine of original sin, following our Fall; in Eastern doctrines it is *karma*). To breathe autonomously is to regain our lost primordial co-breath, and to be able to transform it into the highest goal that we may have—to live from the reserve of breath as an ontologico-ethical mark of the exuberance of Love. But how can we achieve this spiritual transformation of our being? How can we regenerate again after being infused with, as it were, the inherent ontological Fall?

This is a very deep level of ontology (and theology) indeed, and it is perhaps the most original account or question posited on the cosmological and theological foundation of human being in the entire history of philosophy. Life is born out of the primordial longing of God within itself, which is love, or, more precisely, the breath of love. Within this primordial breath there is a movement, an exhalation and inhalation,[22] as it were, of this ground, which is the archetype of all pulsation and all life (but also of our ontological wound of death). Within Christianity this movement is clearly expressed in the Trinitarian teaching, where God himself must become incarnated and wounded, in order to be able to bring the hope of salvation to the world; and it is precisely in the Holy Spirit, that Father sends his Son to the world.[23] The mysterious logic of the trinitarian co-relationality and co-breathing (*conspiratio*) of three divine persons is visible precisely in this primordial and anarchic exhalation and inhalation of the Ground itself, the pulsation of its archetypal life, for Schelling. It is in *pneuma*, as represented by the Holy Spirit, that every living being receives his/her share of his/her vital breath, as its reserve, which is soul. For Roberto M. Unger, whose experimental pragmatist thinking is in many respects very close to Irigaray's philosophy, Jesus Christ "was a concentrated embodiment of divine energy . . . the activity of spirit that we find in our experience of transcendence and that we rediscover at work in evolving nature."[24] We may say, that this movement is a paradigm of our own becoming— as a progression of difference from the ground of our being, as already being wounded, and finite, to the possibility of our own infinite longing through the awakening and mysterious grace of this primordial breath. But also of our death. This is how we transcend ourselves and become spiritual and how our finite self is becoming awakened, and infinite. But one more step needs to be taken: it is the question of the role of breath and sexual difference as related to the sensible transcendental and feminine divine. For Irigaray, it is no coincidence that Jesus, as our saviour, has been incarnated in a young virgin, since women have a privileged access to the breath:

> Naturally still a virgin, Mary retains the fullness of feminine identity that a little girl has. She is already autonomous in relation to her own mother, and her flesh and breath haven't yet been intimately mingled with those of another human being. Mary is still in communion with herself and with the universe via her breath. She is adolescent, already pubescent, but her way of breathing is still that of a child, or almost. Her body has begun to move and to retain breath in those parts of her that are less in relation with the whole. It is at this moment that the message intervenes.
>
> Before her breath might serve in a simple process of natural reproduction, Mary is called by an angel, the messenger or the embodiment of divine breath, to awaken as a woman not only to her vital but also to her spiritual breath. The angel not only shares breath with her, he also speaks words to her to which she listens and responds. The message of the conception of a child doesn't therefore limit itself to a being-moved or to a sharing that is purely material or physical. It is an exchange of words.[25]

According to Irigaray, the incarnation of Christ in a young woman marks the advent of a new epoch (new age) of our spiritual becoming, now with a mother (a woman) and her male child (a man) being both chosen for this revelatory and redemptive task. We may here only remember another young woman and a virgin—namely, Antigone from the Greek tradition, and Creon who has chosen to follow the diabolic[26] path by literally taking breath and freedom (and the possibility for her to share her life and spiritual breath with others in the future) from her—as a woman. Antigone dies, but her death (by herself; she has withdrawn her breath from this world)[27] is of divine and redemptory character. We know that Hegel and Irigaray both think that her mission might even be higher than that of Christ. Through her radically apolitical and thus ethical act of safeguarding for her brother (a corpse) a symbolic burial, she regains for all of us the lost cosmic order. As Mary has now shared her breath with Jesus, and thus enabled with this sharing a new life—now of a savior, this gesture of hers will open a new possibility for a future epoch (*the Age of the Spirit*), in which, according to Irigaray, we all will become autonomous in our breath, and when we, men and women, will ourselves become linked to divine breath.[28] In this way the essence of religion is now affirmed by Irigaray by acknowledging the special role of women—as being in a closer relation to the breath of life.

But to become enlightened by the power of self-affection is not possible without grace. For Caputo, Jesus dispersed grace all around the world, and if we would be able to touch his garment, Caputo writes, we could *feel* this grace as existing among us, close to us, as an energy, circulating in his body, as filled with *pneuma*, or the divine breath.[29] The pneumatic grace of his body is related to the first breath, which he receives both from the Holy Spirit and from his Mother, being spiritually linked by, as it were, a pneumatic covenant. But the first grace we all receive is in a gesture of sharing the breath in the womb of our mothers, as already beautifully explained by Irigaray. We could now also say that, similarly to Jesus and his birth, Buddha's enlightenment and his redemptory role for the world, on the other side, has been explained in an analogous narrative in *Gandavyuha*, a Mahayana *sutra* from the fourth century CE. We know that in Indian mythology, we have a very strong acknowledgment of sexual difference from the very beginning—as in divine couples throughout the Hindu (also Vedic) cosmology and universe, and later in Yoga and especially Hindu and Buddhist Tantra. Now, in this sacred Buddhist text, Maya, the mother of Shakyamuni Buddha, welcomes in her body the bodhisattva, ascending from the Tushita Heaven into her womb and being born as Buddha into this world. But Maya's womb is able to welcome many other bodhisattvas, and her body "came to embrace the entire world" and "became as expansive as ether."[30] This gesture of the mother of all Buddhas, past, present, and future, is another crucial mark of the pneumatic bond between a young woman and a young man, securing, as Irigaray would say, firstly, respect for life and cosmic order, then for generational order, and, finally, for sexual differentiation.[31] They all represent and embrace all that we need to preserve in order to safeguard *a life* and its breath in their immanence—within the cosmos, within ourselves, and within community.

Toward Sharing of the Divine Breath in Humans

Now it is our wish to wind up this chapter with a meditation on an ethics of breath. First the return to Nietzsche is needed; Gaston Bachelard, in his beautiful and seminal series of books on the four elements, elaborates on Nietzsche in his book on air and depicts him there as an aerial philosopher. For Bachelard, air is intrinsically linked to our imagination and freedom, to the "philosophy of absolute becoming," to the "awareness of the free moment,"[32] to what opens to us in the future. For him, air indeed is a substance of our freedom. In the process of reevaluating all values, air and breathing represent the most crucial parts. For Bachelard, and this now is really important, Nietzsche's doctrine involves the whole being and represents the transformation of its vital energy.[33] We have seen that, for our dwelling in the ontological realm of pure breath, a new self-affection was needed, one able to acknowledge and, as it were, follow the movements of the Holy Breath in Jesus, or another type of Cosmic/Vital Breath (*prana*) in Buddha[34]; one able to abide in silence and listening and closest proximity to the pure breath. We need to nurture, as argued, a space in our interiority (microcosm, the body, *psyche*—as breathing), to be able to empty, or forget in ourselves, all projections that were hindering the ethical encounter with the other, in his/her singularity and difference.

But to move to the ethical world now: here, silence is the principal value of the threshold. It enables us to listen first to the movements of our inner breath, to the pulsation (inspiration and expiration) of life in ourselves (this now is not a path of ontology any more, but of ethics),[35] and at the same moment, in an ethical temporality and an exchange of respiratory energies that shall be explained in this last part, also be attuned to the pulsation of breath and life in the other being. This is how the first memory of our ethical obligation is born. This movement and transformation of our self-affection, and our entire being, really inaugurates a new philosophical discipline—the ethical pneumatology—qua respiration in our being in relation to the other. To enter the plane of ethics let us first reintroduce these words of Irigaray:

> Something has happened—an event, or an advent—an encounter between humans. A breath or soul has been born, brought forth by two others. There are now living beings for whom we lack the ways of approaching, the gestures and words for drawing nearer to one another, for exchanging.[36]

The temporality of ethical encounter is without doubt one of the most difficult questions of ethics. We have already mentioned the Irigarayan concept of the ecstasy of encounter, as a radicalized intersubjective mode of between-two, based on our self-affection, sexual difference, and mutual mesocosmic breathing. In my self-affection (based in silence and listening) I am first infused with my basic ontological attentiveness—toward breath as an exhalation and inhalation of Being, as a paradigm of a progression of first difference (pulsation, life; sexual difference); but in this I am always already wounded with my finiteness, and my ontological link to the pure breath is broken. This wound is our longing to become *more* than what we are in this present moment, and to become awakened in our *spirituality* (*spiritus*=breath and respiration), but this is only possible with the help of the other, as she is transcending my finite world. Ontological attentiveness and my self-affection thus transform into an ethical attentiveness, for which the reserve of breath is needed, one that I will now be able to share with the other. Our task here is to become an embodied soul in which there would be an imagination of the future event, of the advent of the other—for which a revolution of our culture of sentiments indeed is needed. This marks the beginning of any religious gesture, if religion is understood as a horizontal rather than vertical link between two subjects, and as a horizontal order within communities. This shift from verticality does not mean that we could not use the name "God" in this encounter anymore. *God* now is the name for the reserve of breath, or an excess of breath, which as a vital breath-energy is available for us as a gift, or grace of the moment of our encounter with the other.

We have seen that in the Trinity we have an exhalation and inhalation as a mysterious logic of the trinitarian co-relationality and co-breathing (*conspiratio*) of the three divine persons: in Schelling, this is visible in the primordial and anarchic exhalation and inhalation of the Ground itself, the pulsation of its archetypal life. Now let us try to discuss this trinitarian pneumatics in a radicalized ethico-spiritual sense. In Mark 15:37, we read about the death of Jesus Christ: "Then Jesus gave a loud cry and breathed his last [*eksepneusen*]." We shall argue here that, from this moment of His last breath until the moment of resurrection and giving His breath to the disciples, the co-breathing in the Trinity is in crisis. There are two moments we need to acknowledge here: firstly, from the very moment of His last breath breathed into the world, when Jesus dies for us, humanity also partakes in this trinitarian crisis; it is without the reserve of breath and it witnesses the cosmic crisis, or coming of a cosmic night (Mark 15:33: "When it was noon, darkness came over the whole land until three in the afternoon"). Secondly, it is in the faith of a woman—namely, Mary Magdalene—that the resurrected Jesus will first reappear and only later *breathe* the reserve of breath back onto His disciples (John 20:22—"When he had said this, he breathed on them and said to them, Receive the Holy Spirit"). We know that for Irigaray, as Mary is "spiritual ancestor and spiritual mother of Jesus,"[37] analogously now the resurrected Jesus is bringing the Holy Spirit and thus spiritual autonomy to Mary Magdalene, as *mater familias*, or the first apostle (Schüssler-Fiorenza),[38] and then to the entire humanity. In the gospel of John we are witnessing the peak moment of the trinitarian crisis, when in famous *noli me tangere* passage (*me mou haptou*), Jesus says to Mary Magdalene not to hold onto him, because he "has not yet ascended to Father" (John 20:17). According to our interpretation of this passage, the prohibition against touching his body (Jesus is represented by the *neaniskos* in the gospel of Mark) does not relate to the logic of haptology[39] but rather to an original and idiosyncratic pneumatic meaning: it is the touching within an ethico-pneumatic interval between/of two autonomous bodies and breaths that we are witnessing here, an encounter of a divine character, inaugurating a new spiritual bond—the coming of love to this world, when men and women will become spiritual brothers and sisters in love by compassionately sharing their spiritual breaths in the community-to-come. But this touching without touch means that we have two subjectivities, two self-affections (also marked by sexual difference) indeed—one already divine, the other becoming divine, which now for the first time are dwelling within the transcendence of each other; pure love and compassion (*agape, caritas*) can emerge only from this interval of breath between them.

It is precisely this event that marks the advent of the third age of humanity—the age of the Spirit, when the task of humanity will be to "become itself divine breath."[40] The coming of this epoch of breath is thus based on both self-affectivity and love, as visible in this idiosyncratic encounter between Jesus Christ and Mary Magdalene. The reserve of breath has now been regained—one that only can heal the wound of the world as the fracture in the very core of our being. It is our task to get this reserve for ourselves (faith, grace, our soul), to become spiritual in a way to in-breathe or let into ourselves the breath of love, and share it with others, in an encounter of spiritual energies—which now is divine by itself—as an exchange of pure breath in its primordial rhythm of exhalation and inhalation. This now is the co-breathing of two autonomous persons in an atmosphere of freedom and grace.[41]

(Chóra)

In the conclusion of the chapter about the concubine of a Levite and Mary we already indicated that *chóra*, in the Christian context, is in the triadic structure present in the manner of an invisible trace, as a sign of an anarchic pulsation of Life, an impression of its formless presence in the very heart of the Trinity. This place without designation is what was attacked and threatened throughout history by violent modes of dwelling (violent to the whole of creation) and that which could return only through Mary's matrixial essence. This was the essence of her ontological virginity—which is entirely opposed to various theological assumptions or even tests aimed at discovering the (non)interference with the intimacy of her body—as Luce Irigaray also emphasizes—and thereby at the designation of Mary's subordination. Agamben captures this thought about *chóra* in his work *The Coming Community*, when he mentions Amalric of Bena (Amaury de Bène, twelfth-thirteenth century, died c. 1204–1207) and his "heretical" doctrine of God as *chóra*:

> This, and nothing else, was the doctrinal content of the heresy that on November 12, 1210, sent the followers of Amalric of

Bena to burn at the stake. Amalric interpreted the Apostle's claim that "God is all in all" as a radical theological development of the Platonic doctrine of the *chora*. God is in every thing as the place in which every thing is, or rather as the determination and the "topia" of every entity. The transcendent, therefore, is not a supreme entity above all things; rather, *the pure transcendent is the taking-place of every thing.*[42]

The radical and heretical theological Trinitarian message by Amalric is that for him, God incarnated in Abraham, the Son in Mary's lap, and the Holy Spirit in Amalric and his disciples. In this, Amalric is a direct spiritual predecessor to Luce Irigaray, who in her "Age of Breath" presented the same kind of genealogy of development or evolution of the space (or *chóra*) of God. The first age, when God-the-Father created humanity, which fell into sin, was followed by the second, in which Jesus was born from Mary for humanity (Mary and Jesus are thus the new Eve and the new Adam), and this age brought along the hope of redemption. The third age, also referred to as the "Age of Breath," or "Age of the Spirit" (Irigaray uses both), is the oncoming era in which, based on the revelation of God and the incarnation of Jesus as well as through the spiritual/ethical exchange of Breath between man and woman, humanity will become *itself* the divine breath. In complete conformity with Amalric's doctrine, Irigaray writes that in the third age there will be "a moment in which all universe returns to God." In this, her thought is in full agreement with the notion of *chóra* as the primary matrix of God (in the form of subjective and objective genitive). This thought is crucial for the present time, as it enables the whole of creation to be thought as a process of spiritual exchange of divine energies, including nature and its precious beings, which is the essential constituent part of both Amalric's and Irigaray's teachings.[43]

As previously indicated, to Plato in *Timaeus*, the *chóra* is linked to the so-called third kind ("*Third type* is space, which exists always"; 52a; *chóra* is here an expression for space).[44] In reply to what its nature is (in Plato, *chóra* always resides in the feminine element), he writes as follows:

> What must we suppose it do to and to be? This above all: it is a *receptacle* of all becoming—its wetnurse, as it were. (49a)

> We must always refer to it by the same term, for it does not depart from its own character in any way. Not only does it

> always receive all things, it has never in any way whatever taken on any characteristic similar to any of the things that enter it. (50b–c)

> It is in fact appropriate to compare the receiving thing to a mother, the source to a father, and the nature between them to their offspring. (50d)

Chóra is thus the nurturer and wet nurse of the universe (88d), the primordial matrix/womb of dwelling, "the receptacle" (53a) in the process of coming to being.

But how should we now think the *chóra* on the horizon of Luce Irigaray and her interpretation of Mary's atmosphere of freedom and grace? In the foreground among those who thought it in philosophical terms are, of course, Jacques Derrida and Julia Kristeva. The latter first understands *chóra* in the Greek sense as that within which our discourse moves and which can never be given an axiomatic form. To Kristeva, *chóra* thus comes before the sign or the signifier, and is in the difference between the semiotic and symbolic on the side of the former. To Kristeva—and this is important for us—it is semiotically closer to the body and the discreet quantities of energy movements in it.[45] Hence, the *chóra* can be situated, yet is impossible to position. Derrida goes a step farther and sets the *chóra* at the very heart of questioning about God and our profession about Him (we are using the male form of address here intentionally). That *chóra* is situated in the proximity of the feminine is unmistakably clear since as early as Plato (the metaphors of receptacle, receiver, wet nurse, genetrix, mother), and in Derrida, too, *chóra* is referred to with female pronouns.[46] This is what Derrida says about *chóra*:

> It does not give place [*elle ne donne pas lieu*] as one would give something, whatever it may be; it neither creates nor produces anything, not even an event insofar as it takes place. It gives no order and makes no promise. It is radically ahistorical, because nothing happens through it and nothing happens to it. Plato insists on its necessary indifference: to receive all and allow itself to be marked or affected by what is inscribed in it, the *khora* must remain without form and without proper determination.

[. . .]

If one wishes to respect the absolute singularity of the *khora* (there is only one *khora*, even if it can be pure multiplicity of places), it is necessary always to refer to it in the same manner. Not to give it the same name, as one French translation suggests, but to call it, address oneself to it in the same manner.[47]

Hence, *chóra* is in closest proximity to the area of the formless (*cháos* as the archetype of primordial dwelling), but creative, and thereby of a mysterious absence, promise, and hope; in short—of dwelling in peace.[48] *Chóra* is, as a metaphor for space and for the order of dwelling of a substantiating (sexual) *différance*,[49] finally, present as an invisible trace (T) and (co)eternal origin of matrixiality. *Chóra*: cosmic womb, shelter of becoming and dwelling, *invulnerable to the evil of this world*.[50]

tracing matrixiality

POSTLUDE

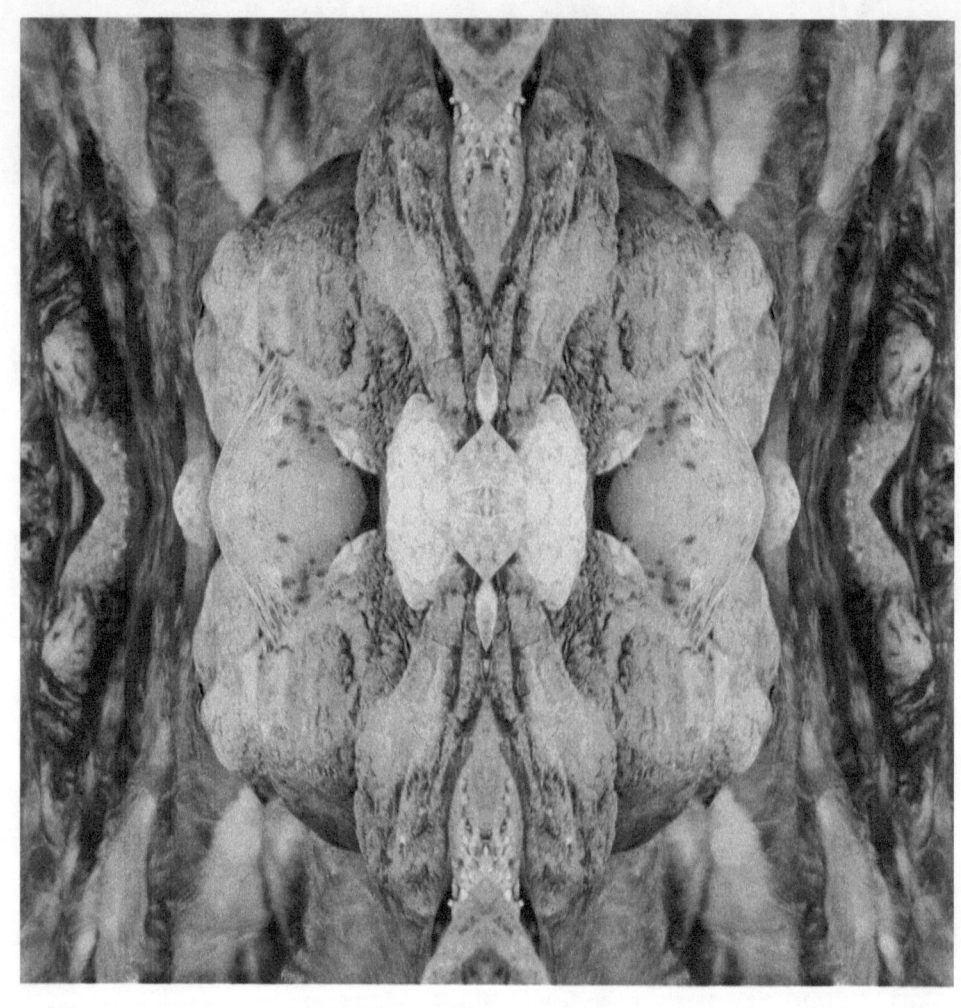

shared-sisterly

Jesus / Antigone

We have seen in our previous chapters that Antigone's dwelling place is close to ancient pre-Olympian and chthonic goddesses, protectresses of the spheres of fertility, birth, life, love, and the ancient matrixial orders of being—Metis, the Earth goddess, Erinyes, Demeter, Kore/Persephone, and Aphrodite. We have also seen that, by redeeming her dead brother, Antigone brings to this world an alien law, that is neither accessible to her sister (as a paradigmatic woman) nor to Creon (as a paradigmatic man). But the question remains—and it is the question about the origin and about the destiny of Antigone and her sisterly act. Three interpretations have been vital for this book: Antigone as understood by Irigaray, Kristeva, and Ettinger.[1] In her beautiful and tender interpretation of Antigone, Julia Kristeva (who, like Irigaray and Ettinger, are protectresses and not enemies of Antigone, like so many other interpreters, both men and women), wrote in two important passages the following words:

> Christ and Mary, differently and together, recognize, in short, the sovereign lucidity of Antigone. . . . And they invite all women, natural mothers of the species, not to halt the flow of childbearing but to join with them (Jesus and Mary) at one of the possible crossroads of Greek and Jewish memory. . . . [T]he Virgin Mary accomplishes this displacement spectacularly in an eternal return that culminates in the Pieta that attaches her to Jesus, such a young woman, a descendant of the Sulamite who would have dreamt of Antigone.[2]

According to Kristeva, Antigone stands in the closest vicinity of Jesus and Mary. But, before we reflect upon this co-relationality of these three divine persons, again and again we have to ask ourselves the same question: From whence did Antigone come and where is she bound in her protest and irrevocable deed, coming out of her powerful yet calm auto-affection?

With Hölderlin, we can observe in Sophocles's Antigone the highest trait of a personality—the most highly evolved phenomenon of a human being, indeed—of mysterious activity of the soul, in its auto-affection or self-knowledge (*autognotos*; poetic thought, pre-Socratic thought)[3] being in the closest vicinity of the god/s, yet still remaining faithful to her *own* audacious potentiality of the spirit.[4] By calling her "Queen,"[5] Hölderlin offers an idiosyncratic, yet perhaps one the most profound understandings of the Greek heroine. Besides being an *epikleros*—an heiress to the throne of the royal house of Thebes (her first son from the marriage with Haimon would have become the next king, and Creon obviously cannot live with such an option)—and thus considering herself on the same political level as a princess or even a ruler, Queen Antigone now also inaugurates a new possibility of an even more comprehensive feminine identity than that of a political actor in the midst of the masculinized Greek society: according to Rosenfield's beautiful insight, Antigone is "kin to everything—human, super-human, sub-human."[6] Antigone's mission is therefore not of this world, though neither is it of the nether world: within the precarious lifeworld of a young woman, moving, as it were, toward the edge of a precipice, she now appears as a mighty Heroine, offering with her voluntary death a hope of redemption not only to the community of Thebes, but also to humanity.[7] And it is in this view that Antigone stands in the closest vicinity of Jesus—now in an elemental constellation of their encounter. At the moment of her second arrival on the stage of the ethics of unwritten laws, as it were—for the second rite of burial of her deceased brother—Antigone appears in front of the guards in the following way, clearly marking her appearance with elementally cosmic signifiers of wind/air:

> A sudden whirlwind upraised
> A cloud of dust that blotted out the sky,
> And swept the palion, and stripped the woodlands
>   bare,
> and shook the firmament. We closed our eyes
> And waited till the heaven-sent plague should pass.
> At last it ceased, and lo! there stood this maid.[8]

Appearing in front of these men with closed eyes, Antigone is now incarnated on this earth as a creature of an ancient elemental cosmic world, and, with another powerful metaphor, now also as a mother bird coming to a stripped nest and crying bitterly over her lost children. The performance of the burial rites for her brother—now for the second time—will lead to an inevitable climax of the tragedy. Antigone is

> led along that *forgotten path* and there is *walled up* alive in *a hole* in the rock, shut off forever from the light of the sun. Alone in her crypt, her cave, her den, her womb, she is given just enough food by those who hold power to ensure that the city is not soiled and shamed by her decay. . . . She will cut off her breath—her voice, her air, blood, life—with the veil of her belt, returning into the shadow (of) a tomb, the night (of) death.[9]

This now shows the inverse genealogical proximity of Antigone and Jesus: in the vicinity of key elemental and cosmic markers—of wind, air, breath, and spirit—it is destined for both Antigone and Jesus to accomplish their ethical tasks with their most sacred gestures—both alone and together. Jesus calls his Father (but whom could the fatherless and motherless Antigone have called; who could have been expected to save her?)—*My God, my God why have you forsaken me* (Matt. 27:46), cries with a loud voice, and breathes his last. Mary Magdalene and the other Mary enter the rock-hewn tomb of Jesus, with stones having already been rolled away, and they see there a young man—an angel dressed in a white robe (Mark 16:5). Jesus dies, but he returns from his tomb/*womb* (which opens and thus enlivens a new future matrixial space) to his disciples—and then he breathes on them the Holy Spirit, a sign of new life (John 20:22). Jesus now returns—first by resuscitating cosmic breath as being already clandestinely protected and safeguarded by Antigone for the future—by reinstating and pouring it back into this world, and thus illuminating the cosmic darkness from within their tombs with a new splendor of the divine breath to be shared (co-breathing): first between him and Mary Magdalene, but then also with his disciples, and with the rest of humanity.

Jesus and Antigone, Antigone and Jesus: *O ye shared-sisterly Head!*[10] Antigone and Jesus—how close are you then? Jesus's disciples Joseph and

Nicodemus took his body and wrapped it with the spices in linen clothes (John 19:40)—but who could have taken care of Antigone after she had dedicated—by offering her body—all her care to the preservation of the most ancient unwritten laws? Antigone had to take care of the past, so as to preserve it for the future ethical mission of Jesus. But, again, who could have helped Antigone, who had already accomplished her highest spiritual/maternal/matrixial gestures in her sacred acts in protection of the unwritten laws and ancient and future god(desse)s, as both visible and traceable in her "maternal vocation of tenderness and care?"[11] Could it have been Metis, or Aphrodite? Reaching the very precipice of the ancient unwritten laws, Antigone mourns:

> To fade and wither in a living tomb,
> An alien midst the living and the dead.
> [. . .]
> Not one friend left to share my bitter woe,
> And o'er my ashes heave one passing sigh.[12]

But there is a friend in this future past, already waiting for Antigone—yes, it is He. Jesus has dreamt of sister Antigone and of her highest cosmico-ethical dedication. They've known each other from the beginning. Jesus has prayed and cried for her, and their co-breathing now enlivens and accomplishes the destiny of both—by reinstating the highest ethical laws of Antigone and Jesus into this world. Their highest cosmico-ethical co-breathing enables us to understand their mysteriously sacred and alien language. This is expressed in their co-breath as here revealed in dual: "Antigona in Jezus sodihata."[13] In a spiritual sense, as found in Franz Von Baader, the two beings, who embrace within their spiritual bond, are "truly united in a breath, common to them both."[14] According to Baader, this unification represents a higher spiritual kiss—now thought of as a sacred *conspiration* of two divine beings.[15]

In her reading of Antigone, Ettinger argued that matrixial love (now as the mutual love of Jesus and Antigone) is "care-full and compassionate, yet painful."[16] In their highest ethical conspiracy, based on the love and pain they experienced, both Jesus and Antigone have revealed and inaugurated a new matrixial covenant for this world.[17] This mutual wombing forth[18] of cosmic justice by Antigone and Jesus is a mark of the eternal divine protection of unwritten ethical laws and genealogies of life.

In their spiritual embrace,
Christ and Antigone form
the eternal matrix,
an ultimate sign of the
divinely infused
conspiration in love.

loving embrace in co-breath

NOTES

Prelude

1. We have borrowed this term both from Jakob Böhme and Bracha L. Ettinger. Böhme refers to "Matrice" as follows: "This is the blessing of Mary among all women, / that she was the first from Adam / in which this heavenly matrix was disclosed" (cit. from Ernst Benz, *Der Vollkommene Mensch nach Jacob Böhme* [Stuttgart: Kohlhammer, 1937], 109). In German, Böhme's words read as: "Das ist Marien Benedyung unter allen Weibern / daß sie die erste von Adam her ist / in welcher ist die himlische Matrix wieder eröfnet werden." Cf. also: "Und eben in dieser heiligen Matrice, welche GOttes Wort und Kraft in dem süssen Namen JEsu / in dem Samen MARIAE im Ziel des Bundes wieder erweckt / ward der Schlangen-Gift in der Selen und Fleische zerbrochen" (ibid.). But it was Bracha L. Ettinger who actually invented and developed in her numerous writings the "Matrix" and the "matrixial" as philosophical and psychoanalytical concepts. See (among other works) the following books and essays: *The Matrixial Borderspace*; "From Proto-Ethical Compassion to Responsibility: Besideness and the Three Primal Mother-Phantasies of Not-enoughness, Devouring and Abandonment," *Athena* 2 (2007): 100–35; "The Becoming Threshold of Matrixial Borderlines," in *Travelers' Tales: Narratives of Home and Displacement*, ed. George Robertson, Melinda Mash, Lisa Tickner, and Jon Bird (London: Routledge, 1994), 38–62; "Matrix: Beyond the Phallus," *Women's Art Magazine* 56 (1994): 12–15; and "Matrix and Metamorphosus," *Trouble in the Archives*, special issue of *differences* 4, no. 3 (1992): 176–208.

2. Ettinger, "Transgressing," 198, 199, 203. This text brings Ettinger's interpretation of Sophocles's *Antigone*—as a testimony of Antigone's suffering that comes from "the tearing apart of her principal partner-in-difference" (ibid., 210). For Antigone, the death and a potential nonburial of her brother "inflicts the horrible cut in the matrixial web" (ibid.) More from her reading later in this book.

3. Cf. Ettinger, "Transgressing," 204: "*Women have some privileged access to a paradoxical time of future-past and a paradoxical space of outside-inside*. Men however are in contact with this time and space, as women are too, by compassionate matrixial jointing-in-difference with the m/Other, with others and with particular art presences—whether art-objects, art-actions, art-gestures, music—as transjects."

4. The thought that, out of respect for the dignity of the victims, cannot appear in the prologue to this book, is described in the report on the rapes that took place in South Sudan and Congo at the beginning of this millennium. See the article in *Time* (March 21, 2015) titled "War and Rape," by Aryn Baker: "After the soldiers killed her husband and sons, five of them held her down and forced her to watch as three others raped her 10-year-old daughter. Her name was Nyalaat. When the men were done, Mary says, 'I couldn't even see my little girl anymore. I could only see blood.' Then the men took turns with Mary. Nyalaat died a few hours later. 'I wanted to die too'" (Baker, "War and Rape," 20). This violence is somehow directed against all of us, and without us assuming our share of responsibility for these amoral and tragic events, no future social, cultural, and ethical change is possible. In this sense, the ideologically substantiated sexual violence is a symptom of the nihilism of our common, so-called civilizational humanity. But it is also a sign of a long process in history—of the repressed orders of femininity (the orders of procreation, life, and growth)—that originated in the times of ancient Greek religion (the eclipse of ancient chthonic goddesses, Antigone's fate), Semitic religions (sexual violence and rapes in the Old Testament, also the attitude toward women in Islam), and Asian religions (castes and disclaimed sexual difference in religion), as well as other religions and cultures of the world.

5. Cf. *Feminist Readings of Antigone*, ed. Fanny Söderbäck (Albany: State University of New York Press, 2010), with, among others, seminal essays on Antigone by Tina Chanter, Luce Irigaray, Judith Butler, Bracha Ettinger, and Julia Kristeva.

6. *Sophocles in Two Volumes: I: Oedipus the King, Oedipus at Colonus, Antigone*, trans. F. Storr (Cambridge: Harvard University Press, 1981), 355.

7. A seminal book for the philosophy of natality is without any doubt the volume edited by Robin May Schott, *Birth, Death, and Femininity* (Bloomington and Indianapolis: Indiana University Press, 2010).

8. See Luce Irigaray, *To Be Born: Genesis of a New Human Being* (New York: Palgrave, 2017).

9. Gilles Deleuze, *Pure Immanence: Essays on a Life*, trans. Anne Boyman (New York: Zone Books, 2005), 30.

10. In a chapter from *Borders and Debordering: Topologies, Praxes, Hospitableness*, written as an ethical meditation upon the death of three-year-old Syrian boy Alyan Kurdi in 2015, we contended: "[W]hen we make our sorrowful

lamentations upon the death of a child, we already—precognitively and in compassion with the child—know that all three existential borders or layers have been radically displaced from their homely and maternal presence into the disruption of a cosmic event, disruption of an elementary peace or primeval home; displaced then into the *chaotic* darkness, or even death. The death of a child, drowned in the waters, is thus more than just a tragedy, countable in numbers of victims—it is a loss for all of us, who are *sharing this world in a way of our dwelling*. The death of any child is a transgression, an intrusion of cosmic disorder into our world. . . . For us, of greatest urge today is to have the strength of imagining of new ethical laws, being able to protect the most vulnerable of all—the children—and among them primarily little girls and boys, being at war, or migrants, being radically expelled from their *dwelling*." Lenart Škof, "Lamentation of a Child: On Migration, Vulnerability, and Ethics of Hospitality," in *Borders and Debordering: Topologies, Praxes, Hospitableness*, ed. Tomaž Grušovnik, Eduardo Mendieta, and Lenart Škof (Lanham, MD: Lexington Books, 2018), 185 and 188.

11. Clemens Sedmak, "Peace, Vulnerability, and the Human Imagination," in *The Poesis of Peace: Narratives, Cultures, and Philosophies*, ed. Klaus-Gerd Giesen, Carool Kersten, and Lenart Škof (New York and London: Routledge, 2017), 27–40.

12. Cf. Sedmak, "Peace, Vulnerability, and the Human Imagination," 32ff.

13. See, about this, Paulo Freire's *Pedagogy of Freedom: Ethics, Democracy, and Civic Courage* (Lanham, MD: Rowman and Littlefield, 2001) and, of course, his work *Pedagogy of the Oppressed* (New York and London: Continuum, 2005).

14. Sedmak, "Peace, Vulnerability, and the Human Imagination," 33.

15. Elizabeth Grosz, *The Incorporeal: Ontology, Ethics, and the Limits of Materialism* (New York: Columbia University Press, 2017), 7.

16. See Schott, *Birth, Death, and Femininity*, especially Sigridur Thorgeirsdottir's reflections on Nietzsche's philosophy of birth (171ff.). My reflections on the margins of birth and death and related intersubjective ethics aim at surpassing ontologically extremely disrupting constellations as explained already by Simone de Beauvoir about the Woman-Mother as "the chaos," and about woman's womb "as the origin of all life" but also an origin which "condemns man to death" (ibid., 28).

Chapter 1

1. Upon referring to the "we," it would be necessary to address what Jean-Luc Nancy refers to in his *Being Singular Plural* (Stanford: Stanford University Press, 2000), 5ff, thinking of a coexistence, communication as a very essence of Being, which, for Nancy, ultimately is material—i.e., as an ontology

of bodies, filling the empty space in ethics between the areas of Heidegger's/Irigaray's on one, and Levinas's thought on the other side. Let us add that close to this constellation is the position of American pragmatism's processual and communicative ethics (Mead and Dewey).

2. Luce Irigaray, *Una nuova cultura dell'energia: Al di là di Oriente e Occidente* (Torino: Bollati Boringheri, 2013).

3. Luce Irigaray, *In the Beginning, She Was* (London: Bloomsbury, 2013), ch. 5, "Between Myth and History."

4. Friedrich Nietzsche, *Thus Spoke Zarathustra: A Book for All and None*, ed. Adrian del Caro and Robert B. Pippin, trans. Adrian del Caro (Cambridge: Cambridge University Press, 2006), 57–58.

5. Nancy, *Being Singular Plural*, xiii.

6. Jean-Luc Nancy, *Corpus*, trans. Richard A. Rand (New York: Fordham University Press, 2008), 53.

7. Ibid., 103. See also: "Since the *First World War* (in other words, the simultaneous invention of a new juridical space for an international political economy, *and* a new combat-space for a whole new number of victims) these bodies, crowded wherever they go, are bodies primarily sacrificed" (79).

8. Max Statkiewicz and Valerie Reed, "Antigone's (Re)Turn: The Ēthos of the Coming Community," *Analecta Husserliana* 85 (2005): 788.

9. Georg Wilhelm Freidrich Hegel, *Lectures on the Philosophy of Religion*, part 2, ed. Peter C. Hodgson, trans. R. F. Brown, P. C. Hodgson, and J. M. Stewart (Berkeley: University of California Press, 1984), 1087.

10. On the history of *agrapta nomima* see Rosalind Thomas, "Writing, Law, and Written Law," in *The Cambridge Companion to Ancient Greek Law*, ed. Michael Gagarin and David Cohen (Cambridge: Cambridge University Press, 2005), 41–60.

11. Rémi Brague, *La loi de Dieu: Histoire philosophique d'une alliance* (Paris: Editions Gallimard, 2005), 43. Original passage: "Mais c'est seulement Sophocle qui permet de comprendre ce que signifie le caractère divin d'une loi. Dans le célèbre passage de l'*Antigone*, l'héroïne dit des lois dont elle se réclame contre le décret de Créon que 'personne ne sait d'où elles sont apparues.' C'est qu'elles ne sont en fait jamais apparues du tout, elles sont si manifestes qu'elles n'ont pas de point d'émergence."

12. On the very concept of *ethical anatomy* (with its elements: eye, heart, lungs, stomach, skin . . .), see my book *Breath of Proximity: Intersubjectivity, Ethics, and Peace* (Dordrecht: Springer, 2015).

13. Mary Douglas, *Leviticus as Literature* (Oxford and New York: Oxford University Press, 2000), 67ff. It is an important observation of Douglas for our purpose, namely, that "Leviticus focuses its metaphysical resources on that very point between life and death" and also "that there has always been in the Jewish culture a strong association between body and tabernacle in respect of fertility" (67, 80).

14. Ibid., 188.
15. Ibid., 190.
16. Emmanuel Levinas, *Outside the Subject* (London: Continuum, 1993), 91, 98.
17. Walter F. Otto, *Die Götter Griechenlands: Das Bild des Göttlichen im Spiegel des griechischen Geistes* (Frankfurt am Main: Klostermann, 1987). See chapter 2 on the ancient religion and myth.
18. John D. Caputo, *The Insistence of God: A Theology of Perhaps* (Bloomington and Indianapolis: Indiana University Press, 2013), 251. In this sense, Caputo's cosmic Jesus "is a man of flesh and blood, with animal companions and with animal needs . . . a Judeo-pagan prophet and healer, in tune with the animals and the elements, in whose body the elements dance their cosmic dance, supplying as it does a conduit through which the elements flow, and I treat the elements as a cosmic grace which is channelled by the body of Jesus" (251–52).
19. Walter Burkert seems to be more critical or at least reserved of this view in his *Griechische Religion der archaischen und klassischen Epoche* (Stuttgart: Kohlhammer, 2011). Burkert here contrasts chthonic religion with "die Epiphanie der Gottheit von oben her im Tanz," which, for him, testifies for a different religious principle (70). Yet, he admits the importance of chthonic order in particular as related to the nutrition and life circle (306). From Burkert one still gets the general impression that he was not willing to grant any greater importance to the deities of chthonic origin.
20. In our reading of Hegel, we draw on an excellent critique of Hegel's understanding of Antigone by Patricia J. Mills, "Hegel's *Antigone*," *The Owl of Minerva* 17, no. 2 (Spring 1986): 131–52. According to Mills, Hegel's interpretation of this play "does not consider the play in its entirety," and moreover, his reading is "an over simplification made to fit his view of the tragic character of pagan life as a conflict between equal and contrary values" (137).
21. Georg Wilhelm Friedrich Hegel, *Phenomenology of Spirit*, trans. A. V. Miller (Oxford and New York: Oxford University Press, 1977), 288. See chap. "BB. Spirit A. The *true* Spirit. The ethical order."
22. Patricia J. Mills, of course, rejects this ethical constellation of Hegel and affirms that in her acts, "Antigone has a moral courage which allows her to *choose* a course of action even though it condemns her to death. Whereas Hegel claims that the sister's intuition of ethical life is not open to the daylight of consciousness, the chorus in Sophocles' play cries out to Antigone: 'Your death is the doing of your conscious hand'" (Mills, "Hegel's *Antigone*," 141). And the final judgment of Hegel's misrepresentations of Antigone as defined by Mills reads as follows: "With the limitation of woman there is a limitation of the Hegelian system. Hegel's universal is necessarily male and male is *not* universal. Humanity is both male and female and the claim to encompass the universality of human experience must allow for woman's experience and participation outside the sphere of the family: it must allow for a more comprehensive account of the

Antigone than Hegel provides" (152). Curiously enough, for Bernard Henri Lévy's reading of Sophocles's play (in *The Testament of God*, trans. George Holoch, New York: Harper and Row, 1980), Creon stands for the state *and* cosmic order while Antigone represents its negative, nihilistic aspect.

23. Cf. Sean Ireton, *An Ontological Study of Death: From Hegel to Heidegger* (Pittsburgh: Duquesne University Press, 2007), 55: "The act of Antigone is therefore dialectical, for it preserves the annuled existence of her kin, raising the singular family member to the level of universal Spirit."

24. Ibid., 143. Interestingly enough, and as presented by Hannes Charen in his "Hegel Reading Antigone," (*Monatshefte* 103, no. 4 [2001]: 504–16), and, as always, as revealed by Derrida (in his *Glas*), Hegel himself transgressed this dichotomy between the family and the state: after ten years of uncertainty he admitted his illegitimate son Ludwig into his family. Namely, Hegel's third (actually his firstborn, yet illegitimate) son, Georg Ludwig Friedrich Fischer (1807–1831), was the result of an affair with his landlady Christiana Burkhardt (his two legitimate sons were Karl Friedrich Wilhelm, b. 1813, and Immanuel Thomas Christian, b. 1814). Ludwig was born in the year of the publication of *Phenomenology of Spirit*, and not "redeemed," as it were, by his father until 1817. Derrida now relates to Hegel's son Ludwig and hints to Antigone by stating: "Isn't there always an element excluded from the system that assures the system's space of possibility?" (cit. in Charen, "Hegel Reading Antigone," 510; see Jacques Derrida, *Glas* [New York: University of Nebraska, 1990], 162). Hegel therefore brings his son back to the family although this is strictly against the human laws, forbidding extramarital children. This is why, in Hegel's system, "Antigone marks what the system cannot sustain, the failure of the position, the failure of judgement. Antigone is too much" (Charen, "Hegel Reading Antigone," 514).

25. Cf. Charen, "Hegel Reading Antigone." Related to "remembrance" and "forgiveness," we are referring here to J. M. Bernstein's essay on Antigone ("the celestial Antigone, the most resplendent figure ever to have appeared on earth," in *Feminist Readings of Antigone*, 111–30). Bernstein's reading of Hegel's Antigone appears as much more favorable to Hegel's account than Mills's and related feminist critiques of Hegel's philosophical appropriations of Sophocles's *Antigone*. For us, the most important insight from Bernstein's essay is his claim that by her autonomous act she enacted and inaugurated the community of the living and the death—it is for this reason that, finally, "Antigone models and anticipates the work of phenomenological memory" (128).

26. Irigaray, *In the Beginning, She Was*, 118–19.

27. Ibid., 119.

28. Martha C. Nussbaum, *The Fragility of Goodness: Luck and Ethics in Greek Tragedy and Philosophy* (Cambridge: Cambridge University Press, 2001), 63. In his work *Oneself as Another*, trans. Katherine Blamey (Chicago and London: The University of Chicago Press, 1994), Paul Ricoeur devotes a short chapter

("Interlude: Tragic Action—*for Olivier again*," 241–49) precisely to Antigone. In this chapter dedicated to his son, who died tragically, Ricoeur contemplates Antigone's ethics and draws on Nussbaum and her above-mentioned book, as he clearly puts Antigone in the context of tragic dichotomy with Creon and mutual "narrowness" (243) in their allegedly absolute engagement. On the other hand, Ricoeur is willing to recognize Antigone, whom he now understands in the sense of her "sisterhood" (244ff; as an expression of absolute commitment to her family), a certain advantage or special place based on ancient, unwritten law. However, in the conclusion of his brief interpretation, Ricoeur again defines her act as a reductive gesture based (merely) on the request for the burial of her brother: "Antigone's vision of the world is no less restrictive and subject to internal contradictions than that of Creon," writes Ricoeur (244). With this, in his opinion, the very limit of the sphere of the human has been reached, which also delimits Antigone's act.

29. Nussbaum, *Fragility of Goodness*, 64.

30. Ibid., 77.

31. *Sophocles in Two Volumes*, I, v. 523 (Οὔτοι συνέχθειν, ἀλλὰ συμφιλεῖν ἔφυν).

32. Statkiewicz and Reed, "Antigone's (Re)Turn," 788.

33. For Irigaray, silence is the speaking of the threshold. Already for Heidegger, the meaning of the threshold lies in difference. Difference between two subjectivities and other differences, which all, for Irigaray, have been inaugurated in the most basic of all differences, sexual difference. Upon her/him coming to my world, at the very threshold, silence is what must be "preserved before meeting the other," it is also "openness that nothing occupies or preoccupies—no language, no values, no pre-established truth." Luce Irigaray, "Ethical gestures toward the other," *Poligrafi* 15, no. 57 (2008): 10. This securing of the place for silence in ourselves and in spaces of *between-us* presupposes that we remain two and demands from us a new kind of *self-affection*—one respectful to my self, for the difference and being attentive toward the needs of others.

34. Jacques Derrida, *Of Hospitality*, Rachel Bowlby (Stanford: Stanford University Press, 2000), 85. On law and justice see also Jacques Derrida, *Acts of Religion*, ed. Gil Anidjar (New York and London: Routledge, 2002), in particular chapters "Force of Law: The 'Mystical Foundation of Authority'" and "Hostipitality."

35. See A. Dufourmantelle invocation of Jan Patočka and his thought in *Of Hospitality*: "She is one of those who love, not one of those who hate," wrote Patočka, but this love is not Christlike. It signifies "love as foreign to the human condition, deriving from the portion of night which is the portion of the gods" (42). It seems that the difference between Antigone and Christ lies in their relation to the ancient religion. While Christ (as a man) revolutionized the ancient Judaic religion, it was Antigone's sacred duty that first came out

from her sexual identity as a key cosmico-ethical impetus and was thus also closely related to the cosmic interiority of the divine law.

36. *The Story of Sāvitrī*, in *Selections from Classical Sanskrit Literature*, trans. John Brough (London: Luzac, 1951), 43. In this book, we are using diacritical signs for Sanskrit only with certain more relevant terms from Indian philosophy and religion.

37. The *Gayatri mantra* reads as follows: "Might we make our own that desirable effulgence of god Savitar, / who will rouse forth our insights." *The Rigveda*, trans. Stephanie W. Jamison and Joel P. Brereton (Oxford: Oxford University Press, 2014), 554.

38. See *Story of Sāvitrī*. Here we also rely on Asko Parpola, "The Religious Background of the Savitri Legend," in *Harānandalaharī—Volume in Honour of Professor Minoru Hara on His Seventieth Birthday*, ed. R. Tsuchida and A. Wezler (Reinbeck: Dr. Inge Wezler Verlag für orientalische Fachpublikationen, 2000), 193–216; see also the extended version of the essay "Savitri and Resurrection," in *Changing Patterns of Family and Kinship in South Asia*, ed. Asko Parpola and Sirka Tenhunen (Helsinki: Finnish Oriental Society, 1998), 167–312; and, additionally, Renukadas Yeshwantrao Deshpande, *The Ancient Tale of Savitri* (Pondicherry: Sri Aurobindo International Centre of Education, 1995). The story of Savitri appears in different sources—in the *Vedas* (where we can trace its ancestral lineage to the *Savitri-mantra*) and the *Mahabharata* (*Aranyaka-parvan* 3.277–83), as well as some of the *Puranas*. In the *Mahabharata*, the story is set in the context of a wife's loyalty (*pativrata*) and is narrated by the sage Markandeya to comfort Yudishthira, who, after his beloved wife Draupadi was kidnapped, found himself alone, robbed of the support of his devoted spouse, in whom he would always find his strength.

39. In relation to Vedic theology, see my work on Vedic thought, including the translation and commentary of two key Upanishads, titled *Besede vedske Indije* (Ljubljana: Nova revija, 2005).

40. *Story of Savitri*, 55.

41. Cf. the afterword of her translation of the story into Slovene: *Zgodba o Savitri* (Branik: Abram, 2002), 68ff.; for Deshpande, *Ancient Tale of Savitri*, 73. Compassion for the captured enemies is mentioned specifically (strophe 162 of the poem).

42. Subhash Anand, *Story as Theology: An Interpretative Study of Five Episodes from the* Mahābhārata (New Delhi: Intercultural Publications, 1996), 117ff.

43. Deshpande, *Ancient Tale of Savitri*, vi.

44. Sri Aurobindo, *Savitri: A Legend and a Symbol* (Twin Lakes, WI: Lotus Press, 2003), 8–9.

45. See Luce Irigaray, *To Be Two* (New York: Routledge, 2001), 34: "a woman gives birth to a woman."

46. See Parpola, "Religious Background of the Savitri Legend," 200. One of the possible interpretations of this story is also, naturally, that it echoes the

practice of *sati* (the funeral ritual in which the widow is burned on the pyre of her dead husband). This interpretation could easily be substantiated by the many glorifying words that the loyal and devoted wife uses when speaking about her husband. But the comprehensive framework of the story, which focuses on the special role of woman/Goddess in the process of Satyavan's return from the homeland of the dead, and the placement of the two in the contexts of the logic of divine couples and of cooperation between the masculine and feminine principles divest this interpretation of the more staid, moving the story in its communicative essence in a different, even opposite, direction from a ritual associated with demands deriving from the later Hindu environment of exclusive religious domination by men.

47. On the argumentative autonomy of Upanishadic women see Amartya Sen, *The Argumentative Indian: Writings on Indian History, Culture, and Identity* (New York: Farrar, Straus and Giroux, 2005), 7–9.

48. Ibid., 197.

49. Here we should point out the interpretation of Savitri by Asko Parpola, one of the greatest living Indologists. Parpola reviewed all the sources featuring Savitri and studied the complex historical and mythological contexts of this legend. In dealing with *The Story of Savitri*, Parpola was highly critical of the role of gender within the framework of ancient Indian religion. After presenting the legend as it can be understood from the various sources in which it appears (with the *Mahabharata* as the earliest testimony, also in Parpola's opinion), he deals with the question of its potential role and meaning in the religious and cultural contexts of the period. Parpola is not willing to understand the legend of Savitri outside of the role of the *Savitri Vrata* ritual, to this day one of the principal rituals of Indian women who hope to avoid widowhood through it (the ritual is, of course, part of the Brahmanic tradition, which sees women in an ideological/religious perspective as essentially—i.e., ontologically—inferior and subordinate to men). In his Indologist study, exceptional in every other aspect, Parpola fails to assign Savitri the role that would construe her as a guardian of primeval cosmic laws. Although he mentions these ancient and pre-Vedic—i.e., proto-Shaktist traditions (e.g., Parpola, "Savitri and Resurrection," 216)—he does not appreciate this aspect, even completely disregarding it at key points. This is particularly interesting as it is clear that according to Parpola, the goddess Savitri is a variant of the goddess Durga from northwest India (in the former Madra area in today's Rajasthan, as well as in Kashmir). Parpola goes farther and, based on proven contacts between the Pakistan area of that period (the Indus Valley Civilization) and Mesopotamia, he compares Durga with the Sumerian-Akkadian goddess Innana/Ishtar, who probably served—so Parpola—as a model for Durga (the Canaanite equivalent of this goddess was Astarte). So here we have an extremely interesting link between ancient Middle Eastern cults of female deities (part of which, in the context of contemporary feminist theology, is also the figure of Mary) and the ancient Indus Valley Civilization as well as its Aryan (Vedic)

legacy (cf. about this ibid., 224ff). In the end, Parpola engages in an explication of Savitri as a prototype sati in her ritual of following the husband to death (*sahagamana*, in the sense of "going (into death) with" or "dying with"). Here he also relies on Herman Lommel (see 272), who saw Savitri primarily in one role: that of a faithful wife willing to sacrifice for her husband. Sati has been dated back to the time of Alexander the Great, when the historians who accompanied him recorded the customs of certain Indian tribes, including that their wives, after the death of their husbands, voluntarily immolated themselves on their pyres (an earlier variant found in the broader area of the present North India before 1900 BCE was of women taking their own lives by hanging themselves from a fig tree; for this reason, the fig or banyan tree in the earlier culture of the Harappan religion was defined as the tree of Death) (274). Similar practices were also observed among other Indo-European peoples of that period (there is evidence that they were present among the Greek, Germanic, and Slavic peoples and the Scythians, and were also related to the women's fear of humiliation and rape, as well as kidnapping as consequences of campaigns and defeats). Still—based on the interpretation of the text as well as Indian commentaries—it would be incorrect to classify Savitri solely in this genealogy and thereby deprive her of her own ontological and sexual structures, which indisputably belong to her. My interpretation also departs from Parpola's at the point where Savitri is linked to incestuous (similarly as Antigone is classified in J. Butler) familial relationships. To conclude: Parpola, in his otherwise brilliant study, considers Savitri's role to be prevalently instrumental (303).

50. Irigaray makes particular mention of these traditions in her work *Between East and West: From Singularity to Community*, trans. Stephen Pluhácek (Delhi: New Age Books, 2005), 9: "To go back and meditate starting from practices and texts of Eastern cultures, especially pre-Aryan aboriginal ones, can show us a way to carry on our History." Interestingly, her book commences with a well-known sentence about the human incomprehensibility from the first choral ode in *Antigone*.

51. Luce Irigaray, *Il mistero di Maria* (Roma: Paoline, 2010), 20. Cf. also about the link between Mary and Indian goddesses in the tradition of Shaktism (24): "If one removes Mary from her simply maternal role, if one considers her as woman, one might compare her to one of the feminine partners of the Indian god, Shiva, the god who corresponds to our era. . . . In fact, Mary appears to be the woman who represents and safeguards wisdom traditions in a universe of men, where fire often predominates, and is destructive. It is she who succeeds even in appeasing the anger of God, transforming his need or desire for vengeance into compassion and love. Mary is the mediator between God and humans." For the relation between fire and breath see my *Breath of Proximity*, the chapters about Feuerbach and, especially, Heidegger.

52. Irigaray relates of this bodily-spiritual gesture as follows: "She also often holds her hands crossed at this place, as if she might seek to protect a treasure

there: the site of the transformation of her vital breath into an amorous, spiritual breath able to be shared. In certain icons, the baby Jesus is also depicted here" (Irigaray, *Il mistero di Maria*, 14). Thus, adds the philosopher, "it will be the breath of the woman that will birth that of the man in terms of the redemption of the world" (19).

53. Ibid., 10.

54. See Paul Claudel, *Feuilles de Saints* (Paris: Gallimard, 2002), 70f. Fr. original: "Continuellement occupé à respire pour ne pas mourir . . . Thérèse resplendissante dans le souffle du Saint-Esprit."

55. Deshpande, *Ancient Tale of Savitri*, 44.

56. On Alcestis see studies by Richard Garner, "Death and Victory in Euripides' Alcestis," *Classical Antiquity*, 7, no. 1 (1988): 58–71, and Charles Segal, *Euripides and the Poetics of Sorrow: Art, Gender, and Commemoration in Alcestis, Hippolytus, and Hecuba* (Durham: Duke University Press, 1993).

57. Euripides, *Medea and Other Plays*, trans. E. P. Coleridge (Lawrence, KS: Digireads, 2012), 5.

58. Ibid., 17.

59. Svetlana Slapšak, accompanying text in the theatre program for the play *Alkestida* (Ljubljana: SNG Drama, 2013), 21.

60. Euripides, *Medea and Other Plays*, 26.

61. Plato, *Symposium*, 179b, in *Complete works*, ed. John M. Cooper (Indianapolis and Cambridge: Hackett, 1997), 464.

62. Cf. Euripides, *Medea and Other Plays*, 35.

63. See Jan Kott, *Eating of the Gods*, trans. Boleslaw Taborski and E. J. Czerwinski (Evanston: Northwestern University Press, 1987), 108 (chapter "The Veiled Alcestis").

64. These words are our tribute to Jean Anouilh's excellent version of *Antigone*. See his *Plays: One (Antigone, Léocadia; The Waltz of the Toreadors; The Lark; Poor Bitos)* (London: Methuen, 1991).

Chapter 2

1. In Slovenian: "*Kaj boš ti dete počeva, / k na boš matere jméva. . . . / Vida je pa svet kríž striva, / na sred murja je noter skočiva.*" For the mythical story of Fair Vida and its varied motifs see an extraordinarily extensive monograph by Irena Avsenik Nabergoj, *Hrepenenje in skušnjava v svetu literature: motiv Lepe Vide* (Ljubljana: Mladinska knjiga, 2010). For the Ihan version, see ibid., 386ff. The author defines Fair Vida's death as a heroic death of a kidnapped woman (388ff.). Cf. also note 407 in relation to the so-called Maiden's plunge (*Devin skok*, ibid., 390).

2. Shé Hawke, "The Exile of Greek Metis: Recovering a Maternal Divine Ontology," *Poligrafi* 23, no. 91/92 (2018): 70.

3. Hawke, "Exile of Greek Metis," 69. Hesiod versified the myth as such: "Zeus as king of the gods made Metis his first wife. The wisest among gods and mortal men. But when she was about to give birth to the pale-eyed Athene, he tricked her deceitfully with cunning words and put her away in his belly"; and, "And by himself, out of his head, he fathered the pale-eyed Tritogeneia" (Hesiod, *Theogony and Works and Days*, trans. Martin L. West [Oxford: Oxford University Press, 2008], 29–30). The "Tritogeneia" here refers to Athena's birth from water and thereby to her filial origin as the daughter of Metis; whereas it is clear that *-geneia* means "born from," the first element *Trito-* has been interpreted as referring to the sea (Triton is a sea god), Lake Tritonis, described in several ancient texts, or even river Triton, which the historian Herodotus assumed flowed into the lake. For more about this antimatrixial motif and the accompanying matrixial thought see our chapter on the concubine of a Levite.

4. For this notion, see farther on. The term refers to the supplanting of the primal matrix with a new, violence-based genealogy.

5. Hawke, "Exile of Greek Metis," 48.

6. For this genealogy and the issue of dating ancient sources associated with Orphic theology see G. S. Kirk, J. E. Raven, and M. Schofield, eds., *The Presocratic Philosophers* (Cambridge: Cambridge University Press, 1999), 24; and *Ancilla to the Pre-Socratic Philosophers*, trans. Kathleen Freeman (Cambridge: Harvard University Press, 1996), 3. The fact that Chaos is connected to the waters can be deduced from the variants of this cosmogony, where water appears as the source of all things even before the formation of the Cosmic Egg and the Heaven and Earth created out of it, cf. also Hesiod, *Theogony*.

7. Hawke, *Aquamorphia*, 1.

8. Walter F. Otto, *The Homeric Gods*, trans. Moses Hadas (London: Thames and Hudson, 1954), 30; continuing: "It was women too who held the highest divine rank. . . . This primal world of gods is pervaded by a maternal strain, which is as characteristic of it as is the paternal and masculine strain in the Homeric world of gods. . . . In the antique stories of Uranus and Gaia and of Cronus and Rhea, to which we shall address ourselves presently, the children are wholly on the side of the mother, and the father seems to be a stranger with whom they have nothing to do. Things are very different in the realm of Zeus; there the outstanding deities describe themselves emphatically as children of their father."

9. Marcel Detienne and Jean Pierre Vernant, *Cunning Intelligence in Greek Culture and Society*, trans. Janet Lloyd (Chicago and London: The University of Chicago Press, 1991), 133–35.

10. Hawke, "Exile of Greek Metis," 44.

11. Cf. about this Elena Tzelepis and Athena Athanasiou, eds., *Rewriting Difference: Luce Irigaray and the Greeks* (Albany: State University of New York Press, 2010), esp. ch. 6 by G. Schwab. The work deals first with *Oresteia*,

then Sophocles's *Antigone* and *Electra* and the myth about Demeter and Kore-Persephone. Thus, to Luce Irigaray, "Athena is not conceived in a womb, nor born of woman, she is a divinity conceived in the head of the God of gods. . . . A phantasy of the father of the gods" (ibid., 87). This quote refers to Luce Irigaray, *Marine Lover of Friedrich Nietzsche*, trans. Gillian C. Gill (New York: Columbia University Press, 1991), 94–95.

12. Mills, "Hegel's *Antigone*," 146.

13. Otto, *Homeric Gods*, 24.

14. Enrique Dussel, *Ethics of Liberation in the Age of Globalization and Exclusion* (Durham and London: Duke University Press, 2013). In this work Dussel chronologically introduces four stages of the "interregional system" (3): the Egyptian-Mesopotamian, Indo-European (with Persian, Hellenistic, Indian, and Mediterranean centers), Asiatic-Afro-Mediterranean (with Persian, Chinese, African, and Byzantine-Russian centers), and modern world system (with its center in Western Europe and "periphery" in Latin America, Africa, Muslim world, India, Southwestern Asia, and Eastern Europe).

15. We refer to Lewis R. Gordon's dichotomy between "just justice" and "unjust justice" from *Her Majesty's Other Children: Sketches of Racism from a Neocolonial Age* (Lanham, MD: Rowman and Littlefield, 1977), 166.

16. Sophocles, *Antigone*, vv. 1064–77, in *Sophocles in Two Volumes*.

17. Homer, *The Odyssey*, ed. Louise Loomis, trans. Samuel Butler (New York: Wildside, 2007) XXI, 28.

18. Martin Heidegger, *Hölderlin's Hymn "The Ister,"* trans. William McNeill and Julia Davis (Bloomington and Indianapolis: Indiana University Press, 1996), 109.

19. Otto, *Die Götter Griechenlands*.

20. Aeschylus, "Prometheus Bound," in *Aeschylus: Suppliant Maidens. Persians. Prometheus. Seven Against Thebes*, trans. Herbert W. Smyth, Loeb Classical Library, vol. 145 (Cambridge: Harvard University Press, 1926).

21. Immanuel Kant, *Groundwork of the Metaphysics of Morals*, ed. Mary J. Gregor (Cambridge: Cambridge University Press, 1998).

22. Dussel, *Ethics of Liberation*, 1.

23. Ibid., 218.

24. Friedrich Wilhelm Joseph Schelling, *The Grounding of Positive Philosophy*, trans. Bruce Matthews (Albany: State University of New York Press, 2007), 114. "Negative" philosophy, for Schelling, is determination and is grounded in Spinoza's *omnis determinatio est negatio* (24).

25. Ibid., 169, 198. Negative philosophy is, on the contrary, linked with the *Academy*.

26. Friedrich Wilhelm Joseph Schelling, *Clara, or, On Nature's Connection to the Spirit World*, trans. Fiona Steinkamp (Albany: State University of New York Press, 2002), 76.

27. Jacques Derrida, *The Gift of Death*, trans. David Wills (Chicago and London: The University of Chicago Press, 1995), 55.

28. For an exposition of this form of compassion, see my "Metaphysical Ethics Reconsidered: Schopenhauer, Compassion and World Religions," *Schopenhauer Jahrbuch* 87 (2006): 101–17.

29. Derrida, *Gift of Death*, 55.

30. Ibid.

31. Guy Newland, *Compassion: A Tibetan Analysis* (London: Wisdom Publications, 1984), 57.

32. Cf. the ancient Indian tale of Savitri.

33. Martin Heidegger, *Poetry, Language, and Thought*, trans. Albert Hofstadter (New York: Harper and Row, 1971), chap. "Language."

34. And also: "Hospitality and compassion . . . are not only the direct path to the connection between sacrifice and redemption but also the direct path to the connection between grace, solace, care and misericord" (Ettinger, "From Proto-Ethical Compassion to Responsibility," 114).

35. Luce Irigaray, *Sharing the World* (London: Continuum, 2008), 26.

36. Ibid., 24. Irigaray states: "To be sure, the other will be sheltered, but in an enclosed space, a place already defined by our norms, our rules, our lacks and our voids. The other will have the possibility of dwelling only in a loop of the interlacing of relations where we ourselves are situated by our culture, our language, our surroundings. Blind to our lack of freedom" (26).

37. Newland, *Compassion*, 74.

38. The excerpt is from Chandrakirti's *Madhyamakavatarabhasya*.

39. On hearth of being see my chapter in *Borders and Debordering: Topologies, Praxes, Hospitableness*, in which the meaning of the hearth in Heidegger (from §18 of Hölderlin's Hymn "The Ister," "Der Herd als das Sein"; Gr. *hestia*) is presented in the context of his well-known reflection on the homely and unhomely: "[W]e initially know only that unhomely one who, among beings and through his or her own activity in each case, seeks a way out toward the homely and seeks the site of beings. . . . Does this mean that the hearth—around which alone everything, and especially human beings, can be homely—is being?" (Heidegger, *Hölderlin's Hymn "The Ister,"* 109). Being is the hearth, and as such is the *place*, to which all beings (all world, in an ancient cosmological sense) are drawn. It is that which "gathers everything around it—that wherein all beings have their site and are at home as beings" (ibid., 112–13). This place has been safeguarded by the gods/Gods, which are its guardians.

40. Derrida, *Acts of Religion*, 244.

41. Levinas, *Outside the Subject*. Of course, this thought originates from Emmanuel Levinas, *Totality and Infinity*, trans. Alphonso Lingis (Pittsburgh: Duquesne University Press, 1969), 89.

42. On the root *mat-* and its ethical meaning see Jean-Paul Martinon, *After "Rwanda:" In Search for a New Ethics* (Amsterdam and New York: Rodopi, 2013), 36. Here, Martinon refers to Lyotard's genealogies; see ibid., 79.

43. This appendix is based on stories and narratives from Pietro Bartolo and Lidia Tilotta, *Tears of Salt: A Doctor's Story of the Refugee Crisis* (Toronto: W. W. Norton, 2019).

44. Pope Francis, *Visit to Lampedusa: Homily of the Holy Father* (Rome: Libreria Editrice Vaticana, 2013).

45. Cf. the notion of "wombing motherliness" of Wu. See "The third presence" in the "Bethlehemite Concubine/Mary" chapter.

46. See on this Emma Seppala, Emiliana Simon-Thomas, Stephanie L. Brown et al., eds., *The Oxford Handbook of Compassion Science* (Oxford: Oxford University Press, 2017).

47. Cf. Jamie Ward, Patricia Schnakenberg, and Michael J. Banissy, "The Relationship between Mirror-touch Synaesthesia and Empathy: New Evidence and a New Screening Tool," *Cognitive Neuropsychology* 35, no. 5/6 (2018): 314–32; doi:10.1080/02643294.2018.1457017. Synaesthetic touch can be regarded as an extreme form of compassion and it is a form of synesthesia where individuals feel the same sensation that another person feels (such as touch).

48. In his *The Arcades Project*, Benjamin wrote: "On the question of incompleteness of history, Horkheimer's letter of March 16, 1937: 'The determination of incompleteness is idealistic if completeness is not comprised within it. Past injustice has occurred and is completed. The slain are really slain. . . . If one takes the lack of closure entirely seriously, one must believe in the Last Judgement. . . . Perhaps, with regard to incompleteness, there is a difference between the positive and the negative, so that only the injustice, the horror, the sufferings of the past are irreparable. . . . The corrective to this line of thinking may be found in the consideration that history is not simply a science but also and not least a form of remembrance <Eingedenken>. What science has 'determined,' remembrance can modify. Such mindfulness can make the incomplete (happiness) into something complete, and the complete (suffering) into something incomplete. That is theology; but in remembrance we have an experience that forbids us to conceive of history as fundamentally atheological, little as it may be granted us to try to write it with immediately theological concepts'" (Walter Benjamin, *The Arcades Project*, trans. Howard Eiland and Kevin McLaughlin [Cambridge and London: The Belknap Press of Harvard University Press, 2002], 471). Remembrance could be related to the *criterion of a cohabitation*, which is stronger and is tied to the two ethico-political principles of preserving the lives and lamenting the deaths. This is what Jean-Luc Nancy portrayed in his *The Inoperative Community* with the following words: "Millions of deaths, of course, are justified by the revolt of those who die: they are justified as a rejoinder

to the intolerable, as insurrections against social, political, technical, military, religious oppression. But these deaths are not *sublated*: no dialectic, no salvation leads these deaths to any other immanence than that of . . . death" (Jean-Luc Nancy, *The Inoperative Community*, ed. Peter Connor [Minneapolis: University of Minnesota Press, 1991], 13).

Chapter 3

1. See Lenart Škof and Shé M. Hawke, eds., *Shame, Gender Violence, and Ethics: Terrors of Injustice* (Lanham/Boulder/New York/London: Lexington Books, 2021) with the opening words by Yezidi survivor of ISIS enslavement and genocide Farida Khalaf: "I believe in the voices of women, girls, youth, and students—because the power we have is genuine. It is not centered around self-interest or geopolitical interests. We have to act because what makes us human is how we treat each other. When justice is absent, violence becomes cyclical. This is very obvious in Iraq. In the absence of justice every day dozens of crimes are committed against innocents. Everyone in our country has suffered because we live in a cycle of violence" (viii).

2. On the meaning of cultural transmodernity see Enrique Dussel in his excellent study, "Transmodernity and Interculturality," *Poligrafi* 11, no. 41/42 (2006): 16.

3. See on the word *matrixial* also in Ettinger's essay "From Proto-Ethical Compassion to Responsibility," 101. For Ettinger, as a Levinasian, the term *matrixial* (*womb matrix*) is related to the compassionate emotion of the maternal womb (from the Hebrew "wombs" as *rakhamim*; cf. ibid., 101). Cf. on the etymological possibilities of the term *matrix* in Jean-Paul Martinon's work *After "Rwanda,"* 36: "Maternity—Matrix—Material—Maturity—Matrimony—Matter—Materiel. The root *mat-* has two origins: the *immaterial* Latin *mater*, something from which something develops or takes form and the materiel Sanskrit: *mât*, to make by hand, to build." In his explication, Martinon is following Lyotard and his exhibition *Les Immateriaux* in the Pompidou Centre in 1985. See Reesa Greenberg, Bruce Ferguson, and Sandy Nairne, eds., *Thinking about Exhibitions* (London: Routledge, 1997), 159–73; see also n. 79 in Martinon's book *After "Rwanda,"* and especially pp. 37ff. on the African ethics of *ubuntu*, which will be highly relevant in our further explications on relationality later in this chapter.

4. Irigaray, *Il mistero di Maria*, 58.

5. Laurel C. Schneider, *Beyond Monotheism: A Theology of Multiplicity* (London: Westminster Press, 2008), 1ff, 159ff.

6. On a problem of "single divine incarnation in a human being of a male sex" see Emily A. Holmes, *Flesh Made Word: Medieval Women Mystics,*

Writing, and the Incarnation (Waco, TX: Baylor University Press, 2013), 2, see also ibid., "Introduction," 1–25, on incarnation in various Christologies. In the first chapter of her book Holmes proceeds toward a critique of "dualistic [sic!] and essentialist metaphysics and thinking" of the incarnation toward a more inclusive (feminist) interpretation since the publication of Grace Jantzen's *Becoming Divine: Towards a Feminist Philosophy of Religion* from 1999 (see on this ibid., 32ff). For Holmes, the inclusive Christology lies in an understanding of incarnation as "the embodiment of God more generally"—that is, in a way "that God is present in the world" (45).

7. Emily Pennington, *Feminist Eschatology: Embodied Futures* (London and New York: Routledge, 2017), 12f.

8. Ibid., 13. Pennington offers an excellent overview of scholarship on embodiment and feminist eschatologies in chapter 1 of her book. Here, she posits and analyzes various problems as outlined by feminist theologians, such as that eschatology was omnipotently realized by God alone (and Carol Christ's interrogation of this claim), or of eschatology as realized by God through Jesus (and, among others, Rosemary Radford Ruether, echoing Mary Daly's argument that "when God is male, the male is God"; ibid., 36), and finally, claims of divine power that is more intimate as well as that redemption flows through community.

9. See, on this, Irigaray, *In the Beginning, She Was*, 136.

10. See, for example, the article on conflict rape in South Sudan in the *Time* magazine: Aryn Baker, "The Secret War Crime." See on this issue also Martinon, *After "Rwanda."*

11. See the chapter "The Redemption of Women," in Luce Irigaray, *Key Writings* (London: Bloomsbury, 2004), 152.

12. See Schott, *Birth, Death, and Femininity* for four narratives related to sexual violence against women—the rape of the Sabines, the rape of Lucretia, the rape of the Concubine, and the myth about the founding of the city on the Bojana River (in today's Albania). Schott interprets these narratives in the framework of Girard's theory of sacrificial violence (cf. ibid., 28–39).

13. See on this article by David Z. Moster, "Levite of Judges 19–21," *JBL* 134, no. 4 (2015): 721–30; and chapter 2, titled "Patriarchs and Their Women, Some Inaugural Intertexts of Hospitality: The Odyssey, Abraham, Lot, and the Levite of Ephraim," from Judith Still, *Derrida and Hospitality* (Edinburgh: Edinburgh University Press, 2000), 51–92. See also Lauren A. S. Monroe's paper on child and female sacrifice in the Hebrew Bible, "Disembodied Women: Sacrificial Language and the Deaths of Bat-Jephthah, Cozbi, and the Bethlehemite Concubine," *Catholic Biblical Quarterly* 75 (2013): 32–52.

14. Cf. 1 Sam. 11:7.

15. Ettinger, "From Proto-Ethical Compassion to Responsibility," 127. Ettinger here explains Hebrew "Good full of mercy" (*El Maleh Rakhamim*) as "God full of wombs."

16. Judith Still argues that we are actually dealing with two sexual taboos: firstly, the anus should not be penetrated at all, and in both stories (of Lot and of Levite) we are dealing with the even more powerful taboo of wanting to penetrate the priest's anus; secondly, "the hymen-protected vagina" may be entered and penetrated only upon a paternal invitation and this marks the above mentioned substitution of one sexual taboo for the other. See Still, *Derrida and Hospitality*, 74.

17. Ibid., 77.

18. Judg. 21: 10–11.

19. Phyllis Trible, *Texts of Terror: Literary Feminist Readings of Biblical Narratives* (Minneapolis: Fortress Press, 1984), 79, 65, ch. 3 ("An Unnamed Woman: The Extravagance of Violence").

20. By "*matrixial* identity" we understand the ontologico-ethical core of the feminine sexual identity, in a way of a respect for sexuate (and not sexual or sexualized) differentiation, as proposed by Irigaray. In her *In the Beginning, She Was*, Irigaray writes: "Between sister and brother, genealogy becomes the generation of two different horizontal identities: appearance of the transcendence of sexuate identity with respect to the body" (Irigaray, *In the Beginning, She Was*, 133). In this sense matrixial (i.e., bodily) identity supplies us with the possibility of a different understanding of trinitarian relationality, as this topic is discussed later on. If, in Levinasian terms, the other necessarily is the *son*, the transcendence of the other, for Irigaray, is only possible from within two different horizontal (and thus not hierarchical) identities, with sister(s) and brother(s) being the paradigms of such a transcendence *in* relationality (cf. her reading of the *Antigone* in *In the Beginning, She Was*, ch. 5.).

21. Trible, *Texts of Terror*, 87.

22. Monroe, "Disembodied Women," 41.

23. Ludwig Feuerbach, *The Essence of Christianity*, trans. G. Eliot (New York: Harper and Row, 1957), 72.

24. Ibid.

25. See Plato's *Timaeus*, 52a, in Plato, *Complete Works*.

26. Ettinger, "From Proto-Ethical Compassion to Responsibility," 101.

27. Ibid., 100. On Moses and motherhood, see Lisa Guenther, "'Like a Maternal Body': Emmanuel Levinas and the Motherhood of Moses," *Hypatia* 21, no. 1 (2006): 119–36. Guenther interprets Moses's maternity as follows: "Moses is not literally a mother, but he was born to a woman and borne by several other women who substituted for him 'like a maternal body,' even though they had 'neither conceived nor given birth' to him" (124).

28. Cf. Monroe, "Disembodied Women," 32ff.

29. Holmes, *Flesh Made Word*. Cf. among others Rosemary Radford Ruether's seminal book *Goddesses and the Divine Feminine: A Western Religious History* (Berkeley and Los Angeles: University of California Press, 2005).

30. Irigaray, *Il mistero di Maria*, 20.

31. Feuerbach, *Essence of Christianity*, 71.

32. Ibid., 69–70.

33. In semiotics, the first account on triadic logic is to be found in Peirce's philosophical writings, beginning with his early writings on categories from 1867, followed by "Nomenclature and Divisions of Triadic Relations as Far as They are Determined" from his *Syllabus* (1903), and his essay on three categories from "The Principles of Phenomenology" (part 2—"The Categories: Firstness, Secondness and Thirdness," where he states: "My view is that there are three modes of being"); see Justus Buchler, ed., *Philosophical Writings of Peirce* (New York: Dover, 1955), 75–78. On Peirce's triadic theory of semiotics (sign-object-interpretant, or also interpreter-interpretant-interpretee) see Hermann Deuser, *Religionsphilosophie* (Berlin and New York: Walter de Gruyter, 2008), §10; especially see Deuser's original table on semiotic triads and trichotomies; ibid., 268.

34. Josiah Royce, *War as Insurance: An Address* (New York: Macmillan Company, 1914). See part two of this essay, titled "The Neighbor: Love and Hate" where Royce—based upon Peirce's theory of semiotics—beautifully describes the very essence of triadic logic: "[D]yadic, the dual, the bilateral relations of man and man, of each man to his neighbor, are relations fraught with social danger. A pair of men is what I may call an essentially dangerous relation" (30). Finally, for Royce, the third element (a community or an international system of insurance) is needed to intervene between dyadically established relations and thus to mediate among hostile parties.

35. Jonathan Rutherford, "The Third Space: Interview with Homi Bhabha," in *Identity, Community, Culture, Difference*, ed. Jonathan Rutherford (London: Lawrence and Wishart, 1990), 211.

36. Jay Johnston, *Angels of Desire: Esoteric Bodies, Aesthetics and Ethics* (London and New York: Routledge, 2014), 51 (for ternary structure) and 92 (for the citation).

37. Schneider, *Beyond Monotheism*, 4.

38. Ibid.

39. See Plotinus, *The Enneads*, trans. Stephen MacKenna (London: Penguin, 1991), xxxv. On triangels and their cosmic role see Plato's *Timaeus*, 53d, in *Complete Works*.

40. On various trinitarian theologies in the non-Western world see *The Trinity*, ed. Peter C. Phan (Cambridge: Cambridge University Press, 2001), chaps. 16–20. In these chapters we can see the rich variety of triadic thinking in Confucianism (Heaven, Earth, and Humanity) and Daoism (i.e., the dynamics and relationality within Dao—as One, producing Two (yin-yang), and having their offspring as Three), and, of course, within both Hinduism as well as Buddhism (*triguna, tridosha, trikaya* . . .).

41. Schneider, *Beyond Monotheism*, 32.

42. A. Okechukwu Ogbonnaya, *An African Interpretation of the Trinity* (New York: Paragon House, 1994).

43. Ibid., 8.

44. Plato, *Timaeus*, 49a and 52a, in *Complete Works*.

45. According to Plato's *Timaeus*: "The new starting point in my account of the universe needs to be more complex than the earlier one. Then we distinguished two kinds, but now we must specify a third, one of a different sort. The earlier two sufficed for our previous account: one was proposed as a model, intelligible and always changeless, a second as an imitation of the model, something that possesses becoming and is visible. We did not distinguish a third kind at the time, because we thought that we could make do with the two of them. Now, however, it appears that our account compels us to attempt to illuminate in words a kind that is difficult and vague. What must we suppose it do to and to be? This above all: it is a *receptacle* of all becoming—its wetnurse, as it were" (*Timaeus* 49a, in Plato, *Complete Works*, 1251).

46. Kuang-Ming Wu, *On Chinese Body Thinking: A Cultural Hermeneutics* (Leiden: Brill, 1997), 140–42; my emphasis. Wu refers to *Dao de jing*, ch. 6: "The spirit of the valley never dies. / It is called the subtle and profound female./ The gate of the subtle and profound female/ is the root of Heaven and Earth./ It is continuous, and seems to be always existing./ Use it and you will never wear it out" (139f). For more about Wu's idiosyncratic notion of "wombing motherliness"and thus his relation to our notion of matrixiality see ch. 6 of our book.

47. Ibid., 141.

48. Yvonne Sherwood and Kevin Hart, eds., *Derrida and Religion: Other Testaments* (New York: Routledge, 2005), 298.

49. Jürgen Moltmann, *Trinität und Reich Gottes* (Gütersloh: Gütersloher Verlagshaus, 1994), 164–65; see, on this, Phan, *The Trinity*, 229.

50. Feuerbach, *Essence of Christianity*, 71. In German: "Die Maria paßt veilmehr ganz in die Kategorie der Dreieinigkeitsverhältnisse weil sie ohne *männliche* Befruchtung den Sohn gebar, wie Gott Vater ohne *weiblichen* Schoß den Sohn erzeugte, so daß also die Maria eine notwendige, innerlich herausgeforderte, ergänzende Antithese zum Vater im Schoße der Dreieinigkeit bildet." Ludwig Feuerbach, *Das Wesen des Christentums* (Frankfurt am Main: Suhrkamp, 1976), 83. English translation is not accurate here: it does not translate the most important word in this sentence—namely, we read in German "wie Gott Vater ohne *weiblichen Schoß* den Sohn erzeugte" (my emphasis; cf. Engl. translation: "On the contrary, the Virgin Mary fits in perfectly with the relations of the Trinity, since she conceives without man the Son whom the Father begets without woman; so that thus the Holy Virgin is a necessary, inherently requisite antithesis to the Father in the bosom of the Trinity" (*Essence of Christianity*, 71).

51. Ibid., 69. See on this topic also teachings about Mother in Heaven by various Mormon theologians and thinkers. Since the 1854 revelation of Sister Eliza R. Snow about Mother in Heaven in her "O My Father" hymn, this topic

developed into an (un)official doctrine of the LDS. On this, and related dogmatic controversies over the decades see David L. Paulsen and Martin Pulido, "'A Mother There:' A Survey of Historical Teachings about Mother in Heaven," *BYU Studies* 50, no. 1 (2011): 71–97; see also an excellent study written by Taylor G. Petrey, "Rethinking Mormonism's Heavenly Mother," *Harvard Theological Review* 109, no. 3 (2016): 315–41. Petrey's essay is especially important for its comparison with Irigaray's teachings on divine women. In his concluding remarks, Petrey cherishes the capacity of Mormonism to highlight "the benefits of a pluralistic heaven such as what Mormonism can offer," including "making space for a plurality of gendered performances" (340)—beyond divine or human dichotomies, based on heteronormativity. Interestingly enough, it is precisely the Mormon thought that in its current pluriformity can "reveal the fluid and plural nature of sexual difference" as well as "be useful in the analysis of race, ability, and other morphological, social, and historical categories" (341).

52. Irigaray, *Key Writings*, 163.

53. Epiphanius of Salamis, for example, even thinks that chapter 12 of Revelation could already testify to this; Stephen J. Shoemaker, ed., *Ancient Traditions of the Virgin Mary's Dormition and Assumption* (Oxford: Oxford University Press, 2002), 12.

54. Taken from Antoine Wenger, *L'Assomption de la T. S. Vierge dans la tradition byzantine du VIe au Xe siècle* (Paris: Institut français d'études byzantines, 1955) and two other editions of this earliest Greek dormition narrative; cf. ibid., 351 n.1.

55. Ibid., 365.

56. Ibid., 38. On Mary and Christ see Peter Sloterdijk, *Bubbles* (*Spheres I*), trans. Wieland Hoban (South Pasadena, CA: Semiotexte, 2011), 619–624 ("*Matris in gremio*").

57. Moltmann, *Trinität und Reich Gottes*, 179: "Gottvater-Kirchenvater-Landesvater-Familienvater." The paragraph we refer to is titled "Die immanente Trinität."

58. Ibid., 181: "zweigeschlechtlich bzw. transgeschlechtlich."

59. Ibid., 164–65.

60. This citation from the Eleventh Council of Toledo is from online collection, available at https://sourcebooks.fordham.edu/halsall/source/toledo.txt; accessed February 25, 2020; the section reference for this citation is 309; originally this collection comes from J. Neuner and J. Dupuis; *The Christian Faith in the Doctrinal Documents of the Catholic Church* (New York: Alba House, 1982), 102–106. Cf. on this "gynecology of God" in Moltmann, *Trinität und Reich Gottes*, 181 n. 67. For Moltmann, this undoubtedly marks a radical digression from the old patriarchal thinking on God toward a new theology that can acknowledge the importance of introducing sexual difference into the very concept of God.

61. Radford Ruether, *Goddesses and the Divine Feminine*, 155.

62. *New Testament Apocrypha*, ed. Wilhelm Schneemelcher (Philadelphia: Westminster Press, 1963).

63. Irigaray, *Key Writings*, 175.

64. Feuerbach, *Essence of Christianity*, 71.

65. Richard Kearney, *Anatheism: Returning to God After God* (New York: Columbia University Press, 2010), 25: "And this empty receptacle at the core of the circle is, arguably, none other than the womb-heart of Mary itself (*khora*)." According to Kearney, *chóra* also appears as an empty center, around which the persons of the Trinity are moving endlessly in the movement of *perichoresis* (cf. ibid., 56).

66. Wu, *On Chinese Body Thinking*.

67. "[A] woman clothed with the sun, with the moon under her feet, and on her head a crown of twelve stars. She was pregnant and was crying out in birthpangs, in the agony of giving birth" (Rev. 12:2).

68. Sherwood and Hart, *Derrida and Religion*, 93.

69. Phyllis Trible, *God and the Rhetoric of Sexuality* (London: SCM Press, 1992), 34.

70. Ibid., 36.

71. Irigaray, *Il mistero di Maria*, 21–25 (chap. "La verginità di Maria").

72. Cf. Jungian levels of anima in Eve, Helen, Mary and Sophia—the latter being the final phase of anima development. For Jung and Sophia see an excellent paper by Lance S. Owens, "C. G. Jung and Erich Neumann: The Zaddik, Sophia, and the Shekinah" (conference paper, 2016; accessed via ResearchGate on February 5, 2020). In this paper, Owens also shows how important a friendship with Erich Neumann was for Jung: "In *Answer to Job*, Jung forcefully confronted the God-image of Christian theology, the canonical God of his ancestral tradition. He admitted to Neumann that in his nakedness he had 'to insult even God.' The Jehovah of Christian dogma was incomplete and imbalanced. It needed Sophia" (11). And Erich Neumann responded to Jung with these words: "In reality, you believe in the feminine Sophia as the highest authority without admitting it. Perhaps it only seems to me to be so because this is how it is for me personally. . . . Although long suppressed by patriarchal Jewish orthodox, she was the immanence of divinity rising over the horizon of consciousness at this 'turn of time.' In a later essay, Neumann noted her reappearance in the Shekinah as something essentially new in the outlook of Jewish mankind, which hitherto with its ethic and spirit seemed so fundamentally patriarchal that the feminine, repressed and almost despised, could speak to it only through subterranean channels" (15). On the evolution of Sophia's myth in Jewish religious history and Gnostic mythology see 16ff. of this lecture. The story of Sophia also bears close resemblances to the fate of the Greek Metis: "At a catastrophic point, Sophia was separated from her twin, the Logos; she fell into exile, into the depths, into the realm of chaos. How that happened is told in myriad ways. The result was that Sophia entered into what eventually became material reality. Embedded in the existential origin of cosmos, she

became the animating factor, the *anima mundi*—she was the spark of supernal reality present in cosmos. She is often designated in ancient Gnostic texts as the Mother of Life. In Gnostic mythology, Sophia is the one who breathed life and spirit into the first man, Adam" (19).

73. See about the hymn Ciril Sorč and Anton Strle, "Teilhard de Chardin o 'večni ženskosti' in njegov pomen za naš čas," *Bogoslovni vestnik* 33 (1973): 130–38.

74. Teilhard de Chardin, *The Future of Man*, trans. Norman Denny (New York and London: Image Books, 1964), 307.

75. Sorč and Strle, "Teilhard de Chardin," 133.

76. Pierre Teilhard de Chardin, *The Eternal Feminine*, in *Writings in Time of War*, trans. René Hague (New York and Evanston: Harper and Row, 1968), 192, 202.

77. Henri de Lubac, *The Eternal Feminine: A Study of the Poem by Teilhard de Chardin, followed by Teilhard and the Problems of Today*, trans. René Hague (New York: Harper and Row, 1971), 19.

78. Ibid., 95.

79. Teilhard de Chardin, *The Eternal Feminine*, 200.

80. See, about this, the excellent treatise by Karel Sládek, "Sophiology as a Theological Discipline according to Solovyov, Bulgakov and Florensky," *Bogoslovni vestnik* 77, no 1 (2017): 109–16. See pp. 111 and 112 about this, but particularly about the dispute concerning Bulgakov and his doctrine of Sophia.

81. See Brenda Meehan, "Wisdom/Sophia, Russian Identity, and Western Feminist Theology," *CrossCurrents* 46, no. 2 (Summer 1996): 149–68. Meehan says as follows: "Starting with the concept of ultimate reality, Solov'ev argues that the One must differentiate itself internally (and eternally) into three hypostases which are nonetheless one Absolute, one God, in virtue of each having the same divine substance. Solov'ev speaks of that substance as Sophia, the essential wisdom of God" (156). See also the now classic works of feminist theology: Elizabeth A. Johnson, *She Who Is: The Mystery of God in Feminist Theological Discourse* (New York: Crossroad, 1993) and Rosemary Radford Ruether, *Sexism and God-Talk. Toward a Feminist Theology* (Boston: Beacon, 1983). Precisely in the interpretation of Western feminist theology dedicated to Wisdom does Meehan point to the similarities as well as certain delimitations within Russian Sophiology. For contemporary ecofeminism and the creative-processual immanence of God see Nadja Furlan Štante, "Transcendence in (Eco)feminist Christian Hermeneutics," *Bogoslovni vestnik* 77, no. 3/4 (2017): 589–99.

82. Meehan, "Wisdom/Sophia," 156, 157. The second quote is from Solovyov's *Lectures on Divine Humanity*.

83. Sládek, "Sophiology as a Theological Discipline," 113.

84. Meehan, "Wisdom/Sophia," 159–60. The citation within the quote is from Bulgakov (*Sophia, The Wisdom of God*; see ibid., note 39).

85. John O'Donnell, "The Trinitarian Panentheism of Sergej Bulgakov," *Gregorianum* 76, no. 1 (1995): 32ff. The observation made here by this interpreter is extraordinary.

86. Sládek, "Sophiology as a Theological Discipline," 114.

87. Meehan, "Wisdom/Sophia," 160.

88. See Christopher Pramuk, *At Play in Creation: Merton's Awakening to the Feminine Divine* (Collegeville, MI: Liturgical Press, 2015). I thank Shé Hawke for this link.

89. Ibid., 27.

90. Ibid., 31f.

91. Ibid., 32.

Interlude

1. Arthur Schopenhauer, *On the Basis of Morality*, trans. E. F. J. Payne (Indianapolis and Cambridge: Hackett, 1998), 214. See more on this in my essay on Schopenhauer and Pragmatism, "'The Second Philosophy' of Arthur Schopenhauer: Schopenhauer and Radical Empiricism," *Schopenhauer-Jahrbuch* 91 (2010): 55–64.

2. Ibid., 163.

3. George Lakoff and Mark Johnson, *Philosophy in the Flesh: The Embodied Mind and Its Challenge to Western Thought* (New York: Basic Books, 1999).

4. Steve Odin, "The Social Self in Japanese Philosophy and American Pragmatism: A Comparative Study of Watsuji Tetsurō and George Herbert Mead," *Philosophy East and West* 42, no. 3 (1992): 475–501.

5. Chrétien, *The Call and the Response.*

6. Mark J. Nearman, trans., "Kakyō: Zeami's Fundamental Principles of Acting: Part Two," *Monumenta Nipponica* 37, no. 4 (1982): 461f.

7. "Let us assume that everybody has depth, i.e. has three dimensions, and that if two bodies have a third body between them they cannot be in contact with one another; let us remember that what is liquid is not independent of body and must be or contain water, and that if two bodies touch one another under water, their touching surfaces cannot be dry, but must have water between, viz. the water which wets their bounding surfaces; from all this it follows that in water two bodies cannot be in contact with one another. The same holds of two bodies in air—air being to bodies in air precisely what water is to bodies in water—but the facts are not so evident to our observation, because we live in air, just as animals that live in water would not notice that the things which touch one another in water have wet surfaces. The problem, then, is: does the perception of all objects of sense take place in the same way, or does it not;

e.g. taste and touch requiring contact (as they are commonly thought to do), while all other senses perceive over a distance?" (Aristotle, *The Complete Works of Aristotle*, vol. 1., ed. Jonathan Barnes [Princeton: Princeton University Press, 1984], 673).

8. G. H. Mead, *Mind, Self, and Society* (Chicago and London: University of Chicago Press, 1967), 14. See also n. 9. On this aspect see W. Bergmann and G. Hoffmann, "G. H. Mead und die Tradition der Phänomenologie," in *Das Problem der Intersubjektivität*, ed. Hans Joas (Frankfurt am Main: Suhrkamp, 1985), 93–130.

9. David L. Miller, *The Individual and the Social Self: Unpublished Work of George Herbert Mead* (Chicago: University of Chicago Press, 1982), 65.

10. I am indebted to Roman Madzia for kindly reminding me of this remark (on "haptic" see Miller's "Introduction" to *Individual and the Social Self*, 12, 22.).

11. K. J. Booth "Embodied Mind and the Mimetic Basis for Taking the Role of the Other," in *George Herbert Mead in the Twenty-First Century*, ed. F. Thomas Burke and Krzysztof Piotr Skowroński (Lanham, MD: Lexington Books, 2013), 137.

12. Hans Joas, *G. H. Mead: A Contemporary Re-Examination of His Thought*, trans. Raymond Meyer (Cambridge: The MIT Press, 1985), 2.

13. For citations and elaboration on this see Škof, *Breath of Proximity*, 78.

14. For this reason, Joas is probably not perfectly accurate in his statement that Feuerbach in his thought is only encountering the other in a *contemplative* way (Joas, *G. H. Mead*, 13). We think that the constitution of intersubjectivity in Feuerbach already opens a path toward practical ethics, which, of course, is cosmologically underpinned. But Joas is certainly right in pointing at the corporeality of subjects, being in their everyday practical intersubjective relations (ibid., 14).

15. Karl Löwith, "Ludwig Feuerbach," in *Ludwig Feuerbach*, ed. Erich Thies (Darmstadt: Wissenschaftliche Buchgesellschaft, 1976), 49.

16. Chrétien, *The Call and the Response*, 84.

17. Ibid., 85.

18. Earlier in his phenomenological constitution of the touch, Chrétien mentions W. Wundt and his elaboration of touch as *Gefühlssinn*, and stresses the inappropriateness of the term *Tastsinn* for touch (ibid., 120).

19. Ibid.

20. Ibid., 130.

21. Mead, *Mind, Self, and Society*, 62.

22. Odin, "The Social Self"

23. In this chapter, we will also refer to Tetsuro Watsuji, *Fūdo: Wind und Erde*, trans. Dora Fischer-Barnicol and Okochi Ryogi (Darmstadt: Wissenschaftliche Buchgesellschaft, 1992).

24. Odin, "The Social Self," 479.

25. It can, of course, be no coincidence that Mead's closest pragmatist colleague, John Dewey, was warmly accepted by Chinese philosophers and even entitled "Second Confucius" upon his visit to China. On this, see David L. Hall and Roger T. Ames, *The Democracy of the Dead: Dewey, Confucius, and the Hope for Democracy in China* (Chicago and Lasalle, IL: Open Court, 1999); see also Joseph Grange, *John Dewey, Confucius, and Global Philosophy* (Albany: State University of New York Press, 2004); John Dewey, *John Dewey, Lectures in China, 1919–1920*, ed. Robert W. Clopton, trans. T.-C. Ou (Honolulu: The University Press of Hawaii, 1973); Jessica Wang Ching-Sze, *John Dewey in China: To Teach and to Learn* (Albany: State University of New York Press, 2007).

26. Odin, "The Social Self," 490f.

27. Watsuji, *Fūdo*, 495.

28. Norman Wirzba, "The Witness of Humility," in *Words of Life, New Theological Turns in French Phenomenology*, ed. Bruce E. Benson and Norman Wirzba (New York: Fordham University Press, 2010), 233–51.

29. Ibid., 235.

30. Ibid., 247.

31. Watsuji, *Fūdo*, 12–20.

32. Jacques Derrida, "Given Time: The Time of the King," *Critical Inquiry* 18, no. 2 (1992) 166.

33. On this space and Kierkegaard as related to Mead, see my exploration in *Breath of Proximity* (ch. 4.5 on Mead).

34. Arthur Schopenhauer, *The World as Will and Representation*, vol. 1, trans. E. F. J. Payne (New York: Dover, 1969), 404.

35. "For just what the Christian mystics call the *effect of grace* and the *new birth*, is for us the only direct expression of the *freedom of the will*" (Schopenhauer, *World as Will and Representation*, 404).

36. Miller, *The Individual and the Social Self*, 62.

Chapter 4

1. Jean-Luc Marion, *The Erotic Phenomenon*, trans. Stephen E. Lewis (Chicago and London: University of Chicago Press, 2007).

2. Luce Irigaray, *The Way of Love* (London: Continuum, 2002), 11.

3. For the chronology of Schelling's middle works cf. Fiona Steinkamp, "Schelling's Clara: Editors' Obscurity," *Journal of English and Germanic Philology* (2002): 478–96. Steinkamp writes in her "Introduction" to the translation of *Clara*: "*Clara* is unique in the philosophical literature. It is a discussion told as a story, its very structure reflects its content, and it has a woman as one of its central characters" (Schelling, *Clara*, vii).

4. Ludwig Feuerbach, "Über Spiritualismus und Materialismus," in *Kritiken und Abhandlungen III, 1844–1866* (Frankfurt am Main: Suhrkamp, 1975).

5. Ibid., 394.

6. Jason M. Wirth, ed., *Schelling Now: Contemporary Readings* (Bloomington: Indiana University Press, 2005), 6. Wirth thinks that it is between the 1810 *Stuttgart* lectures and 1821 *Erlangen* lectures that we find "a Schelling with whom we are still coming to terms" (4).

7. Ibid., 7.

8. Schelling, *Clara*, 9.

9. Derrida, *Gift of Death*, 55.

10. Schelling, *Clara*, 9.

11. Ibid.

12. Ibid.

13. Alexander Grau, "Clara: Über Schellings gleichnamiges Fragment," *Zeitschrift fur philosophische Forschung*, 51, no. 4 (1997): 590.

14. Schelling, *Clara*, 590.

15. Ibid., 596. Apart from the resemblance of the name Clara to Clara of Assisi, and Schelling's revitalization of the philosophy of nature, Grau also notes that one of Schelling's pseudonyms was Bonaventura and mentions Schelling's idea that, among all monastic orders, one should only preserve the Carthusian one (ibid.).

16. Ibid., 61.

17. Caputo, *Insistence of God*, 231–32.

18. Ibid., 237.

19. Holmes, *Flesh Made Word*, 6.

20. Ibid., 12.

21. Judith Butler, *Frames of War: When Is Life Grievable?* (London and New York: Verso, 2010), 7.

22. Caputo, *Insistence of God*, 254.

23. Schelling, *Clara*, 76.

24. This is from the unpublished collection titled "The Red Geranium and Its Almost Taste of Pepper." I am thankful to Jeff Stewart for sharing this tender prose piece with me.

25. We refer to Hans Herlof Grelland's unpublished conference paper "A Case for Heideggerian Phenomenology: Edvard Munch's 'The Sick Child'" (presented in Riga in 2019; the manuscript is with the author). Edvard Munch first painted this scene in 1886, and then repeatedly throughout his life—the latest version of "The Sick Child" is from 1925. Grellund writes following words about the temporality as an indispensable part of this artwork: "We should be aware of the light in the picture, the light around and in front of Sophie's face. It is difficult not to think of Heidegger's thoughts about the clearing, in German, die Lichtung. In German, as in Norwegian, the word expresses the aspect

of a clearing in a forest that it is a place where the light comes in. So, in a dark forest, the clearing is first seen as light, and a place for light in contrast with the darkness prevailing the darkness of the trees. So, die Lichtung has the double meaning of open space and a place where things can be seen. The light in the painting is like a clearing in front of Sophie. She is not looking at her grieving aunt, she is looking at the clearing in front of her, die Lichtung. It is as if she has her awareness directed towards the future, represented as light, as clearing. Thus the dimension of future is present in the painting as light in the darkness of the situation, as a clearance in the closedness of the situation Sophie finds herself in."

26. F. W. J. Schelling, *Philosophical Inquiries into the Nature of Human Freedom*, trans. J. Gutman (La Salle, IL: Open Court, 1989), 88–89.

27. Ibid., 79.

28. Ibid.

29. Ibid., 89.

30. F. W. J. Schelling, *Ages of the World* (second draft, 1813), trans. Judith Norman (Ann Arbor: University of Michigan Press, 2001), 135.

31. Ibid.

32. Ibid., 150. See also: "For these reasons, anyone who attempts a merely dynamic construction of matter must be led to conclude that its original condition was spiritual" (151).

33. Cf. Jason M. Wirth, *The Conspiracy of Life: Meditations on Schelling and His Life* (Albany: State University of New York Press, 2003), 187: "Love (A^3) holds together and embraces the inertia of the past (the A^1) with the mystery of the future (the A^2). In this sense, one can speak of love as the affirmation of the Augenblick, the present moment, as the 'everlasting, self-overcoming' drive of the determinate past into the mystery of the future (WA, 85)."

34. Ibid., 135.

35. Ibid.

36. Ibid., 212. On reading *Clara* through *Hamlet*, Wirth also adds: "The dead are somehow living hidden in the earth, claiming—precisely through their absence—the living, as if the past were haunting the present" (193). Also, "Animals leave behind ghosts while humans leave behind spirits. . . . Spirits call us back to the decision by which we have abandoned in our propensity to love ourselves. . . . Spirits call humans to live among the ghosts" (197–98).

37. For Böhme's works we have used the German edition provided by Ernst Benz, *Der Vollkommene Mensch nach Jacob Böhme* (Stuttgart: Kohlhammer, 1937). Apart from having an important (although somewhat hidden) influence on Schelling, we also know that Böhme was the only German thinker included in Feuerbach's *Geschichte der neuern Philosophie (von Bacon bis Spinoza)* from 1833. This is a sign of their high esteem for this early German predecessor of

contemporary feminist theology and thinking of the feminine divine. More on Feuerbach's specific link to this aspect later.

38. Schelling, *Ages of the World*, 164. Benz, *Der Vollkommene Mensch nach Jacob Böhme*, 22. These are the words from Prov. 8:22.

39. Schelling, *Ages of the World*, 164–65.

40. This citation is from Böhme's *Von der Menschwerdung Jesus Christi*: in Sophia "stellt sich der Ungrund dar." Also: in Sophia "ist da Principium aus dem ewigen Ungrund eröffnet" (ibid.; this is from his work *Von Sechs Theosophischen Punkten*).

41. Cf. Irigaray, *Il mistero di Maria*, chap. "La Verginità di Maria." It is impossible for Irigaray to believe that Christianity could be founded on such a problematic event/myth as the appropriation of the body of Mary through a masculine order/rule or domination. For Irigaray, it is thus necessary for Mary to keep and preserve for herself the most fundamental sign of her bodily/spiritual identity—she has kept her most intimate breath (i.e., her spiritual identity, also understood as an *inspiration* for the future—the coming of Jesus) of her present and future autonomy in and with herself. Mary, according to Irigaray, is thus *not* available to the Lord at his request.

42. Benz, *Der Vollkommene Mensch nach Jacob Böhme*, 106.

43. "Darum nahm Christus seine Sele vom Weibe / als von einer Jungfrauen / und ward aber ein Mann." Ibid.

44. Ibid., 109. Additionally, as originally stated by Böhme: "Und eben in dieser heiligen Matrice, welche GOttes Wort und Kraft in dem süssen Namen JEsu / in dem Samen MARIAE im Ziel des Bundes wieder erweckte / ward der Schlangen-Gift in der Selen und Fleische zerbrochen" (ibid). Feuerbach also states in a beautiful passage that: "It is true that the Son, as a natural man, dwells only temporarily in the shrine of this body, but the impressions which he here receives are inextinguishable; the Mother is never out of the mind and heart of the son" (Feuerbach, *Essence of Christianity*, 72). For this very reason, it was necessary for Feuerbach to state that "we find in God the beating of a mother's heart" (ibid.).

45. Schelling, *Philosophical Inquiries*, 87.

46. Ibid., 89.

47. Ibid., 86.

48. Schelling, *Clara*, 14.

49. Cf. Wirth, *Conspiracy of Life*, 2: "In the 1809 *Freedom* essay, perhaps Schelling's most daring work and one of the treasures of the nineteenth-century German philosophical tradition, he spoke of a 'unity and conspiracy,' a *Konspiration* (I/7, 391). When something or someone falls out of the conspiracy, they become inflamed with sickness and fever, as 'inflamed by an inner heat.' Schelling used the Latinate-German *Konspiration*, which stems from *conspīro*, to breathe or blow together. *Spīro*, to breathe, is related to *spīritus* (the German

Geist), meaning spirit, but also breath. *Geist* is the progression of difference, the A^3, the breathing out of the dark abyss of nature into form and the simultaneous inhaling of this ground, the retraction of things away from themselves. The conspiracy is a simultaneous expiration and inspiration, and each thing of nature is both inspired yet expiring. This is what we call the conspiracy of life, that is, the life beyond and within life and death."

50. Grau, "Clara," 608–9.

51. Giacomo Puccini, *Suor Angelica*, Italian libretto by Gioachino Forzano, trans. Edoardo Petri, http://opera.stanford.edu/Puccini/SuorAngelica/libretto_ie.html, accessed Feb. 5, 2018.

Chapter 5

1. *The Eumenides*, vv. 666–73, see Aeschylus, *The Oresteia*, trans. Robert Fagles (reprint, London: Penguin Books, 1977), 260–61. This is, of course, an explanation of the mentioned myth of the birth of Athene from Zeus's head. Cf. Hesiod, *Theogony*, vv. 889–93 and 927–28, in *Hesiod and Theognis* (London: Penguin Books, 2000), 52–53.

2. Ludwig Binswanger, *Grundformen und Erkenntnis menschlichen Daseins* (Heidelberg: Roland Asanger Verlag, 1993), 179.

3. Schelling, *Philosophical Inquiries*, 79.

4. See about this John D. Caputo, "The Absence of Monica: Heidegger, Derrida, and Augustine's Confessions," in *Feminist Interpretations of Martin Heidegger*, ed. Nancy J. Holland and Patricia Huntington (University Park: The Pennsylvania State University Press, 2001), 151. Caputo remarks here that the list of things that *Dasein* does not feel, which already contains hunger, should be expanded to include weeping, as this is something that "authentic *Dasein* does not do in *Being and Time*" (ibid.). Contrary to that, the entirety of Derrida's autobiographical *Circumfession* is pervaded by tears, by the gentle closeness in his relationship with the dying mother, and Derrida's utmost despair for the loss of his name in the process of her leave-taking.

5. On Binswanger and his phenomenology of love see the brilliant treatise by Joeri Schrijvers titled "Ludwig Binswanger: The Transcendence of Love," *Bogoslovni vestnik* 77 (2017): 489–502. Bibliographic data are here quoted from Schrijvers. It was largely his exceptional and subtle analyses of Binswanger that drew my attention to the work of this overlooked phenomenologist.

6. Ibid., 491.

7. For the transition into the treatment of love as friendship see section B of the first part of Binswanger's book, i.e., the chapter titled "Das freundschaftliche Miteinandersein" and following (Binswanger, *Grundformen*, 197ff.).

8. Ibid., 17; see 65 about the logic of forsaking and gaining: "Je mehr ich dir gebe, je mehr habe ich, beides grenzlos."

9. Ibid., 18. Binswanger naturally uses the plural (but on page 69 he mentions the indispensability of the dual; *Dualis*). But the constellation of love is embedded into a triadic structure, which also contains twoness: without Me and You there is no atmosphere of community (this third as "We [two]") that permeates our relationship or encounter (see ibid., 20ff). The relationship between two individuals thus never occurs at the level of plain (or even antagonistic) relationship between the I and the You, but always already resides in an atmosphere of community as the We (*Wir*) mode. This is, of course, first meant with regard to the place of encounter, which Binswanger exemplifies with a geometric/cosmic metaphor of ellipse, whose two foci are you and me (ibid., 21). For the temporality of this encounter see Binswanger's explication, as well as our chapter about the interval in ethics in Mead and Zeami in the present book.

10. Feuerbach, *The Essence of Christianity*, xxxiv.

11. *The Fiery Brook: Selected Writings of Ludwig Feuerbach*, trans. Zawar Hanfi (Garden City, NY: Doubleday, 1972), 143.

12. Cf. Nancy, *Being Singular Plural*.

13. Binswanger, *Grundformen*, 22.

14. Ibid., 69.

15. Ibid., 72.

16. Ibid., 73.

17. Ibid., 74.

18. Ibid., 96.

19. Ibid., 114. This is, in our opinion, the only flaw in Binswanger's theory—as becomes clear in the second part of this chapter, Christian love cannot be thought without a reflection on a co-origin of love in the very Beyng (*Seyn*).

20. Martin Heidegger, *Being and Time*, trans. Joan Stambaugh (Albany: State University of New York Press, 1996), 185, 243.

21. Schopenhauer, *The World as Will and Representation*, 402ff.

22. Binswanger, *Grundformen*, 157.

23. Ibid., 170. The solitariness of a couple designated by *Zweisamheit* here could also be described as *selbzweit*, with an expression coined on the example of the well-known German art historical term *selbdritt* (e.g., Anna Selbdritt— meaning part of a threesome).

24. Ibid., 170ff.

25. Ibid., 179.

26. See our chapter on *Clara*; Schelling, *Clara*, 14.

27. On this point, Binswanger was criticized by Michael Theunissen in his work *Der Andere: Studien zur Sozialontologie der Gegenwart* (Berlin: W. de Gruyter, 1965), chap. "Ludwig Binswangers Phänomenologie der erotischen Liebe." Theunissen first claims that Binswanger is dependent on his fundamental thesis, which he nevertheless negates. Theunissen also doubts that the phenomenology of love can be evolved in the direction of transcending in-the-world existence and at the same time deprive it of language and logos on this path

(the completion of love as silence in Binswanger). Thus, for Theunissen, the exuberance of love (as *Überschwang*) cannot reach beyond the boundaries of intentionality, as in his opinion in Binswanger it does (see Theunissen, *Der Andere*, 448). The problem with his interpretation, of which Theunissen is, of course, aware, is that in his critique he remains all the time on the plane of phenomenology, while Binswanger moves within the borderline ontological and theological fields (grace), where no one, with the exceptions of Feuerbach and Schelling, had trod before him.

28. Irigaray's *The Way of Love*, first published in 2002, marks this philosopher's transition into so-called (neo)cosmological thought.

29. Cf. Tine Hribar, *Dar biti* (*The Gift of Being*) (Ljubljana: Slovenska matica 2003), 5: "Without the mother, there would be none of us. From this point of view, we are a gift to ourselves, bestowed on us by her. As if the gift of Being, which I receive, were her own gift. But Being was a gift given to the mother, too. By whom? By her own mother? By the ancestors of humanity? By—if we turn to the beginning of all beginnings—God as Creator of the world? . . . Being is a gift from Being itself." In this passage, Hribar, in effect, thoroughly describes what future ontology should be.

30. Euripides, *The Suppliants*, trans. E. P. Coleridge, http://classics.mit.edu/Euripides/suppliants.html; accessed March 20, 2019.

31. Alain Badiou, "The Scene of Two," trans. Barbara P. Fulks, *Lacanian Ink* 21 (2003): 42–55. In this paper, Badiou follows the logic of the erotic in love, which also dominates Marion's work *The Erotic Phenomenon*.-

32. Schelling, *Clara*, 9, 14.

33. Irigaray, *To Be Born*, v.

34. See note 304 of this chapter.

35. Cf. Irigaray, *To Be Born*, 1.

36. Cf.: "Through its autonomous breathing and its sexuation, the little human gives birth to itself, it brings into the world a singular living being of which it will have to cultivate life, a life irreducible to any other, towards its achievement for itself and for the world into which it takes place" (Irigaray, *To Be Born*, 5).

37. Ibid., 76.

38. Ibid., 77.

39. Swedenborg devoted his work to this very question. When he speaks about children and their innocence, he distinguishes between children's and adults' spirituality, with the former being still incomplete or formless and thereby not yet developed. Although, according to his visionary words, in heaven, "infants are specially under the auspices of the Lord," this is still an imperfect form of love, which Swedenborg, proceeding from the Greek tradition, understands as an expression of *storge* or so-called parental love, which essentially differs from *agape*, *eros*, and *philia*. See Emmanuel Swedenborg, *Heaven and Its Wonders and*

Hell, trans. John C. Ager (West Chester: Swedenborg Foundation, 2009), §277. My derivations, on the contrary, will argue that the Trinitarian mystery contains the *archetype* or *matrix* of a perfect parental-matrixial or genealogical love, which is thus in the ontological sense a prerequisite or paradigm of all love.

40. Jürgen Moltmann, *The Trinity and the Kingdom: The Doctrine of God* (Minneapolis: Fortress Press, 1993), 57, 73.

41. Cf. Anselm Kyongsuk Min, "God as the Mystery of Sharing and Shared Love: Thomas Aquinas on the Trinity," in *The Cambridge Companion to The Trinity*, ed. Peter C. Phan (Cambridge: Cambridge University Press, 2011), 110.

42. Moltmann, *Trinity and the Kingdom*, 1745.

43. Irigaray points out in this regard the importance of (gentle) touch or caress in this relationship. Irigaray, *Una nuova cultura dell'energia*, 89.

44. In light of this constellation it is easy to recognize the absurdity (and cynicism) of Žižek's remark in the Introduction to his work *Antigone*, which is essentially a drama about an anti-genealogy of love, that Sophocles's Antigone "acts as a freakish and ruthless abomination; there definitely is something cold and monstrous about her, as is rendered by the contrast between her and her warmly human sister Ismene" (Slavoj Žižek, *Antigone* [London and New York: Bloomsbury Academic, 2016], 24). Cf. the chapter "The Three Lives of Antigone": "By dread things I am compelled. I know that. / I see the trap closing. Now I know what I am. / But while life is in me I ask only one thing: / let me go mad in my own way. In this madness of mine / I will try to imagine how events could be unwound / even further back, to avoid this horror I'm in . . ." (61). Here, Žižek also mocks Antigone's famous words, deliberately adding the expression *repeating* in the stage directions that introduce "My nature is to love. I cannot hate . . ." (59) to make them sound pathological and thus utterly stultify and trivialize "his" Antigone. This problem has been most extensively treated by Tine Hribar in *Ena je groza* (*One Is Fury*) (Ljubljana: Študentska založba, 2010), chap. IX ("Why Antigone Is a Nagging Issue to Žižek"). Hribar correctly points out the problem of Žižek's equating Christ and Antigone in what he terms their "death drive" (322), which stands in complete contrast to how Irigaray or Kristeva see the two.

45. Hribar, *Ena je groza*, 347ff.

46. Binswanger, *Grundformen*, 72.

47. Martin Heidegger, *The History of Beyng*, trans. Jeffrey Powell and William McNeill (Bloomington: Indiana University Press, 2015), 98–99, 8. All the brackets in the quoted text containing the original phrasing are mine.

48. Cf. ibid., §§ 89 and 90.

49. Ibid., 116.

50. Martin Heidegger, *Basic Writings*, ed. David Farrell Krell (London: Harper, 2008), 353.

51. Heidegger, *History of Beyng*, 60.

52. Cf. ibid., § 58.

53. See Otto, *Homeric Gods*, 102: "This goddess of the eternal miracle of love, says Lucretius at the opening of his poem, alone has the power to bestow peace upon the world. Deeply wounded by love, the war-god himself seeks her embrace and fixes hungry eyes on Aphrodite and gluts them with love. Then must the goddess lovingly whisper in his ear a sweet prayer for peace." Here, too, we can see the embrace (as in Binswanger and Irigaray) represents the primary means of this relationship of affection.

54. Ibid., 101.

55. Jacques Derrida, "Geschlecht: Sexual Difference, Ontological Difference," in *Feminist Interpretations of Martin Heidegger*, ed. Nancy J. Holland and Patricia Huntington (University Park: Pennsylvania State University Press, 2001), 60.

56. Trish Glazenbrook, "Heidegger and Ecofeminism," in *Feminist Interpretations of Martin Heidegger*, ed. Nancy J. Holland and Patricia Huntington (University Park: Pennsylvania State University Press, 2001), 221.

57. Carol Bigwood, "Sappho: The She-Greek Heidegger Forgot," in *Feminist Interpretations of Martin Heidegger*, ed. Nancy J. Holland and Patricia Huntington (University Park, PA: Pennsylvania State University Press, 2001), 165: "Heidegger and she? At first sight, they seem to be unpaired and awkward as two left shoes. . . . Women in Heidegger's corpus are disappointingly trivial and stereotypical, offered up as inconsequential examples that could just as easily be dropped."

58. Ibid., 176.

59. Otto, *Homeric Gods*, 24. Also: "Here is a maternal realm of forms, tensions, and ordinances whose holiness penetrates the entire human existence. At the center stands earth itself, as primal goddess, under many names. Out of her bosom well forth all life and all abundance, and into it they sink again. Birth and death both belong to her, and in her they close the sacred circle" (22–23). For the fragment by Epimenides see *Ancilla to the Pre-Socratic Philosophers*, 11.

60. Martin Heidegger, *Hölderlin's Hymn "The Ister,"* 51. "Unheimlich" in the sense of "tremendous," "fearful," "terrific" (within the latter, also with the sub-meaning "beautiful," see Tine Hribar, *Tragična etika svetosti* (*The Tragic Ethics of Holiness*) [Ljubljana: Slovenska matica, 1991], 136ff.).

61. *Sophocles in Two Volumes*, v. 523. Some have translated this line: "I was born to join in love, not in hate—that is my nature." See *The Three Theban Plays: Antigone; Oedipus the King; Oedipus at Colonus*, trans. Robert Fagles (London: Penguin Books, 1984), 86.

62. Hribar, *Tragična etika svetosti*, 124ff.

63. Irigaray, *Una nuova cultura dell' energia*, 103.

64. Seth Bernardete, *Sacred Transgresssions: A Reading of Sophocles' Antigone* (South Blend, IN: St. Augustine Press, 1999), 96ff.

65. Ibid., 98.
66. Heidegger, *History of Beyng*, 60.
67. We are following the translation of Richard C. Jebb, trans., *The Tragedies of Sophocles: Antigone* (London: Cambridge Universtity Press, 1904), 154 (v. 800). F. Storr's translation of this verse goes as follows: "For as consort still, enthroned with Justice above" (*Sophocles in Two Volumes*, 377; πάρεδρος ἐν ἀρχαῖς θεσμῶν / ἄμαχος γὰρ ἐμπαίζει θεὸς Ἀφροδίτα).
68. See Irigaray, *In the Beginning, She Was*, 126 (the chapter about Antigone).
69. Ibid., 127.
70. Tzelepis and Athanasiou, *Rewriting Difference*, 85. We can now view Mary's relationship toward Jesus in much the same light. See our chapter about Mary as *chóra*. This interruption of the primary order of life is the root not only of the divine Zeus's and later the human Creon's power, but all patriarchal (male or female) power that would establish itself by violence.
71. Hawke, *Aquamorphia*, ix, x (introduction by V. Karalis). See here the numerous mythological examples of triadic goddesses from the rich Indo-European legacy—cf. in particular the so called "matronae" (in the sense of "mothers'" or "belonging to mothers") in the Celts, especially in the depictions of triads of Goddesses associated with fruitfulness or fertility (even in the form of nursing mothers), mainly from the first century onward; see in this regard an exhaustive chapter about goddesses in ancient Indo-European (primarily Germanic) cultures—"Goddesses in Celtic Religion: The Matres and Matronae," by Noémie Beck, retrievable in full at: http://brewminate.com/goddesses-in-celtic-religion-the-matres-and-matronae/.
72. Cf. Heidegger, *The History of Beyng*, 330: "Truth, however, prevails in essence in the silence of beyng. This silence is the nearness of the last god." (Or goddess?). This is what Heidegger says about the event of appropriation (*Ereignis*) in his paper titled "The Way to Language": "There is nothing else from which the Appropriation itself can be derived, even less in whose terms it can be explained. . . . [Appropriation] is itself the most inconspicuous of inconspicuous phenomena, the simplest of simplicities, the nearest of the near, and the farthest of the far in which we mortals spend our lives." Martin Heidegger, *On the Way to Language*, trans. P. D. Hertz and J. Stambaugh (San Francisco: Harper and Row 1971), 135–36.
73. See Plato's *Timaeus*, 49a and 52a, in Plato, *Complete Works*.
74. "The new starting point in my account of the universe needs to be more complex than the earlier one. Then we distinguished two kinds, but now we must specify a third, one of a different sort. The earlier two sufficed for our previous account: one was proposed as a model, intelligible and always changeless, a second as an imitation of the model, something that possesses becoming and is visible. We did not distinguish a third kind at the time, because we thought that we could make do with the two of them. Now, however, it appears that

our account compels us to attempt to illuminate in words a kind that is difficult and vague. What must we suppose it do to and to be? This above all: it is a *receptacle* of all becoming—its wetnurse, as it were" (*Timaeus*, 49a, in Plato, *Complete Works*, 1251).

75. Kuang-Ming Wu, *Chinese Body Thinking*, 140–42; emphasis mine.

76. Ibid., 141.

77. Caputo, "The Absence of Monica," 160. For Heidegger's seminal work from the period 1936–38, see Martin Heidegger, *Contributions to Philosophy (of the Event)* (Bloomington: Indiana University Press, 2012).

78. Cf. Caputo, "The Absence of Monica," 161. The work referenced is *Stone*, by John Sallis (Bloomington: Indiana University Press, 1994).

79. Irigaray, *In the Beginning, She Was*, 23.

80. See Empedocles's fragments, in Kirk, Raven, and Schofield, *Presocratic Philosophers*, 290.

81. "Opposites are said with regard to the same or the same ones." Irigaray, *In the Beginning, She Was*, 28.

82. See Geoffrey Bennington and Jacques Derrida, eds., *Jacques Derrida*, trans. Geoffrey Bennington (Chicago: University of Chicago Press, 1993), chap. "The Mother: Chóra." Linking his discourse to Plato's *chóra* as "nurse, matrix, receptacle, mother" (209), Bennington describes the structure of this relationship in Derrida with the following words: "Everything that we have said implies that the mother is not a woman." (213) As this, ontologically speaking, locates Derrida's thought of *mother/woman/chóra* outside the (simple) father-mother or male-female dichotomy, it opens the possibility of linking this thought to the previously presented Moltmann's Trinitarian concept.

83. Binswanger, *Grundformen*, 22, 69.

84. My interpretation draws on ch. 5 of the book *Japanese Classical Theater in Films* by Keiko I. McDonald (Rutherford, NJ: Fairleigh Dickinson University Press; London and Toronto: Associated University Presses, 1994), 114ff.

85. Ibid., 119.

86. Food is explicitly present as one of the *elements* only in ancient Indian philosophy. See more about that in my article "Food in Ancient Indian Philosophy," in *Encyclopedia of Food and Agricultural Ethics*, ed. P. B. Thompson, D. M. Kaplan, K. Millar, L. Heldke, and R. Bawden (Dordrecht: Springer, 2014). The Indian language knows two expressions—*anna* (Eng. *food*) and *attr* (Eng. *eater*). They both derive from the same root of the word *ad*. Food and eater are, of course, firstly basic biological categories: plants and animals produce or represent food for one another throughout the eternal cycle of life. In ancient Indian thought we thus have four elements (air, water, earth, and fire) and food, and the latter became the most important element even in early Vedic philosophy, particularly in connection to the water cycle. Water is the principal source of life—from the rain falling onto the earth and "feeding" the plants, animals, humans and producing juices in them, to the humans, in whom it provides

for growth and reproduction (through semen). Food is hence the material substratum or substance of all beings, becoming the fundamental element of every living thing. Food is here in the philosophical sense more than just a biological ingredient or something we eat, drink, etc. We can distinguish between (1) food as primary matter or substance; (2) food as empirical food produced by beings (plants and animals) eating one another.

87. McDonald, *Japanese Classical Theater in Films*, 119.
88. Ibid., 121.

Chapter 6

1. Caputo, *The Insistence of God*.
2. On Feuerbach, see my *Breath of Proximity*, ch. 5.
3. Friedrich Nietzsche, *Ecce homo*, trans. D. Large (Oxford: Oxford University Press, 2007), 88.
4. Cf. Feuerbach, *Essence of Christianity*, 91–92: "Flesh and blood is life, and life alone is corporeal reality. But flesh and blood is nothing without the oxygen of sexual distinction."
5. See Friedrich Nietzsche, *The Anti-Christ: Curse of Christianity*, in *The Nietzsche Reader*, ed. K. A. Pearson and D. Large (Oxford: Blackwell, 2006), 486–99. Cf. also his praise of Islamic Spain in ch. 60 of the same book.
6. Schopenhauer was without doubt the first Western philosopher to deconstruct Hegelian Eurocentrist thought on the progression of world cultures on a horizontal East-West civilizational axis. But Schopenhauer's methodological problem lay in his inability to escape his metaphysical presuppositions that fully captured his otherwise beautiful and informed knowledge (and respect) of Hinduism, Buddhism, and other Eastern and Southeastern religious traditions. Cf. on this my paper on Schopenhauer and world religions: Škof, "Metaphysical Ethics Reconsidered." On Upanishads see ch. 2 of my *Breath of Proximity*.
7. In this chapter we will not discuss analogous developments in classical American pragmatism (Peirce, James, Dewey, Mead). More on this in my book *Pragmatist Variations on Ethical and Intercultural Life* (Lanham, MD: Lexington Books, 2012).
8. We think of breath in Merleau-Ponty's philosophy. See on this important relation Petri Berndtson, "The Possibility of a New Respiratory Ontology," in *Atmospheres of Breathing*, ed. Lenart Škof and Petri Berndtson (New York: State University of New York Press, 2018), 25–50.
9. Irigaray, *In the Beginning, She Was*, 159.
10. Irigaray, *Sharing the World*, 78ff.
11. In this chapter, the term *mesocosm* is used in the sense in which it is propounded and defended throughout my *Breath of Proximity*. Mesocosm was there interpreted as "a sign of our awakening of an ethical and spiritual

breath, which is the task and ontological property of each individual" (Škof, *Breath of Proximity*, 36). As a term, the "mesocosm" originates from a book on Newar religion authored by Robert I. Levy and Kedar Raj Rajopadhyaya, titled *Mesocosm: Hinduism and the Organization of a Traditional Newar City of Nepal* (Berkeley: University of California Press, 1990). In his beautiful exposition of a Vedic ritual, Michael Witzel argues for the reconstruction of this term within the Vedic magical interpretation of the world. (Michael Witzel, *Kaṭha Āraṇyaka* (Cambridge: Harvard University Press, 2004), xl, n. 129; cf. also Michael Witzel, "Macrocosm, Mesocosm, and Microcosm: The Persistent Nature of 'Hindu' Beliefs and Symbolic Forms," *International Journal of Hindu Studies* 1, no. 3 (1997): 501–39.

12. In this chapter, we will mostly refer to Luce Irigaray's most recent books, i.e., those forming the so called "third stage" of her thought, among them especially: *The Way of Love* (2002), *Between East and West* (2005), *Sharing the World* (2008), *In the Beginning, She Was* (2013), and *Una nuova cultura dell'energia* (2013).

13. Irigaray, *Way of Love*, xiv.

14. Irigaray, *In the Beginning, She Was*, 160.

15. Ibid., 161f.

16. Irigaray, *Una nuova cultura dell'energia*, 31; our translation.

17. Lenart Škof, "Breath of Hospitality: Silence, Listening, Care," *Nursing Ethics* 23, no. 8 (2016): 902–909.

18. Paul Celan, *Poems of Paul Celan*, trans. Michael Hamburger (New York: Persea Books, 2002), 209; from Paul Celan, *Atemwende* (Frankfurt am Main: Suhrkamp, 1967).

19. Irigaray, *Una nuova cultura dell'energia*, 29; our translation.

20. Schelling, *Philosophical Inquiries*, 70. Schelling uses here the rare Latinate-German word *Konspiration*, which he takes from Lat. *conspīro* ("to breathe together;" this word is of course related to *spiritus*). See on this Wirth, *Conspiracy of Life*, 2.

21. Hermann Spreckelmeyer, *Die philosophische Deutung des Sundenfalls bei Franz Baader* (Würzburg: C. J. Becker Universitäts Druckerei, 1938), 278. Translated by Robert Faas (previously unpublished translation owned by the author).

22. Ibid., 2f. In one of the most ancient speculative Vedic hymns "Creation" (*Rigveda* X.129, from the around the tenth century BC), we find the most precise explanation of this cosmic *breathing* of the Ground/Foundation of Being (That One, or *tad ekam*) itself: "That One breathed without wind by its independent will. There existed nothing else beyond that" (*The Rigveda*, 1608). We have analyzed this Vedic hymn and compared it with Schelling's ontology in detail at many different occasions, cf. especially Škof, *Breath of Proximity*, ch. 3. The poet-philosopher of this hymn argues that even before there were any signs of the existent or nonexistent, of death or life proper, there breathed this first One—by its own mysterious and "independent will" (ibid.).

23. Cf. Matt. 1:18, Luke 1:35. Also, for Schelling, "God must become Man in order that man may be brought back to God" (Schelling, *Philosophical Inquiries*, 57). But he also knows that man "is formed in his mother's womb" (35).

24. Roberto Mangabeira Unger, *The Religion of the Future* (Cambridge: Harvard University Press, 2014), 261. Cf. also his previous book *The Self Awakened: Pragmatism unbound* (Cambridge and London: Harvard University Press, 2007). On cosmic Jesus, see Caputo's *The Insistence of God*: "I treat Jesus as a Judeo-pagan prophet and healer, in tune with the animals and the elements, in whose body the elements dance their cosmic dance, supplying as it does a conduit through which the elements flow, and I treat the elements as a cosmic grace which is channeled by the body of Jesus" (Caputo, *Insistence of God*, 251f.). This indeed is a simply a beautiful depiction of Jesus in his cosmico-theological role. Of course, among the four elements, *pneuma* holds the most exquisite position, since his entire body is filled with this cosmic wind, or spiritual energy: "Yeshua was the sort of man whose *pneuma* filled any room that he entered" (254).

25. Irigaray, *Il mistero di Maria*, 13f.

26. Creon is a paradigm for the progression of evil (the politics of power, tyranny, authority) into the world of free and living breath: "Miming the living, the diabolic does not breathe, or does not breathe any longer. It takes away the air from the others, from the world. It suffocates with its sterile repetitions, its presumptuous imitations, with its wishes deprived of respect for life" (Irigaray, *Key Writings*, 166).

27. Antigone's justice and her life are of a cosmic origin. With his deed, Creon has inflicted this world with the diabolic, an evil that cosmic order. Cf. Job 34:14–15: "If he should take back his spirit to himself, / and gather to himself his breath, / all flesh would perish together, and all mortals return to dust." Verse 15 reads better in French translation: "toute chair expirerait à la fois . . . ;" *La Bible, TOB* (Paris: Editions de Cerf, 1988). This precisely is God's spiritual breath *as reserve* for the humanity, as we shall see later.

28. Irigaray, *Key Writings*, 168. Also, Irigaray states: "God is us, we are divine if we are woman and man in a perfect way" (169).

29. Ibid., 252.

30. *Buddhist Scriptures*, ed. Donald S. Lopez Jr. (London: Penguin, 2004), 132.

31. Irigaray, *In the Beginning, She Was*, 119–35. "The maternal genealogy favours the values of life, of generation, of growth" (127).

32. Gaston Bachelard, *Air and Dreams: An Essay on the Imagination of Movement*, trans. Edith R. Farrell and C. Frederick Farrell (Dallas: The Dallas Institute of Humanities and Culture, 2011), ch. 5, "Nietzsche and the ascensional psyche," 136–37.

33. Ibid., 127.

34. See about Buddha's and Jesus's roles for the future of humanity in Irigaray, *Una nuova cultura dell'energia*, 120. They represent, for her, a paradigm of a new global community, based on heart, breath, listening, language, and thinking.

35. On respiratory ontology in Bachelard and especially in Merleau-Ponty's thought see Petri Berndtson, "The Inspiration and Expiration of Being: The Immense Lung and the Cosmic Breathing as the Sources of Dreams, Poetry, and Philosophy," in *Thinking in Dialogue: Paths into the Phenomenology of Merleau-Ponty*, ed. Karel Novotný, Taylor S. Hammer, Anne Gléonec, and Petr Špecián (Bucharest: Zeta Books, 2010), 281–93. See, on Merleau-Ponty's phenomenology of breathing, Berndtson, "The Possibility of a New Respiratory Ontology." Merleau-Ponty writes in his *Eye and Mind*: "We speak of 'inspiration,' and the word should be taken literally. There really is inspiration and expiration of Being, respiration in Being, action and passion so slightly discernable that it becomes impossible to distinguish between who sees and who is seen, who paints and what is painted" (cit. after Berndtson, "The Inspiration and Expiration of Being," 282).

36. Irigaray, *Sharing the World*, 31.

37. Irigaray, *Key Writings*, 152 ("The Redemption of Women"). See also her insightful thoughts on the *Assumption of Mary* on 163, "whose virginity allows her to rise into heaven without any death or resurrection similar to those of her son."

38. Cf. Elizabeth Schussler-Fiorenza, *In memory of Her: Feminist Theological Reconstruction of Christian Origins* (Minneapolis: Fortress, 1983), 333.

39. Cf., on haptology as related to the dead body of Christ in the tomb, Gregg Lambert, "Untouchable," in *Derrida and Religion*, ed. Yvonne Sherwood and Kevin Hart (New York and London: Routledge, 2005), 363–74.

40. Irigaray, *Key Writings*, 168 ("The Age of the Breath").

41. In chapter 70 of his main work, Schopenhauer argues that this faith does not originate in ourselves, but "like something coming to us from outside" (Schopenhauer, *World as Will and Representation*, 406). This new birth is grace, which, for Schopenhauer, constitutes our freedom (freedom of the will), based on faith (which is knowledge, for Schopenhauer). With this effect, our motives, previously based on the "kingdom of nature," are thus a part of the "kingdom of grace" (408). This is precisely what Irigaray wanted to say with her statement, namely, that "our breath is not dependent only to some necessities we are facing" (Irigaray, *Una nuova cultura dell'energia*, 29).

42. Giorgio Agamben, *The Coming Community*, trans. Michael Hardt (Minneapolis and London: University of Minnesota Press, 2009), 14ff. This is a reference to a passage from Paul's First Epistle to the Corinthians (1 Cor. 15:28: "After everything is under the power of God's Son, he will put himself under the power of God, who put everything under his Son's power. Then God will mean everything to everyone"). For Amalric see *Encyclopaedia Britannica*, vol. 1 (1911 edition), 779, entry Amalric (Fr. Amaury) of Bena (d. c. 1204–07): "French theologian, was born in the latter part of the 12th century at Bena, a village in the diocese of Chartres. He taught philosophy and theology at the University of Paris and enjoyed a great reputation as a subtle dialectician; his lectures developing the philosophy of Aristotle attracted a large circle of hearers.

In 1204 his doctrines were condemned by the university, and, on a personal appeal to Pope Innocent III., the sentence was ratified, Amalric being ordered to return to Paris and recant his errors. His death was caused, it is said, by grief at the humiliation to which he had been subjected. In 1209 ten of his followers were burnt before the gates of Paris, and Amalric's own body was exhumed and burnt and the ashes given to the winds. The doctrines of his followers, known as the Amalricians, were formally condemned by the fourth Lateran Council in 1215. Amalric appears to have derived his philosophical system from Eriugena (q.v.), whose principles he developed in a one-sided and strongly pantheistic form. Three propositions only can with certainty be attributed to him: (1) that God is all; (2) that every Christian is bound to believe that he is a member of the body of Christ, and that this belief is necessary for salvation; (3) that he who remains in love of God can commit no sin. These three propositions were further developed by his followers, who maintained that God revealed Himself in a threefold revelation, the first in Abraham, marking the epoch of the Father; the second in Christ, who began the epoch of the Son; and the third in Amalric and his disciples, who inaugurated the era of the Holy Ghost. Under the pretext that a true believer could commit no sin, the Amalricians indulged in every excess, and the sect does not appear to have long survived the death of its founder.

43. Irigaray, *Key Writings*, "The Age of Breath," 168. See also: "God is us, we are divine if we are woman and man in a perfect way" (169). For more about Amalric of Bena see my paper "The Third Age: Reflections On Our Hidden Material Core," *Sophia* 59:1 (2020), 83–94.

44. All quotes from Plato, *Complete Works*.

45. See Toril Moi, ed., *The Kristeva Reader* (Oxford: Blackwell, 1996), 91ff.

46. See Luka Trebežnik, "Odnos med dekonstrukcijo in religijo pri Jacquesu Derridaju: med nihilizmom in mesijanizmom" (PhD diss., University of Ljubljana, 2016), ch. 1.3.3.3: "Chóra je ženska" (*Chóra* is feminine). Trebežnik writes: "Philosophy wants to speak about *chóra*, it wants to speak about the woman, but its phallogocentric nature makes it impossible. Analogously with the cosmos, the *chóra* brings forth philosophy, as it enables representations of opposition. Just as we people cannot remember our birth, philosophy cannot speak about its wet nurse, at least not philosophically. What remains is an alternative—whether to speak in a non-philosophical manner or not speak at all. Philosophy always speaks about the father and the sons, with the woman representing the trap and the temptation of philosophy" (83). Cf. also Derrida's fragmentary paper *Khóra*, in *On the Name*, ed. Thomas Dutoit (Stanford: Stanford University Press, 1995).

47. Jacques Derrida, "How to Avoid Speaking: Denials," in *Derrida and Negative Theology*, ed. Harold Coward and Toby Foshay (Albany: State University of New York Press, 1992), 107.

48. Cf. on this point Graham Ward, "Deconstructive Theology," in *The Cambridge Companion to Postmodern Theology*, ed. Kevin J. Vanhoozer (Cambridge: Cambridge University Press, 2003), 85. But Ward is extremely critical here and

compares this constellation of undecidability to Hegel's bad infinite or nihilism: "The future is endlessly coming; the hope is then never arrived at. It is always only arriving. . . . *Différance* on such a reading is a form of what Hegel would call the bad infinite. If this third position is correct, then we are close again to a nihilism, for, while decisions can be made and acted upon, decisions as such are rendered local, pragmatic, and fundamentally, arbitrary." Ward seem to have become ensnared in a deconstruction trap and did not let himself be touched by the atmosphere or conspiracy of peace taking place through *chóra* and its silent absence.

49. I am indebted to Jack Caputo for referring me to the link between *chóra* (as I developed it in the chapter about the concubine of a Levite) and *différance*.

50. An interesting parallel to this thought can be found in *Untie the Strong Woman*, by Clarissa Pinkola Estés (Boulder: Sounds True, 2013). This book, entirely dedicated to the Great Mother Goddess and the power of her compassionate affection (as well as to various folk varieties of Mary and her worship such as the Black Virgin Mother), features Xilonen (Chicomecoatl) as the Goddess Mother of Maize in the chapter about the Aztec emperor Moctezuma. In the opinion of the author, this Great Mother of the ancient Aztec peoples was the one who loved and fed all her children. On the three aspects of the Goddess (Virgin Goddess—Mother Goddess—Black Goddess), see Marko Pogačnik's excellent book *The Daughter of Gaia: Rebirth of the Divine Feminine* (Findhorn: Findhorn Press, 2001). Pogačnik—a Slovenian UNESCO artist for peace and environmental thinker—testifies to an urgent need for our global "civilization" to re-acknowledge and revive the suppressed orders of femininity, so greatly needed to reestablish our lost partnership with gods, nature, and ourselves.

Postlude

1. Cf., for Ettinger, her essay "From Proto-Ethical Compassion to Responsibility," and also the essay on Antigone, "Transgressing With-In-To the Feminine," in *Feminist Readings of Antigone*, ed. Fanny Söderbäck (Albany: State University of New York Press, 2010), 195–214. For Antigone see also Ettinger's essay "Antigone with(out) Jocaste," in *Interrogating Antigone*, ed. S. E. Wilmer and Audrone Žukauskaite (Oxford: Oxford University Press, 2010), 212–28.

2. Kristeva, "Antigone," 225.

3. See Kathrin H. Rosenfield, *Antigone: Sophocles' Art, Hölderlin's Insight* (Aurora, CO: The Davies Group, 2010), 20f. (Sophocles's *basilida* would otherwise be translated as being the last of the royal house, "daughter/child of kings," or perhaps "princess"; cf. ibid., 95).

4. See, "Anmerkungen zur Antigone," in Friedrich Hölderlin, *Werke in zwei Bänden*, bd. 2, ed. Günther Mieth (München and Wien: Carl Hanser

Verlag, 1982), 451–58. The passage goes as follows: "Es ist ein großer Behelf der geheimarbeitenden Seele, daß sie auf dem höchsten Bewußtsein dem Bewußtsein ausweicht und, ehe sie wirklich der gegenwärtige Gott ergreift, mit kühnem, oft sogar blasphemischem Worte diesem begegnet und so die heilige lebende Möglichkeit des Geistes erhält" (453). See also Kathrin H. Rosenfield, "Hölderlins' Antigone und Sophokles' tragisches Paradox," *Poetica* 33, no. 3/4 (2001): 465–501.

5. Cf. *Antigone*, in Hölderlin, *Werke in zwei Bänden*, 434: "Die Königin, Thebes Herrn!"

6. Rosenfield, *Antigone*, 96.

7. In conclusion, Rosenfield writes the following: "So much, then, for the idea that Antigone harbors an incestuous passion for her dead brother. . . . As the fruit of a unique incest, she has no proper father or mother, belongs to no proper generation, has no proper status in the world. She is at once too much and too little, wandering through a world that has no place for her" (146).

8. *Sophocles in Two Volumes*, 347.

9. Luce Irigaray, *Speculum of the Other Woman*, trans. Gillian C. Gill (Ithaca: Cornell University Press, 1985), 218f.

10. Hölderlin begins his translation of *Antigone* with Antigone's famous words to her sister Ismene ("Ismene, sister of my blood and heart"; cf. *Sophocles in Two Volumes*, 315), and translating the Greek Ὦ κοινὸν αὐτάδελφον Ἰσμήνης κάρα, with an idiosyncratic "Gemeinsamschwesterliches! O Ismenes Haupt!" For the English rendering of this beautiful neologism by Hölderlin we are using Rosenfield's equally insightful translation with "shared-sisterly . . . head." In a more extensive version, and by following Wolfgang Schadewaldt's modern translation of *Antigone* from 1974 with "Gemeinsames, der eignen Schwester, o Ismenes Haupt!" this now reads as: "Shared (Head,) of a true sister, o head of Ismene" (Rosenfield, *Antigone*, 34, 36).

11. Kristeva, "Antigone," 222.

12. *Sophocles in Two Volumes*, 381 and 383 (vv. 850 and 880).

13. "Antigone and Jesus co-breathe" (expressed in Slovenian dual). Rosenfield namely points to Hölderlin's efforts "into recovering the feel of the Greek dual, a middle-term between singular and plural that has no equivalent in modern languages . . . to express the intimate association of two beings *melted together* . . . into a *single thing* or a single principle."(*Antigone*, 39). We may add that in modern Slovenian language actually dual is wholly preserved and thus enables us to express this highest ethical conspiracy of Antigone and Jesus also grammatically.

14. See John Trinick, *The Fire-Tried Stone: An Enquiry into the Development of a Symbol* (London: Wordens of Cornwall Limited in association with Vincent Stuart and John M. Watkins, 1967), 102. Baader points out that already St Bernard called the Holy Spirit "the kiss of Father and the Son" (ibid.). The

book of Franz von Baader referred to is titled *On the Emancipation of Catholicism*. On Antigone as compared (but *not* identified) to Christ see Manfred Függe, *Verweigerung oder Neue Ordunung. Jean Anouilhs Antigone im politischen und ideologischen Kontext der Besatzungszeit 1940–1944, I* (Rheinfelden: Shäuble Verlag, 1982), 390.

15. In a PhD dissertation written by Finnish respiratory philosopher and my fellow co-breather Petri Berndtson, we find the following note on the phenomenon of the breath-kiss: "It is also important to mention here in relation to this Christian context of conspiracy that originally the Christian notion of 'conspiratio' has its beginning already in the first century Christianity as Ivan Illich writes: 'In the Christian liturgy of the first century, the *osculum* [kiss] assumed a new function. It became one of two high points in the celebration of the Eucharist. *Conspiratio*, the mouth-to-mouth kiss, became the solemn liturgical gesture by which participants in the cult-action shared their breath or spirit with one another. It came to signify their union in one Holy Spirit, the community that takes shape in God's breath. The *ecclesia* came to be through a public ritual action, the liturgy, and the soul of this liturgy was the *conspiratio*. Explicitly, corporeally, the central Christian celebration was understood as a co-breathing, a con-spiracy, the bringing about of a common atmosphere, a divine milieu. . . . [In the early Christian celebration of the Eucharist] [c]*onspiratio* became the strongest, clearest and most unambiguously somatic expression for the entirely nonhierarchical creation of a fraternal spirit in preparation for the unifying meal.'" This beautiful passage appears in Ivan Illich, "The Cultivation of Conspiracy," in *The Challenges of Ivan Illich: A Collective Reflection*, ed. Lee Hoinacki and Carl Mitcham (Albany: State University of New York Press, 2002), 240. Cf. Berndtson, "Phenomenological Ontology of Breathing," 230 n. 890.

16. Ettinger, "Transgressing With-In-To the Feminine," 205.

17. For the matrixial covenant see Ettinger, "The Becoming Threshold of Matrixial Borderlines," 44. Cf. also *The Matrixial Borderspace*, 112–13.

18. As stated by Kuang-Ming Wu in *On Chinese Body Thinking*: "[E]very human relation worthy of its name is a mothering and wombing—your being vacuous draws me forth, lets me become as I am. . . . The inner personal touch fills the void in me and in you, making us one. Yet we remain two, for two-ness enables touch. We are thus two in one, and one in two, thanks to our personal void and touch inside. All this describes mutual fulfilment. Personal void generates love—inner touch—that *mothers us* to grow into ourselves" (Wu, *On Chinese Body Thinking*, 140–42).

BIBLIOGRAPHY

Aeschylus. *The Oresteia*. Translated by Robert Fagles. Reprint, London: Penguin Books, 1977.

———. "Prometheus Bound." In *Aeschylus: Suppliant Maidens. Persians. Prometheus. Seven against Thebes*. Translated by Herbert W. Smyth. Loeb Classical Library, vol. 145. Cambridge: Harvard University Press, 1926.

Agamben, Giorgio. *The Coming Community*. Translated by Michael Hardt. Minneapolis and London: University of Minnesota Press, 2009.

Anand, Subhash. *Story as Theology: An Interpretative Study of Five Episodes from the Mahābhārata*. New Delhi: Intercultural Publications, 1996.

Ancilla to the Pre-Socratic Philosophers. Translated by Kathleen Freeman. Cambridge: Harvard University Press, 1996.

Anouilh, Jean. *Plays: One (Antigone, Léocadia; The Waltz of the Toreadors; The Lark; Poor Bitos)*. London: Methuen, 1991.

Aristotle. *The Complete Works of Aristotle*. Vol. 1. Edited by Jonathan Barnes. Princeton: Princeton University Press, 1984.

Avsenik Nabergoj, Irena. *Hrepenenje in skušnjava v svetu literature: motiv Lepe Vide*. Ljubljana: Mladinska knjiga, 2010.

Bachelard, Gaston. *Air and Dreams: An Essay on the Imagination of Movement*. Translated by Edith R. Farrell and C. Frederick Farrell. Dallas: The Dallas Institute of Humanities and Culture, 2011.

Badiou, Alain. "The Scene of Two." Translated by Barbara P. Fulks. *Lacanian Ink* 21 (2003): 42–55.

———, and Slavoj Žižek. *Hvalnica ljubezni*. Translated by Stojan Pelko and Alenka Zupančič Žerdin. Ljubljana: Analecta, 2010.

Baker, Aryn. "The Secret War Crime." *Time*, March 21, 2015.

Bartolo, Pietro, and Lidia Tilotta. *Tears of Salt: A Doctor's Story of the Refugee Crisis*. Toronto: W. W. Norton, 2019.

Benjamin, Walter. *The Arcades Project*. Translated by Howard Eiland and Kevin McLaughlin. Cambridge and London: The Belknap Press of Harvard University Press, 2002.

Bennington, Geoffrey, and Jacques Derrida, eds. *Jacques Derrida*. Translated by Geoffrey Bennington. Chicago: University of Chicago Press, 1993.

Benson, Bruce E., and Norman Wirzba, eds. *Words of Life*. New York: Fordham University Press, 2010.

Benz, Ernst. *Der Vollkommene Mensch nach Jacob Böhme*. Stuttgart: Kohlhammer, 1937.

Bergmann, Werner, and Gisbert Hoffman. "G. H. Mead und die Tradition der Phänomenologie." In *Das Problem der Intersubjektivität*, edited by Hans Joas, 93–130. Frankfurt am Main: Suhrkamp, 1985.

Bernardete, Seth. *Sacred Transgressions: A Reading of Sophocles' Antigone*. South Bend, IN: St. Augustine, 1999.

Berndtson, Petri. "The Inspiration and Expiration of Being: The Immense Lung and the Cosmic Breathing as the Sources of Dreams, Poetry, and Philosophy." In *Thinking in Dialogue: Paths into the Phenomenology of Merleau-Ponty*, edited by Karel Novotný, Taylor S. Hammer, Anne Gléonec, and Petr Špecián, 281–93. Bucharest: Zeta Books, 2010.

———. "Phenomenological Ontology of Breathing: The Phenomenologico-Ontological Interpretation of the Barbaric Conviction of We Breathe Air and a New Philosophical Principle of Silence of Breath, Abyss of Air." PhD diss., University of Jyväskylä, 2018.

———. "The Possibility of a New Respiratory Ontology." In *Atmospheres of Breathing*, edited by Lenart Škof and Petri Berndtson, 25–50. Albany: State University of New York Press, 2018.

Bible, La, TOB. Paris: Editions de Cerf, 1988.

Bigwood, Carol. "Sappho: The She-Greek Heidegger Forgot." In *Feminist Interpretations of Martin Heidegger*, edited by Nancy J. Holland and Patricia Huntington, 165–95. University Park: Pennsylvania State University Press, 2001.

Binswanger, Ludwig. *Grundformen und Erkenntnis menschlichen Daseins*. Heidelberg: Roland Asanger Verlag, 1993.

Booth, Kelvin J. "Embodied Mind and the Mimetic Basis for Taking the Role of the Other." In *George Herbert Mead in the Twenty-First Century*, edited by F. Thomas Burke and Krzysztof Piotr Skowroński, 137–48. Lanham, MD: Lexington Books, 2013.

Brague, Rémi. *La loi de Dieu: Histoire philosophique d'une alliance*. Paris: Editions Gallimard, 2005.

Buchler, Justus, ed. *Philosophical Writings of Peirce*. New York: Dover, 1955.

Buddhist Scriptures. Edited by Donald S. Lopez Jr. London: Penguin, 2004.

Burke, F. Thomas, and Krzysztof Piotr Skowroński, eds. *George Herbert Mead in the Twenty-First Century*. Lanham, MD: Lexington Books, 2013.

Burkert, Walter. *Griechische Religion der archaischen und klassischen Epoche*. Stuttgart: Kohlhammer, 2011.

Butler, Judith. *Frames of War: When Is Life Grievable?* London and New York: Verso, 2010.

Caputo, John D. "The Absence of Monica: Heidegger, Derrida, and Augustine's Confessions." In *Feminist Interpretations of Martin Heidegger*, edited by Nancy J. Holland and Patricia Huntington, 149–164. University Park: Pennsylvania State University Press, 2001.

———. *The Insistence of God: A Theology of Perhaps*. Bloomington and Indianapolis: Indiana University Press, 2013.

Celan, Paul. *Atemwende*. Frankfurt am Main: Suhrkamp, 1967.

———. *Poems of Paul Celan*. Translated by Michael Hamburger. New York: Persea Books, 2002.

Charen, Hannes. "Hegel Reading Antigone." *Monatshefte* 103, no. 4 (2001): 504–16.

Ching-Sze Wang, Jessica. *John Dewey in China: To Teach and to Learn*. Albany: State University of New York Press, 2007.

Chrétien, Jean-Louis. *The Call and the Response*. Translated by Anne A. Davenport. New York: Fordham University Press, 2004.

Claudel, Paul. *Feuilles de Saints*. Paris: Gallimard, 2002.

———. *Five Great Odes*. Translated by Edward Lucie-Smith. Chester Springs: Dufour Editions, 1970.

Coward, Harold, and Toby Foshay, eds. *Derrida and Negative Theology*. Albany: State University of New York Press, 1992.

Deleuze, Gilles. *Pure Immanence: Essays on a Life*. Translated by Anne Boyman. New York: Zone Books, 2005.

Derrida, Jacques. *Acts of Religion*. Edited by Gil Anidjar. New York and London: Routledge, 2002.

———. "Force of Law: The 'Mystical Foundation of Authority.'" In *Acts of Religion*, edited by Gil Anidjar, 228–98. New York and London: Routledge, 2002.

———. "Geschlecht: Sexual Difference, Ontological Difference." In *Feminist Interpretations of Martin Heidegger*, edited by Nancy J. Holland and Patricia Huntington, 53–72. University Park: Pennsylvania State University Press, 2001.

———. *The Gift of Death*. Translated by David Wills. Chicago and London: The University of Chicago Press, 1995.

———. "Given Time: The Time of the King." *Critical Inquiry* 18, no. 2 (1992): 161–87.

———. *Glas*. New York: University of Nebraska, 1990.

———. "How to Avoid Speaking: Denials." In *Derrida and Negative Theology*, edited by Harold Coward and Toby Foshay, 73–142. Albany: State University of New York Press, 1992.

———. *Khóra*. In *On the Name*, edited by Thomas Dutoit. Stanford: Stanford University Press, 1995.

———. *Of Hospitality*. Translated by Rachel Bowlby. Stanford: Stanford University Press, 2000.

Deshpande, Renukadas Yeshwantrao. *The Ancient Tale of Savitri*. Pondicherry: Sri Aurobindo International Centre of Education, 1995.

Detienne, Marcel, and Jean Pierre Vernant. *Cunning Intelligence in Greek Culture and Society*. Translated by Janet Lloyd. Chicago and London: The University of Chicago Press, 1991.

Deuser, Hermann. *Religionsphilosophie*. Berlin and New York: Walter de Gruyter, 2008.

Dewey, John. *John Dewey, Lectures in China, 1919–1920*. Edited by Robert W. Clopton. Honolulu: The University Press of Hawaii, 1973.

Douglas, Mary. *Leviticus as Literature*. Oxford and New York: Oxford University Press, 2000.

Dussel, Enrique. *Ethics of Liberation in the Age of Globalization and Exclusion*. Durham and London: Duke University Press, 2013.

———. "Transmodernity and Interculturality." *Poligrafi* 11, no. 41/42 (2006): 5–40.

Estés, Clarissa Pinkola. *Untie the Strong Woman*. Boulder, CO: Sounds True, 2013.

Ettinger, Bracha L. "The Becoming Threshold of Matrixial Borderlines." In *Travelers' Tales: Narratives of Home and Displacement*, edited by George Robertson, Melinda Mash, Lisa Tickner, and Jon Bird, 38–62. London: Routledge, 1994.

———. "From Proto-Ethical Compassion to Responsibility: Besideness and the Three Primal Mother-Phantasies of Not-enoughness, Devouring, and Abandonment." *Athena* 2 (2007): 100–35.

———. "Matrix and Metamorphosus." *Trouble in the Archives*, special issue of *differences* 4, no. 3 (1992): 176–208.

———. "Matrix: Beyond the Phallus." *Women's Art Magazine* 56 (1994): 12–15.

———. *The Matrixial Borderspace*. Minneapolis and London: University of Minnesota Press, 2006.

———. "Transgressing With-In-To the Feminine." In *Feminist Readings of Antigone*, edited by Fanny Söderbäck, 195–214. Albany: State University of New York Press, 2010.

———. "Antigone with(out) Jocaste." In *Interrogating Antigone*, edited by S. E. Wilmer and Audrone Žukauskaite, 212–28. Oxford: Oxford University Press, 2010.

Euripides. *Medea and Other Plays*. Translated by E. P. Coleridge. Lawrence, KS: Digireads, 2012.

———. *The Suppliants*. Translated by E. P. Coleridge. http://classics.mit.edu/Euripides/suppliants.html; accessed March 20, 2019.

Evripid. *Alkestida*. Translated by J. Ivanc. Ljubljana: SNG Drama, 2013.

Feuerbach, Ludwig. *Das Wesen des Christentums*. Frankfurt am Main: Suhrkamp, 1976.

———. *The Essence of Christianity*. Translated by G. Eliot. New York: Harper, 1957.
———. *The Fiery Brook: Selected Writings of Ludwig Feuerbach*. Translated by Zawar Hanfi. Garden City, NY: Doubleday, 1972.
———. "Über Spiritualismus und Materialismus." In *Kritiken und Abhandlungen III, 1844–1866*. Frankfurt am Main: Suhrkamp, 1975.
———. *Werke in sechs Bänden*. Bd. 3. Kritiken und Abhandlungen II, 1839–1843. Frankfurt am Main: Suhrkamp, 1975.
———. *Werke in sechs Bänden*. Bd. 4. Kritiken und Abhandlungen III, 1844–1866. Frankfurt am Main: Suhrkamp, 1975.
Flügge, Manfred. *Verweigerung oder Neue Ordunung. Jean Anouilhs Antigone im politischen und ideologischen Kontext der Besatzungszeit 1940–1944*, I, II. Rheinfelden: Shäuble Verlag, 1982.
Francis, Pope. *Visit to Lampedusa: Homily of the Holy Father*. Rome: Libreria Editrice Vaticana, 2013.
Furlan Štante, Nadja. "Transcendence in (Eco)feminist Christian Hermeneutics." *Bogoslovni vestnik* 77, no. 3/4 (2017): 589–99.
Garner, Richard. "Death and Victory in Euripides' Alcestis." *Classical Antiquity* 7, no. 1 (1988): 58–71.
Giesen, Klaus-Gerd, Carool Kersten, and Lenart Škof, eds. *The Poesis of Peace: Narratives, Cultures, and Philosophies*. New York and London: Routledge, 2017.
Glazenbrook, Trish. "Heidegger and Ecofeminism." In *Feminist Interpretations of Martin Heidegger*, edited by Nancy J. Holland and Patricia Huntington, 221–51. University Park: Pennsylvania State University Press, 2001.
Gordon, Lewis R. *Her Majesty's Other Children: Sketches of Racism from a Neocolonial Age*. Lanham, MD: Rowman and Littlefield, 1977.
Grange, Joseph. *John Dewey, Confucius, and Global Philosophy*. Abany: State University of New York Press, 2004.
Grau, Alexander. "Clara: Über Schellings gleichnamiges Fragment." *Zeitschrift für philosophische Forschung* 51, no. 4 (1997): 590–610.
Greenberg, Reesa, Bruce W. Ferguson, and Sandy Nairne, eds. *Thinking about Exhibitions*. London: Routledge, 1997.
Grosz, Elizabeth. *The Incorporeal: Ontology, Ethics, and the Limits of Materialism*. New York: Columbia University Press, 2017.
Grušovnik, Tomaž, Eduardo Mendieta, and Lenart Škof, eds. *Borders and Debordering: Topologies, Praxes, Hospitableness*. Lanham, MD: Lexington Books, 2018.
Guenther, Lisa. "'Like a Maternal Body': Emmanuel Levinas and the Motherhood of Moses." *Hypatia* 21, no. 1 (2006): 119–36.
Hall, David L., and Roger T. Ames. *The Democracy of the Dead: Dewey, Confucius, and the Hope for Democracy in China*. Chicago and Lasalle, IL: Open Court, 1999.

Hawke, Shé. *Aquamorphia: Falling for Water*. Carindale: Interactive Press, 2014.
———. "The Exile of Greek Metis: Recovering a Maternal Divine Ontology." *Poligrafi* 23, no. 91/92 (2018): 41–75.
Hegel, Georg Wilhelm Friedrich. *Lectures on the Philosophy of Religion*. Part II, 3.αβ. Translated by R. F. Brown, P. C. Hodgson, and J. M. Stewart. Berkeley: University of California Press, 1984.
———. *Phenomenology of Spirit*. Translated by A. V. Miller. Oxford and New York: Oxford University Press, 1977.
Heidegger, Martin. *Basic Writings*. Edited by David Farrell Krell. London: Harper, 2008.
———. *Being and Time*. Translated by Joan Stambaugh. Albany: State University of New York Press, 1996.
———. *Contribution to Philosophy (of the Event)*. Bloomington: Indiana University Press, 2012.
———. *Elucidations of Hölderlin's Poetry*. Translated by Keith Hoeller. New York: Humanity Books, 2000.
———. *The History of Beyng*. Translated by Jeffrey Powell and William McNeill. Bloomington: Indiana University Press, 2015.
———. *Hölderlin's Hymn "The Ister."* Translated by William McNeill and Julia Davis. Bloomington and Indianapolis: Indiana University Press, 1996.
———. *On the Way to Language*. Translated by P. D. Hertz and J. Stambaugh. San Francisco: Harper and Row, 1971.
———. *Poetry, Language, and Thought*. Translated by Albert Hofstadter. New York: Harper and Row, 1971.
Hesiod. *Theogony and Works and Days*. Translated by Martin L. West. Oxford: Oxford University Press, 2008.
Hesiod and Theognis. London: Penguin Books, 2000.
Hölderlin, Friedrich. *Werke in zwei Bänden*. Bd. 2. Edited by Günther Mieth. München and Wien: Carl Hanser Verlag, 1982.
———. *Hyperion, or the Hermit in Greece*. Translated by Howard Gaskill. Cambridge: Open Book Publishers, 2019.
Holland, Nancy J., and Patricia Huntington, eds. *Feminist Interpretations of Martin Heidegger*. University Park: The Pennsylvania State University Press, 2001.
Holmes, Emily A. *Flesh Made Word: Medieval Women Mystics, Writing, and the Incarnation*. Waco, TX: Baylor University Press, 2013.
Holy Bible, The. New Revised Standard Version. Nashville: Thomas Nelson, 1990.
Homer. *The Odyssey*. Edited by Louise Loomis. Translated by Samuel Butler. New York: Wildside, 2007.
Hribar, Tine. *Dar biti*. Ljubljana: Slovenska matica, 2003.
———. *Ena je groza*. Ljubljana: Študentska založba, 2010.
———. *Tragična etika svetosti*. Ljubljana: Slovenska matica, 1991.

Illich, Ivan. "The Cultivation of Conspiracy." In *The Challenges of Ivan Illich: A Collective Reflection*, edited by Lee Hoinacki and Carl Mitcham, 233–42. Albany: State University of New York Press, 2002.
Ireton, Sean. *An Ontological Study of Death: From Hegel to Heidegger*. Pittsburgh: Duquesne University Press, 2007.
Irigaray, Luce. *Between East and West: From Singularity to Community*. Translated by Stephen Pluhácek. Delhi: New Age Books, 2005.
———. "Ethical Gestures toward the Other." *Poligrafi* 15, no. 57 (2008): 3–23.
———. *Il mistero di Maria*. Roma: Paoline, 2010.
———. *In the Beginning, She Was*. London: Bloomsbury, 2013.
———. *Key writings*. London: Bloomsbury, 2004.
———. *Marine Lover of Friedrich Nietzsche*. Translated by Gillian C. Gill. New York: Columbia University Press, 1991.
———. *Sharing the World*. London: Continuum, 2008.
———. *Speculum of the Other Woman*. Translated by Gillian C. Gill. Ithaca: Cornell University Press, 1985.
———. *To Be Born: Genesis of a New Human Being*. New York: Palgrave, 2017.
———. *To Be Two*. New York: Routledge, 2001.
———. *Una nuova cultura dell'energia: Al di là di Oriente e Occidente*. Torino: Bollati Boringheri, 2013.
———. *The Way of Love*. London: Continuum, 2002.
Jebb, Richard C., trans. *The Tragedies of Sophocles: Antigone*. London: Cambridge University Press, 1904.
Joas, Hans. *G. H. Mead: A Contemporary Re-Examination of His Thought*. Translated by Raymond Meyer. Cambridge MA.: The MIT Press, 1985.
———, ed. *Das Problem der Intersubjektivität*. Frankfurt am Main: Suhrkamp, 1985.
Johnson, Elizabeth A. *She Who Is: The Mystery of God in Feminist Theological Discourse*. New York: Crossroad, 1993.
Johnston, Jay. *Angels of Desire: Esoteric Bodies, Aesthetics, and Ethics*. London and New York: Routledge 2014.
Kant, Immanuel. *Groundwork of the Metaphysics of Morals*. Edited by Mary J. Gregor. Cambridge: Cambridge University Press, 1998.
Kearney, Richard. *Anatheism: Returning to God after God*. New York: Columbia University Press, 2010.
Kirk, G. S., J. E. Raven, and M. Schofield, eds. *The Presocratic Philosophers*. Cambridge: Cambridge University Press, 1999.
Kott, Jan. *Eating of the Gods*. Translated by Boleslaw Taborski and E. J. Czerwinski. Evanston, IL: Northwestern University Press, 1987.
Kristeva, Julia. "Antigone: Limit and Horizon." In *Feminist Readings of Antigone*, edited by Fanny Söderbäck, 215–30. Albany: State University of New York Press, 2010.

Lakoff, George, and Mark Johnson. *Philosophy in the Flesh: The Embodied Mind and Its Challenge to Western Thought.* New York: Basic Books, 1999.

Lambert, Greg. "Untouchable." In *Derrida and Religion,* edited by Yvonne Sherwood and Kevin Hart, 363–74. New York and London: Routledge, 2005.

Levinas, Emmanuel. *Outside the Subject.* Translated by Michael B. Smith. London: Continuum, 1993.

———. *Totality and Infinity.* Translated by Alphonso Lingis. Pittsburgh: Duquesne University Press, 1969.

Lévy, Bernard-Henri. *The Testament of God.* Translated by George Holoch. New York: Harper and Row, 1980.

Levy, Robert I., and Kedar Raj Rajopadhyaya. *Mesocosm: Hinduism and the Organization of a Traditional Newar City of Nepal.* Berkeley: University of California Press, 1990.

Löwith, Karl. "Ludwig Feuerbach." In *Ludwig Feuerbach,* edited by Erich Thies, 33–61. Darmstadt: Wissenschaftliche Buchgesellschaft, 1976.

Lubac, Henri de. *The Eternal Feminine: A Study of the Poem by Teilhard de Chardin, followed by Teilhard and the Problems of Today.* Translated by René Hague. New York: Harper and Row, 1971.

Marion, Jean-Luc. *The Erotic Phenomenon.* Translated by Stephen E. Lewis. Chicago and London: University of Chicago Press, 2007.

Martinon, Jean-Paul. *After "Rwanda:" In Search for a New Ethics.* Amsterdam and New York: Rodopi, 2013.

McDonald, Keiko I. *Japanese Classical Theater in Films.* Rutherford: Fairleigh Dickinson University Press; London and Toronto: Associated University Presses, 1994.

Mead, G. H. *Mind, Self, and Society.* Chicago and London: University of Chicago Press, 1967.

Meehan, Brenda. "Wisdom/Sophia, Russian Identity, and Western Feminist Theology." *CrossCurrents* 46, no. 2 (Summer 1996): 149–68.

Miller, David L. *The Individual and the Social Self: Unpublished Work of George Herbert Mead.* Chicago: University of Chicago Press, 1982.

Mills, Patricia J. "Hegel's Antigone." *The Owl of Minerva* 17, no. 2 (Spring 1986): 131–52.

Min, Anselm Kyongsuk. "God as the Mystery of Sharing and Shared Love: Thomas Aquinas on the Trinity." In *The Cambridge Companion to the Trinity,* edited by Peter C. Phan, 87–107. Cambridge Companions to Religion. Cambridge: Cambridge University Press, 2011. doi:10.1017/CCOL9780521 877398.006.

Moi, Toril, ed. *The Kristeva Reader.* Oxford: Blackwell, 1996.

Moltmann, Jürgen. *Trinität und Reich Gottes.* Gütersloh: Gütersloher Verlagshaus, 1994.

———. *The Trinity and the Kingdom: The Doctrine of God.* Minneapolis: Fortress, 1993.

Monroe, Lauren A. S. "Disembodied Women: Sacrificial Language and the Deaths of Bat-Jephthah, Cozbi, and the Bethlehemite Concubine." *Catholic Biblical Quarterly* 75 (2013): 32–52.
Moster, David Z. "The Levite of Judges 19–21." *JBL* 134, no. 4 (2015): 721–30.
Nagy, Gregory. *The Ancient Greek Hero in 24 Hours*. Cambridge, MA: Belknap Press, 2013.
Nancy, Jean-Luc. *Being Singular Plural*. Translated by Robert D. Richardson. Stanford: Stanford University Press, 2000.
———. *Corpus*. Translated by Richard A. Rand. New York: Fordham University Press, 2008.
———. *The Inoperative Community*. Edited by Peter Connor. Minneapolis: University of Minnesota Press, 1991.
Nearman, Mark J., trans. "Kakyō: Zeami's Fundamental Principles of Acting: Part Two." *Monumenta Nipponica* 37, no. 4 (1982): 459, 461–96.
New Testament Apocrypha. Edited by Wilhelm Schneemelcher. Philadelphia: Westminster Press, 1963.
Newland, Guy. *Compassion: A Tibetan Analysis*. London: Wisdom Publications, 1984.
Nietzsche, Friedrich. *The Anti-Christ: Curse of Christianity*. In *The Nietzsche Reader*, edited by K. A. Pearson and D. Large, 486–99. Oxford: Blackwell, 2006.
———. *Ecce Homo*. Translated by D. Large. Oxford: Oxford University Press, 2007.
———. *Thus Spoke Zarathustra: A Book for All and None*. Edited by Adrian del Caro and Robert B. Pippin. Translated by Adrian del Caro. Cambridge: Cambridge University Press, 2006.
Nussbaum, Martha C. *The Fragility of Goodness: Luck and Ethics in Greek Tragedy and Philosophy*. Updated edition. Cambridge: Cambridge University Press, 2001.
Odin, Steve. "The Social Self in Japanese Philosophy and American Pragmatism: A Comparative Study of Watsuji Tetsurō and George Herbert Mead." *Philosophy East and West* 42, no. 3 (1992): 475–501.
O'Donnell, John. "The Trinitarian Panentheism of Sergej Bulgakov." *Gregorianum* 76, no. 1 (1995): 31–45.
Ogbonnaya, A. Okechukwu. *An African Interpretation of the Trinity*. New York: Paragon House, 1994.
Otto, Walter F. *Die Götter Griechenlands: Das Bild des Göttlichen im Spiegel des griechischen Geistes*. Frankfurt am Main: Klostermann, 1987.
———. *The Homeric Gods*. Translated by Moses Hadas. London: Thames and Hudson, 1954.
Parpola, Asko. "Savitri and Ressurection." In *Changing Patterns of Family and Kinship in South Asia*, edited by Asko Parpola and Sirka Tenhunen, 167–312. Studia Orientalia 84. Helsinki: Finnish Oriental Society, 1998.
———. "The Religious Background of the Savitri Legend." In *Harānandala-harī—Volume in Honour of Professor Minoru Hara on his Seventieth Birthday*,

edited by R. Tsuchida and A. Weber, 193–216. Reinbeck: Dr. Inge Wezler Verlag für orientalische Fachpublikationen, 2000.

Paulsen, David L., and Martin Pulido. "'A Mother There': A Survey of Historical Teachings about Mother in Heaven." *BYU Studies* 50, no. 1 (2011): 71–97.

Pennington, Emily. *Feminist Eschatology: Embodied futures*. London and New York: Routledge, 2017.

Petrey, Taylor G. "Rethinking Mormonism's Heavenly Mother." *Harvard Theological Review* 109, no. 3 (2016): 315–41.

Plato. *Complete Works*. Edited by John M. Cooper. Indianapolis and Cambridge: Hackett, 1997.

Plotinus. *The Enneads*. Translated by Stephen MacKenna. London: Penguin, 1991.

Pogačnik, Marko. *The Daughter of Gaia: Rebirth of the Divine Feminine*. Findhorn: Findhorn Press, 2001.

Pramuk, Christopher. *At Play in Creation: Merton's Awakening to the Feminine Divine*. Collegeville, MI: Liturgical Press, 2015.

Puccini, Giacomo. *Suor Angelica*. Italian libretto by Gioachino Forzano. Translated by Edoardo Petri. http://opera.stanford.edu/Puccini/SuorAngelica/libretto_ie.html. Accessed February 5, 2019.

Radford Ruether, Rosemary. *Goddesses and the Divine Feminine: A Western Religious History*. Berkeley and Los Angeles: University of California Press, 2005.

———. *Sexism and God-Talk. Toward a Feminist Theology*. Boston: Beacon, 1983.

Ricoeur, Paul. *Oneself as Another*. Translated by Katherine Balmey. Chicago and London: The University of Chicago Press, 1994.

Rigveda, The. Translated by Stephanie W. Jamison and Joel P. Brereton. Oxford: Oxford University Press, 2014.

Rosenfield, Kathrin H. *Antigone: Sophocles' Art, Hölderlin's Insight*. Aurora, CO: The Davies Group, 2010.

———. "Hölderlin's Antigone und Sophokles' tragisches Paradox." *Poetica* 33, no. 3/4 (2001): 465–501.

Royce, Josiah. *War as Insurance: An Address*. New York: Macmillan, 1914.

Rutherford, Jonathan. "The Third Space: Interview with Homi Bhabha." In *Identity, Community, Culture, Difference*, edited by Jonathan Rutherford, 207–21. London: Lawrence and Wishart, 1990.

Saint Augustine. *Confessions*. Translated by Henry Chadwick. Oxford: Oxford University Press, 2009.

Sallis, John. *Stone*. Bloomington: Indiana University Press, 1994.

Schelling, Friedrich Wilhelm Joseph. *Ages of the World* (second draft, 1813). Translated by Judith Norman. Ann Arbor: University of Michigan Press, 2001.

———. *Clara, or, On Nature's Connection to the Spirit World*. Translated by Fiona Steinkamp. Albany: State University of New York Press, 2002.

———. *The Grounding of Positive Philosophy*. Translated by Bruce Matthews. Albany: State University of New York Press, 2007.

———. *Philosophical Inquiries into the Nature of Human Freedom*. Translated by J. Gutman. La Salle, IL: Open Court, 1989.
Schelling, Karl Friedrich August, ed. *F. W. J von Schellings sämtliche Werke*. Stuttgart: J. G. Cotta, 1856–61.
Schneider, Laurel C. *Beyond Monotheism: A Theology of Multiplicity*. London: Routledge, 2008.
Schopenhauer, Arthur. *On the Basis of Morality*. Translated by E. F. J. Payne. Indianapolis and Cambridge: Hackett, 1998.
———. *The World as Will and Representation*. Vol. 1. Translated by E. F. J. Payne. New York: Dover, 1969.
Schott, Robin May, ed. *Birth, Death, and Femininity*. Bloomington and Indianapolis: Indiana University Press, 2010.
Schrijvers, Joeri. "Ludwig Binswanger: The Transcendence of Love." *Bogoslovni vestnik* 77 (2017): 489–502.
Schussler-Fiorenza, Elizabeth. *In Memory of Her: Feminist Theological Reconstruction of Christian Origins*. Minneapolis: Fortress, 1983.
Sedmak, Clemens. "Peace, Vulnerability, and Human Imagination." In *The Poesis of Peace*, edited by Klaus-Gerd Giesen, Carool Kersten, and Lenart Škof, 27–40. New York: Routledge, 2017.
Segal, Charles. *Euripides and the Poetics of Sorrow: Art, Gender, and Commemoration in Alcestis, Hippolytus, and Hecuba*. Durham: Duke University Press, 1993.
Sen, Amartya. *The Argumentative Indian: Writings on Indian History, Culture, and Identity*. New York: Farrar, Straus and Giroux, 2005.
Seppala, Emma, Emiliana Simon-Thomas, and Stephanie L. Brown et al., eds. *The Oxford Handbook of Compassion Science*. Oxford: Oxford University Press, 2017.
Sherwood, Yvonne, and Kevin Hart, eds. *Derrida and Religion: Other Testaments*. New York: Routledge, 2005.
Shoemaker, Stephen J., ed. *Ancient Traditions of the Virgin Mary's Dormition and Assumption*. Oxford: Oxford University Press, 2002.
Sládek, Karel. "Sophiology as a Theological Discipline according to Solovyov, Bulgakov, and Florensky." *Bogoslovni vestnik* 77, no. 1 (2017): 109–16.
Sloterdijk, Peter. *Bubbles (Spheres I)*. Translated by Wieland Hoban. South Pasadena, CA: Semiotexte, 2011.
Söderbäck, Fanny, ed. *Feminist Readings of Antigone*. Albany: State University of New York Press, 2010.
Sophocles in Two Volumes: I: Oedipus the King, Oedipus at Colonus, Antigone. Translated by F. Storr. Cambridge: Harvard University Press, 1981.
Sorč, Ciril, and Anton Strle. "Teilhard de Chardin o 'večni ženskosti' in njegov pomen za naš čas." *Bogoslovni vestnik* 33 (1973): 130–38.
Spreckelmeyer, Hermann, *Die philosophische Deutung des Sundenfalls bei Franz Baader*. Würzburg: C. J. Becker Universitäts Druckerei, 1938.
Sri Aurobindo. *Savitri: A Legend and a Symbol*. Twin Lakes, WI: Lotus Press, 2003.

Statkiewicz, Max, and Valerie Reed. "Antigone's (Re)Turn: The Ēthos of the Coming Community." *Analecta Husserliana* 85 (2005): 787–811.
Steinkamp, Fiona. "Schelling's Clara: Editors' Obscurity." *Journal of English and Germanic Philology* (2002): 478–96.
Still, Judith. *Derrida and Hospitality*. Edinburgh: Edinburgh University Press, 2010.
Story of Sāvitrī, The. In *Selections from Classical Sanskrit Literature*. Translated by John Brough. London: Luzac, 1951.
Swedenborg, Emmanuel. *Heaven and Its Wonders and Hell*. Translated by John C. Ager. West Chester: Swedenborg Foundation, 2009.
Škof, Lenart. *Besede vedske Indije*. Ljubljana: Nova revija, 2005.
———. "Breath of Hospitality: Silence, Listening, Care." *Nursing Ethics* 23, no. 8 (2016): 902–909.
———. *Breath of Proximity: Intersubjectivity, Ethics and Peace*. Dordrecht: Springer, 2015.
———. "Food in Ancient Indian Philosophy." In *Encyclopedia of Food and Agricultural Ethics*, edited by P. B. Thompson, D. M. Kaplan, K. Millar, L. Heldke, and R. Bawden, Dordrecht: Springer, 2014. doi:10.1007/978-94-007-6167-4_491-1.
———. "Lamentation of a Child: On Migration, Vulnerability, and Ethics of Hospitality." In *Borders and Debordering: Topologies, Praxes, Hospitableness*, edited by Tomaž Grušovnik, Eduardo Mendieta, and Lenart Škof, 181–92. Lanham: Lexington Books, 2018.
———. "The Material Principle and an Ethics of Hospitality and Compassion: Requiem for Lampedusa." *Annales, Series historia et sociologia* 25, no. 2 (2015): 263–72.
———. "Metaphysical Ethics Reconsidered: Schopenhauer, Compassion and World Religions." *Schopenhauer Jahrbuch* 87 (2006): 101–17.
———. "On Sacred Genealogies in Antigone and Sāvitrī." In *The Poesis of Peace*, edited by Klaus-Gerd Giesen, Carool Kersten, and Lenart Škof, 68–78. New York: Routledge, 2017.
———. "The Third Age: Reflections On Our Hidden Material Core," *Sophia* 59:1 (2020): 83–94.
———. *Pragmatist Variations on Ethical and Intercultural Life*. Lanham, MD: Lexington Books, 2012.
———. " 'The Second Philosophy' of Arthur Schopenhauer: Schopenhauer and Radical Empiricism." *Schopenhauer-Jahrbuch* 91 (2010): 55–64.
———, and Shé M. Hawke, eds., *Shame, Gender Violence, and Ethics: Terrors of Injustice*. Lanham/Boulder/New York/London: Lexington Books, 2021.
Teilhard de Chardin. *The Eternal Feminine*. In *Writings in Time of War*. Translated by René Hague. New York and Evanston: Harper and Row, 1968.
———. *The Future of Man*. Translated by Norman Denny. New York and London: Image Books, 1964.

Theunissen, Michael. *Der Andere: Studien zur Sozialontologie der Gegenwart*. Berlin: W. de Gruyter, 1965.
Thies, Erich, ed. *Ludwig Feuerbach*. Darmstadt: Wissenschaftliche Buchgesellschaft, 1976.
Thomas, Rosalind. "Writing, Law, and Written Law." In *The Cambridge Companion to Ancient Greek Law*, edited by Michael Gagarin and David Cohen, 41–60. Cambridge: Cambridge University Press, 2005.
Three Theban Plays, The: Antigone; Oedipus the King; Oedipus at Colonus. Translated by Robert Fagles. London: Penguin Books, 1984.
Trebežnik, Luka. "Odnos med dekonstrukcijo in religijo pri Jacquesu Derridaju: med nihilizmom in mesijanizmom." PhD diss., University of Ljubljana, 2016.
Trible, Phyllis. *God and the Rhetoric of Sexuality*. London: SCM Press, 1992.
———. *Texts of Terror: Literary-Feminist Readings of Biblical Narratives*. Minneapolis: Fortress Press, 1984.
Trinick, John. *The Fire-Tried Stone: An Enquiry into the Development of a Symbol*. London: Wordens of Cornwall Limited in association with Vincent Stuart and John M. Watkins, 1967.
Trinity, The. Edited by Peter C. Phan. Cambridge: Cambridge University Press, 2011.
Tzelepis, Elena, and Athena Athnasiou, eds. *Rewriting Difference: Luce Irigaray and the Greeks*. Albany: State University of New York Press, 2008.
Unger, Roberto Mangabeira. *The Religion of the Future*. Cambridge: Harvard University Press, 2014.
———. *The Self Awakened: Pragmatism Unbound*. Cambridge and London: Harvard University Press, 2007.
Ward, Graham. "Deconstructive Theology." In *The Cambridge Companion to Postmodern Theology*, edited by Kevin J. Vanhoozer, 76–91. Cambridge: Cambridge University Press 2003.
Ward, Jamie, Patricia Schnakenberg, and Michael J. Banissy. "The Relationship between Mirror-Touch Synaesthesia and Empathy: New Evidence and a New Screening Tool." *Cognitive Neuropsychology* 35, no. 5/6 (2018): 314–32. doi:10.1080/02643294.2018.1457017.
Watsuji, Tetsuro. *Fūdo: Wind und Erde*. Translated by Dora Fischer-Barnicol and Okochi Ryogi. Darmstadt: Wissenschaftliche Buchgesellschaft, 1992.
Wenger, Antoine. *L'Assomption de la T. S. Vierge dans la tradition byzantine du VIe au Xe siècle*. Paris: Institut français d'études byzantines, 1955.
Wirth, Jason M. *The Conspiracy of Life: Meditations on Schelling and His Life*. Albany: State University of New York Press, 2003.
———, ed. *Schelling Now: Contemporary Readings*. Bloomington: Indiana University Press, 2005.
Wirzba, Norman. "The Witness of Humility." In *Words of Life, New Theological Turns in French Phenomenology*, edited by Bruce E. Benson and Norman Wirzba, 233–51. New York: Fordham University Press, 2010.

Witzel, Michael. *Kaṭha Āraṇyaka*. Cambridge.: Harvard University Press, 2004.
———. "Macrocosm, Mesocosm, and Microcosm: The Persistent Nature of 'Hindu' Beliefs and Symbolic Forms." *International Journal of Hindu Studies* 1, no. 3 (1997): 501–39.
Wu, Kuang-Ming. *On Chinese Body Thinking: A Cultural Hermeneutics*. Leiden: Brill, 1997.
Zgodba o Savitri. Translated by Vlasta Pacheiner-Klander. Branik: Abram, 2002.
Žižek, Slavoj. *Antigone*. London and New York: Bloomsbury Academic, 2016.

INDEX

abyss, 100–101, 103–104, 199–200n49
abyssal divine feminine, 103
Aeschylus, 111, 183n20, 200n1
Agamben, Giorgio, 14–15, 17, 158, 210n42
agapeistic compassion, 46–47
agrapta nomima, 8, 13, 16, 42, 174n10
ahimsa, 25
Alcestis, 8, 31–34, 181n56, 63
Amalric of Bena, 158
Andrei Rublev, 63
Angela of Foligno, 54
Anouilh, Jean, 181n64, 214n14
antiethical, 32
antimatrixial, 53, 62, 135, 182n3
Aphrodite, 9, 130–35, 139, 165, 168
Apollo, 32
Aristotle, 57, 73, 79, 81, 84, 195n8, 210–11n42
Artemis, 32
Athena, 38–39, 182–83n11
Augustin, 113, 120–21, 200n4

Baader, Franz von, 152, 168, 208n21, 213–14n14
Bachelard, Gaston, 155, 209n32, 210n35
Badiou, Alain, 122, 202n31

Bartolo, Pietro, 46–47, 185n43
being of twoness, 118
Bernardete, Seth, 204n64
Bernstein, Jay M., 176n25
Bethletemite Concubine, 49–69, 185n45, 187n13
Bhabha, Homi, 56, 189n35
Bigwood, Carol, 131–32, 204n57
Binswanger, Ludwig, 111–20, 122–25, 129–31, 137, 19, 200n2, 200n5, n7, 201n7, 201n9, n13, n22, 201–202n27, 203n46, 204n53, 206n83
Böhme, Jakob, 8, 99–106, 171n1, 198–99n37, 199n38, n42, n44
Brague, Rémi, 16, 174n11
Brahma, 23–24, 27
breath of love, 101, 106, 112, 138, 152, 158
breath-energy, 157
breath-kiss, 152
Buddha, 22, 146, 149, 154–55
Bulgakov, Sergei, 65–68, 193n80–n81, n84, 194n85
Burkert, Walter, 175n19
Butler, Judith, 8, 14–15, 95–96, 172n5, 179–80n49, 197n21

Caputo, John D., 8, 17, 47, 94–96, 117, 138, 145, 154, 175n18,

Caputo, John D. *(continued)*
  197n17, n22, 200n4, 206n77–n78, 207n1, 209n24, 212n49
Celan, Paul, 151, 208n18
chakra, 29
Chandrakirti, 45
Chaos, 38, 44, 161, 173n16, 182n6
Chrétien, Jean-Louis, 47, 75–77, 79–81, 83, 146, 194n1, n6, 195n17, n19
Chóra, 5–6, 8, 53, 58–59, 62–64, 102, 131, 137, 158–61, 192n65, 205n70, 206n82, 211n46, 211–12n48, 212n49
Claudel, Paul, 3, 30, 181n54
co-breathing, 152, 157–58, 167–68, 214n15
cohabitation, 185n48
(co)mediatrix, 51
conspiracy, 168, 199–200n49, 211–12n48, 213n13, 214n15
conspiratio, 152, 157, 214n15
contact experience, 75, 77, 79, 81, 83
cosmic
  breathing, 147, 156, 208n22, 210n35
  egg, 38–39, 182n6
  genealogy, 26
  order, 13, 16–17, 19–20, 26, 31, 44, 95, 135–36, 154–55, 175–76n22, 209n27
  waters, 43, 92

Danaë, 21
deceased others, 91
Deleuze, Gilles, 6, 91, 93, 172n9
Demeter, 17, 31, 38, 65, 122, 132, 136, 165, 182–83n11
Derrida, Jacques, 8, 16, 22, 43, 45, 47, 59, 82, 91–92, 121, 131, 137, 140, 160, 176n24, 177n30, 182n27, n29, n40, 187n13, 188n16, 190n48, 192n68, 196n33, 197n9, 200n4, 204n55, 206n82, 210n39, 211n46–n47
Deshpande, R. Y., 25–26, 30–31, 178n38, 41, 43, 181n55
Detienne, Marcel, 39, 182n9
Dewey, John, 81, 173–74n1, 196n26, 207n7
dialectical dyad, 148
différance, 66, 138–39, 161, 201–202n48, 202n49
Dionysius, 132
divine justice, 16
divine-maternal, 26
Dufourmantelle, Anne, 22, 177–78n35
dual subjectivity, 56
Durga (Durgā), 179
Dussel, Enrique, 42, 183n14, n22, 186n2
Dzong-ka-ba, 43

ecofeminism, 131, 193n81, 204n56
elements (Presocratic), 13, 17, 41, 146
embrace, 6, 25, 114–16, 119, 139, 142, 155, 169, 204n53
Erikepaios, 38
Erinyes, 16, 38, 41, 44, 132, 165
Eros, 120, 131, 133–35
eternal Feminine, 8, 65–67
ether, 155
ethical
  anatomy, 47, 91, 174n12
  archeology, 16
  cardiology, 46–47, 117
  gynecology, 47
  humility, 6
  pneumatology, 47, 156
Ettinger, Bracha L., 3–4, 8, 44, 47, 54, 165, 168, 171n1–n2, 172n3,

n5, 184n34, 186n3, 187n15, 188n26, 212n1, 214n16–n17
Ettingerian matrixial core, 4
Euripides, 8, 33, 181n56–n57, n60, n62, 202n30
exuberance of love, 6–9, 34, 66, 108, 117, 119, 137, 139–40, 152, 201–202n27

Fair Vida (Lepa Vida), 8, 37–47, 108, 181n1
feminine body, 16, 51
Feuerbach, Ludwig, 7–8, 17, 42, 47, 53, 55, 60, 63, 74–75, 77–81, 83, 90, 103, 112, 114–15, 146, 149, 180n51, 188n23, 189n32, 190n50, 192n64, 195n15–16, 197n4, 199n44, 201n10–n11, 201–202n27, 207n2, n4
Florensky, Pavel, 65–66, 68, 193n80
fourfold 116, 130–31, 134–35, 138–40
forgiveness, 19, 176n25

Gaia, 16, 182n8
Gargi Vachaknavi, 28
genealogical
 love, 117, 131, 202–203n39
 sisters, 3, 8, 127
Glazenbrook, Trish, 131, 204n56
God's womb, 52
Grau, Alexander, 93, 197n13, n15, 200n50
Gregory Palamas, St., 29
Grelland, Hans Herlof, 99, 197–98n25
Grosz, Elizabeth, 7, 173n15
gynocentric epistemology, 131

Habermas, Jürgen, 78
Hades, 16, 33, 41
Hadewijch of Brabant, 54

haptic, 75, 77–79, 195n11
Hawke, Shé, 38–39, 181n2, 182n3, n5, n7, n10, 186n1, 194n88, 205n71
hearth, 41, 45, 142, 152, 184n39
heavenly matrix, 195, 171n1
Hegel, Georg Wilhelm Friedrich, 4–5, 7–8, 14–21, 29, 39, 51, 133, 147, 154, 174n9, 175n20–n21, 175–76n22, 176n23–n25, 211–212n48
Heidegger, Martin, 8, 16–17, 41, 45, 75, 80, 91, 112–13, 115, 117–18, 120–21, 125–26, 128–32, 137–39, 146–47, 176n23, 177n33, 180n51, 183n18, 184n33, n39, 200n4, 201n20, 203n47, n50–n51, 204n55–n57, n60, 206n66, n72, 206n77
Heracles, 33
heroic
 death, 30, 118, 181n1
 women, 8, 13
Hesiod, 44, 182n3, n6, 200n1
Hestia, 184n39
Hofmannsthal, Hugo von, 116
Hölderlin, Friedrich, 17, 128, 166, 212n4, 213n5, n10
Holy Spirit (Holy Ghost), 30, 59, 63, 67, 69, 126–27, 136, 152–54, 157, 159, 167, 213–14n14, 214n15
Holy Trinity, 55, 62–63, 65, 67–68, 125
horizontal transcendence, 124, 138
hospitality, 7–8, 13–14, 22, 37, 41–46, 51, 61, 63–64, 82, 113, 124, 172–73n10, 177n34, 177–78n35, 184n34, 187n13, 188n16, 208n17
Hribar, Tine, 123, 128, 132, 202n29, 203n44, 204n60, n62

Husserl, Edmund, 29, 146–47
imagination of peace, 6
immortal(ity), 24, 26, 32, 34, 120, 134
Irigaray, Luce, 5, 8–9, 14–17, 19–22, 27–29, 39, 45, 47, 49–51, 54–55, 60–63, 73, 89–91, 95, 104–105, 113, 117, 122–25, 133, 135, 139, 145–61, 165, 172n5, n8, 174n–n3, 176n26, 177n33, 178n45, 180n50–n51, 180–81n52, 182–83n11, 184n35–36, 186n4, 187n9, n11, 188n20, 189n30, 191n52, 192n63, n71, 196n2, 199n41, 202n33, n35–36, 203n43–44, 204n53, n63, 206n79, n81, 207n9–10, 208n13–n16, n19, 209n25–n26, n28–n29, n31, 210n36–n37, n40–41, 211n43, 213n9
Issa Grace, 6

Jesus (of Nazareth), 3–4, 8, 21, 25–26, 29, 50–51, 53–54, 61–64, 69, 95, 100, 102–106, 127, 135, 153–55, 157–59, 165–69, 175n18, 180–81n52, 187n8, 199n40–n41, 205n70, 209n24, n34, 213n13
John of the Cross, 80
Johnston, Elizabeth, 50
Johnston, Jay, 56
Jung, Carl Gustav, 65, 192–93n72
Justus 'Cor' Becker, 208n21

Kant, Immanuel, 183n21
Kearney, Richard, 63, 192n65
Kierkegaard, Søren, 5, 42, 89, 196n34
Kilpinen, Erkki, 74
Kore, 17, 31 125, 132, 136, 165

Kristeva, Julia, 3, 5, 8, 160, 165, 172n5, 203n44, 212n2, 213n11

Lacan, Jacques, 5, 8 14–15, 89
laments, 6, 47
Lazarus, 25, 94–96, 103, 106, 120, 140
Lepa Vida (Fair Vida), 37–47
Levinas, Emmanuel, 16, 22, 28, 42, 44, 47, 91, 112, 115, 125, 146, 173–74n1, 175n16, 184n41, 188n27
Lévy, Bernard Henri, 175–76n22
listening, 7, 149, 155–56, 209–10n34
Lot 52, 187n13, 188n16
loving
  encounter, 115–16, 129
  togetherness, 114, 117, 122
Lucretia (Lucrece), 187n12

Marguerite Porete, 54
Marion, Jean-Luc, 89, 112, 146, 196n1
Martha, 95
Martinon, Jean-Paul, 185n43, 186n3, 187n10
Mary, 3, 8, 28–30, 49–69, 95, 104–105, 131, 137, 153–54, 157–60, 165, 171n1, 172n4, 179–80n49, 180n51, 190n50, 192n65, n72, 199n41, 205n70, 212n50
Mary Magdalene, 103, 157–58, 167
material phenomenology, 111, 119
matricide, 39
matrixial
  bond, 136
  covenant, 168, 214n17
  genealogy/-ies, 62, 137
  identity, 4, 52, 188n20
  ontology, 47
  theology, 50, 55, 58, 60–61
matrix of love, 3–9, 66, 135–36

Maximus the Confessor, 5, 89
Mead, George Herbert, 47, 74–75,
    77–83, 173–74n1, 195n9–n15,
    n22, 196n34, 201n9, 207n7
Medeia (Medea), 32
Merleau-Ponty, Maurice, 28, 146,
    207n8, 210n35
Merton, Thomas, 69
mesocosmic breathing, 147, 156
Metis, 8, 31, 37–47, 132, 136, 165,
    168, 182n3, n5, 192–93n72
mindfulness, 129, 149, 185–86n48
Moltmann, Jürgen, 60, 62–63,
    125–27, 131, 190n49, 191n57–
    n60, 203n40, n42
Mormonism, 190n51
mourning, 49, 91–92, 95–96, 99–100,
    102, 106, 111, 118–19, 121–22
Moses, 188n27
Munch, Edward, 99, 197–98n25

Nancy, Jean-Luc, 15, 53, 61, 112,
    115, 140, 146, 173–74n1,
    174n5–n6, 185–86n48, 201n12
Nietzsche, Friedrich, 7, 15, 42, 132,
    146, 149, 155, 173n16, 174n4,
    207n3, n5
nonviolent dwelling, 129
Nussbaum, Martha C., 20–21,
    176–77n28, 177n29

Ogbonnaya, Adonijah Okechukwu,
    57–58, 190n42
ontology
    of love, 27, 43, 87, 90, 92, 95,
    111–12, 115, 118, 120, 122–23,
    135
    of violence, 3
Orin, 139, 141–42
Otto, Walter F., 17, 39, 130, 175n17,
    182n8, 183n13, n19, 204n53,
    n59

Pacheiner-Klander, Vlasta, 25
Parpola, Asko, 28, 178n38, 178–
    79n46, 179–80n49
Patočka, Jan, 22, 177–78n35
Phanes, 38–39, 57
Peirce, Charles S., 55, 289n33–n34,
    207n7
Persephone, 16, 38, 65, 125, 132,
    136, 165, 182–83n11
Pinkola Estés, Clarisse, 212n50
Plato, 5, 29, 34, 57–58, 63, 67, 89,
    121, 127, 137, 159–60, 181n61,
    188n25, 189n39, 190n44–n45,
    205n73, 205–206n74, n82,
    211n44
pneumatic covenant, 154
Pogačnik, Marko, 212n50
Polyneices, 14, 16–17, 20, 51, 121, 133
Pope Francis, 44, 185n44
primordial encounter, 120, 122,
    129–30, 137, 140
procreatrix, 28, 38
Prometheus, 41, 183n20
Puccini, Giacomo, 107, 200n51
Pythagoras, 57

Radford Ruether, Rosemary, 187n8,
    188n29, 191n61, 193n81
rakhamim, 43, 45, 187n15
rape, 47, 49, 51–52, 172n4, 179–
    80n49, 187n10–n12
Rawls, John, 7
Reed, Valerie, 15, 174n8, 177n33
rehem, 64
reserve of breath, 151–52, 156–58
respiratory ontology, 210n35
resurrection, 25, 28, 61, 92, 94–95,
    127, 158, 210n37
Ricoeur, Paul, 20, 176–77n28
Royce, Josiah, 56, 189n34

Saint Teresa of Avila, 30

Sappho, 9, 128, 131–32, 204n57
Satyavan, 23–26, 30, 178–79n46
Savitar, 23–24, 26, 28, 178n37
Savitri (Sāvitrī), 8, 13–35, 108, 135, 178n40–n45, 178–79n46, 179–80n49, 180n55, 184n32
Schelling, Friedrich Wilhelm Joseph, 8, 17, 42, 90–94, 96, 99–106, 111–12, 118–20, 122–23, 125, 127, 131, 152–53, 157, 183n24–n26, 196n3, 197n6–n15, n23, 198n26–n36, 198–99n37, 199n38–39, n45–n48, 199–200n49, 200n3, 201n26, 201–202n27, 202n32, 208n20, 208n22, 209n23
Schneider, Laurel C., 56, 186n5, 189n37, n41
Schopenhauer, Arthur, 7, 42, 47, 73–74, 79, 83, 113, 118, 146, 184n28, 194n2, 196n35–n36, 201n21, 207n6, 210n41
Schrijvers, Joeri, 113, 200n5
Schüssler-Fiorenza, Elizabeth, 157, 210n38
Sedmak, Clemens, 6–7, 173n11–n12, n14
self-affection, 93, 146–51, 154–56, 158, 158, 166, 177n33
self-sacrifice, 31
self-transcendence, 5–6, 59, 89, 145
sexual difference, 19, 27, 30, 34, 39, 60, 62, 90, 112, 123, 125, 130–31, 139, 146–48, 153–54, 156, 158, 172n4, 177n33, 190–91n51, n60, 204n55
Shekinah, 126, 192–93n72
Shigenori Nagatomo, 74
Sister Angelica (Suor Angelica), 107–109
Śiva (Shiva), 24, 142, 180n51

Škof, Lenart, 172–73n10, 173n11, 186n1, 195n14, 207n6, n8, 207–208n11, 208n17, n22
Slapšak, Svetlana, 33, 181n59
Socrates, 4, 57
Solovyov, Vladimir, 65–67, 193n80, n82
Sophia 8, 64–65, 67–69, 103–105, 192–93n72, 193n80–n82, n84, 194n87, 199n40
Statkiewicz, Max, 174n8, 177n32
Stewart, Jeff, 96, 197n24
Still, Judith, 187n13, 188n16
suicide, 31, 39, 108
Surya, 26
sympathetic gesture, 80
symptomatology, 42–43
synaesthetic touch, 185n47
Swedenborg, Emmanuel, 202–203n39

tactile experience, 83
tears, 6, 43, 46–47, 91–92, 95–97, 100, 106, 111, 119, 121–22, 138, 141, 200n4
Teilhard de Chardin, 65, 95, 193n73–n79
Tertullian, 58
Thales, 57
Theunissen, Michael, 201–202n27
Thomas Aquinas, 5, 26, 203n41
Trible, Phyllis, 52, 64, 188n19, n22, 192n69
trinitarian
  pneumatics, 157
  theology, 57, 125–26

Unger, Roberto Mangabeira, 153, 209n24
unwritten laws, 8, 14, 34, 46, 133, 135–36, 166, 168

Varuna, 17

Virgin Mary, 55, 65–66, 105, 153, 165, 190n50, 191n53
Vishnu, 24
vulnerability, 6–7, 49, 51–52

Watsuji Tetsurō, 75–77, 80–83, 194n5, 195n24, 196n28, n32
Whitehead, Alfred North, 81
wind, 17, 41, 47, 96, 141–42, 151, 155, 166–67, 208n22, 209n24
Wirth, Jason, 91, 100, 197n6, 198n33–n36, 199–200n49, 208n20
Wisdom-Sophia, 69, 193n81–n84, 194n87
Wirzba, Norman, 81, 196n29
Wollstonecraft, Mary, 90

wombing motherliness, 47, 58–59, 62–63, 137–38, 185n45, 190n46
womb-matrix, 53, 62–64
womb-power, 59, 138
wound of knowledge, 7
Wu, Kuang-ming, 47, 58–59, 137, 185n45, 190n46, 192n66, 206n75, 214n18

Xenophanes, 57

Yama, 17, 23–25, 27, 30
Yoga, 29, 142

Zeami Motokiyo, 75
Zeus, 32, 38–39, 182n3, n8, 200n1, 205n70
Žižek, Slavoj, 14–15, 203n44

ABOUT THE AUTHOR

Dr. Lenart Škof is professor of philosophy and head of the Institute for Philosophical Studies at the Science and Research Centre of Koper and dean of Institutum Studiorum Humanitatis of Alma Mater Europaea (Maribor, Slovenia). Lenart Škof received a KAAD grant (Universität Tübingen), a Fulbright grant (Stanford University), and a Humboldt fellowship for experienced researchers (Max Weber Institute for Advanced Studies, Universität Erfurt). His main research interests lie in ethics, new materialism, and feminist philosophy. Dr. Škof has lectured at various universities, including Australian Catholic University, University of Vienna, University of Delhi, Jadavpur University (Kolkata), Linköpings Universitet (Sweden), Russian Academy of Sciences, University of Erfurt and others. His recent books include: *Shame, Gender Violence, and Ethics: Terrors of Injustice*, edited by L. Škof and S. Hawke (Lexington Books, 2021), *Borders and Debordering: Topologies, Praxes, Hospitableness*, edited by E. Mendieta, L. Škof, and T. Grušovnik (Lexington Books, 2018), *Atmospheres of Breathing*, edited by L. Škof and P. Berndtson (SUNY Press, 2018), *Ethik des Atems* (Herder/Karl Alber, 2017), and *Poesis of Peace: Narratives, Cultures, and Philosophies*, edited by K-G. Giesen, C. Kersten, and L. Škof (Routledge, 2017).

Homepage: https://lenartskof.academia.edu/.

www.ingramcontent.com/pod-product-compliance
Lightning Source LLC
Chambersburg PA
CBHW020649230426
43665CB00008B/365